THE OVERSPENT AMERICAN

WHY WE WANT
WHAT WE DON'T NEED

Juliet B. Schor

HarperPerennial
A Division of HarperCollins*Publishers*

ILLUSTRATION CREDITS:

Page 1: Crate and Barrel advertisement as seen in the Boston Globe Magazine, 1993.
Page 25: Courtesy Hartmarr Corporation.
Page 43: Courtesy Hartmarr Corporation.
Page 65: Copyright Shreve, Crump & Low Co., Ltd., 1997.
Page 112: From Adbusters Magazine, 1 (800) 663–1243.
Page 144: Spoof ad contest entry, from Adbusters Magazine, 1 (800) 663–1243.

Cover art derived from American Gothic by Grant Wood
Friends of the American Art Collection
All rights reserved by the Art Institute of Chicago and VAGA, New York, NY

First HarperPerennial edition published 1999.

THE LIBRARY OF CONGRESS HAS CATALOGUED THE HARDCOVER EDITION AS FOLLOWS:
Schor, Juliet B.
The overspent American : why we want what we don't need / Juliet B. Schor.
p.   cm.
Includes bibliographical references and index.
ISBN 0-465-06056-0 (hc)
1. Consumer behavior—United States. 2. Consumption (Economics)—United States.
3. Credit—United States. 4. Debt—United States. 5. Finance, Personal—United States.
6. Lifestyles—United States. 7. Saving and thrift—United States. 8. Values—United States.
I. Title.
HF5415.33.U6S36 1998
339.4'7'0973—dc2197-42493

ISBN 0-06-097758-2 (pbk)

20 19

RRD 06 07 08 09

Also by Juliet B. Schor

The Overworked American

FOR PRASANNAN,

who taught me the value of money

CONTENTS

ACKNOWLEDGMENTS

A great many people and institutions helped me with this book. I am grateful to them. I begin by acknowledging my intellectual debts to those economists whose work on consumption and consumer society has formed the basis for my own thinking: John Kenneth Galbraith, James Duesenberry, Tibor Scitovsky, Robert Frank, Clair Brown, Stephen Marglin, and Amartya Sen. Most of them are friends and colleagues, and I want to thank them for discussions, insights, and support over the years.

For reading and commenting on chapters or the entire manuscript, I would like to thank Russell Belk, Pat Berhau, John Donatich, Don Fehr, Susan Fournier, Cees Goossens, and Hans Mommaas. For sending manuscripts or unpublished papers, I would like to thank Larry Ausubel, Susan Fournier, Douglas Holt, Frank Levy, Tom O'Guinn, Craig Thompson, and Richard Wilk. For helpful conversations, I am grateful to Colin Campbell, Eric Corijn, Brad Googins, Robert J. Gordon, Douglas Holt, Hans Mommaas, Miles Rubin, Betsy Taylor, and Nigel Thrift. For help in gathering materials and citations, I am grateful to Daniel Bregman, Susan Fournier, Mohan Rao, and Amartya Sen. Research from this book has been presented at a number of universities. Thanks to participants in my seminars at the University of Wisconsin, Tilburg University, Harvard Divinity School, Notre Dame, and the New School for Social Research. I would also like to thank my fellow board members at the Center for a New

American Dream, and especially Betsy Taylor, for an ongoing conversation that has taught me a tremendous amount.

I have had an evolving group of research assistants throughout this project. I am grateful to all of them, including Joan Adrianssen, Amy Agigian, Angela Chao, Jeff Chou, Saskia Goedhart, Karen Greve, Marc Haine, Lynn Lu, Tracy Tefertiller, and Dan Winterson. For secretarial and administrative assistance, thanks to Mieke Lustenhouwer and Catherine Cezeaux.

Much of the research I conducted for this book was collaborative. First, thanks to Angela Chao for sharing the cosmetics project with me. For their collaboration on the Telecom survey, I am grateful to Brad Googins and the Center on Work and Family, now of Boston College, and especially to Judi Casey, Marcie Catephores, and Leon Litchfield. Many thanks to officials at Telecom, and at Addison-Wesley, where the questionnaire was piloted. For help with the downshifter survey and analysis, I would like to thank Ron Decker, Jacques Hagenaars, Ethel Klein, Elana Stancanelli, Harald van der Werff, and Jeroen Vermunt. For their help in locating people to be interviewed, I am grateful to Cecile Andrews, Janet Luhrs, Colquitt Meacham and Holly Bruno, and especially Vicki Robin and members of the New Road Map Foundation. I would also like to thank the many individuals who agreed to be interviewed and then gave so generously their time and life stories. Thanks as well to those who filled out my written questionnaire on downshifting and simple living. Finally, I would like to thank Adbusters and the corporations and advertising agencies that allowed me to reproduce their ads.

I received financial assistance from a number of sources, and I want to express a deep debt of gratitude to all of them. First, to the John S. Simon Guggenheim Foundation, for awarding me a fellowship for the writing of the book. Second, to the Merck Family Fund, which helped underwrite many of the expenses of my research and allowed me to participate in and use the results from its February 1995 poll. Third, to Susan Sechler and David Devlin-Foltz of the PEW Global Stewardship Initiative, which funded the Telecom survey. Fourth, to the Work and Organization Research Center (WORC) of Tilburg University for general research support. Finally, I am most grateful to the Leisure Studies Department of Tilburg

University, where I resided for the two years I wrote this book. The department provided me not only with the teaching relief I needed but also with a stimulating intellectual environment and a wonderful community.

I would also like to thank those individuals in the publishing world who helped make this book happen. Gerry McCauley has not only been a wonderful agent, but a true friend. Through the turmoil at Basic Books, he taught me why authors need people like him. Thanks also to Geri Toma for her sage assistance, and to Cindy Buck, who copyedited the manuscript. I am grateful to the staff at Basic, including John Donatich, Marian Brown, and Brian Desmond for all their excellent work, and especially to Jack McKeown for his vision and steadfast support. My greatest debt is to my editor, Susan Rabiner. Having left Basic before my book was published, to start her own literary agency, Susan nevertheless agreed to continue her editing. Her insights were nothing short of brilliant. I will cherish our collaboration always.

Finally, I would like to thank my friends and family. Fred Meisel was, as always, a fount of good advice. My children, Krishnan Dasaratha and Elana Sulakshana, are a daily blessing. My three brothers, Lizzie, and our relatives on both sides are always supportive and encouraging. I dedicate this book to my husband, Prasannan Parthasarathi, whose help, intelligence, good judgment, and love I can always rely on.

Some months after the publication of *The Overworked American*, I gave a public lecture in a church in Harvard Square. At the end of the talk, a young woman, in her thirties, raised her hand. A hospital administrator, she found herself trapped in what I had called in my book "the cycle of work and spend." How can I get out, she asked? While I felt fairly certain about one part of my answer (work less), I was less clear about the other (spend less). Was cutting back feasible for middle-class American consumers? What was driving their spending? How does spending affect the quality of life for people who are materially comfortable? Assuming an individual could break down the institutional barriers to shorter hours that I had discussed in my book, could he or she negotiate the lifestyle obstacles? What were the difficulties of living more simply in our highly consumerist culture?

At the same time that I was ruminating about these issues, I became convinced that America, as a country, *had* to free itself from work-and-spend. The ecological devastation created by the national lifestyle had become unacceptable. Almost any version of global, intergenerational, and class equity pointed to the need to change middle-class consumer patterns. But I also felt that creating a powerful impetus for change would require a better understanding of the social forces that sustained the lifestyle. This book is my effort to contribute to that understanding.

The book is based on a number of different types of research. The first is the development of a new methodology for identifying the presence of status buying in particular consumer products and its application to women's cosmetics. That research, done jointly with Angela Chao, is discussed in chapter 3. The second is a survey I conducted in 1994 and 1995, in collaboration with Brad Googins and the Center for Work and Family, then at Boston University. The survey was done at "Telecom," a large telecommunications company in the southeastern United States. It dealt with a wide range of issues, and is mainly reported on in chapter 4. The research for chapter 5, on downshifting, comes from a national telephone poll I carried out in the fall of 1996, as well as from twenty-six in-depth interviews with various types of downshifters. In addition to the interviews, I gathered written "life histories" of downshifters and spent time in Seattle researching the simple living movement. This qualitative research was not designed to provide a random sample of downshifters but mainly to fill out my understanding of the phenomenon. I was also fortunate to collaborate on an earlier survey by the Merck Family Fund that covered many of the same issues I was interested in. In addition to "piloting" the downshifter questions, the Merck survey included focus groups and answers to a variety of questions about Americans' attitudes toward spending. I have discussed these throughout the book as well. To keep the text as accessible as possible, I have confined details about all this research either to appendices or notes, or I refer the reader to the relevant academic papers. I have also confined to the notes other issues which are mainly of significance to specialists.

Finally, I must explain who this book is about and written for. Unlike *The Overworked American*, which deals with an experience that is common across the workforce, this book is mainly about middle-class and upper-middle-class consumers. As I argue in chapter 2, spending patterns are strongly differentiated by class, and the system of competitive spending I describe is driven by those with discretionary income. While I believe all Americans are deeply affected by consumerism, this book is directed to people, like the hospital administrator in Cambridge, whose incomes afford a comfortable lifestyle. (As a member of this group myself, I have taken the liberty at times of using the pronouns *we* and *us*.) I focus on more affluent consumers not because I believe that inequalities of consuming power are unimportant. Far from it. They are at the heart of the problem. But I believe that achieving an equitable standard of living for all Americans will require that those of us with comfortable material lives transform our relationship to spending. I offer this book as a step in that direction.

In 1996 a best-selling book entitled *The Millionaire Next Door* caused a minor sensation. In contrast to the popular perception of millionaire lifestyles, this book reveals that most millionaires live frugal lives—buying used cars, purchasing their suits at JC Penney, and shopping for bargains. These very wealthy people feel no need to let the world know they can afford to live much better than their neighbors.

Millions of other Americans, on the other hand, have a different relationship with spending. What they acquire and own is tightly bound to their personal identity. Driving a certain type of car, wearing particular designer labels, living in a certain kind of home, and ordering the right bottle of wine create and support a particular image of themselves to present to the world.

This is not to say that most Americans make consumer purchases solely to fool others about who they really are. It is not to say that we are a nation of crass status-seekers. Or that people who purchase more than they need are simply demonstrating a base materialism, in the sense of valuing material possessions above all else. But it is to say that, unlike the millionaires next door, who are not driven to use their wealth to create an attractive image of themselves, many of us are continually comparing our own lifestyle and possessions to those of a select group of people we respect and want to be like, people whose sense of what's important in life seems close to our own.

This aspect of our spending is not new—competitive acquisition has long been an American institution. At the turn of the century, the rich consumed conspicuously. In the early post–World War II decades, Americans spent to keep up with the Joneses, using their possessions to make the statement that they were not failing in their careers. But in recent decades, the culture of spending has changed and intensified. In the old days, our neighbors set the standard for what we had to have. They may have earned a little more, or a little less, but their incomes and ours were in the same ballpark. Their house down the block, worth roughly the same as ours, confirmed this. Today the neighbors are no longer the focus of comparison.

How could they be? We may not even know them, much less which restaurants they patronize, where they vacation, and how much they spent for their living room couch.

For reasons that will become clear, the comparisons we make are no longer restricted to those in our own general earnings category, or even to those one rung above us on the ladder. Today a person is more likely to be making comparisons with, or choose as a "reference group," people whose incomes are three, four, or five times his or her own. The result is that millions of us have become participants in a national culture of upscale spending. I call it the new consumerism.

Part of what's new is that lifestyle aspirations are now formed by different points of reference. For many of us, the neighborhood has been replaced by a community of coworkers, people we work alongside and colleagues in our own and related professions. And while our real-life friends still matter, they have been joined by our media "friends." (This is true both figuratively and literally—the television show *Friends* is a good example of an influential media referent.) We watch the way television families live, we read about the lifestyles of celebrities and other public figures we admire, and we consciously and unconsciously assimilate this information. It affects us.

So far so good. We are in a wider world, so we like to know that we are stacking up well against a wider population group than the people on the block. No harm in that. But as new reference groups form, they are less likely to comprise people who all earn approximately the same amount of money. And therein lies the problem. When a person who earns $75,000 a year compares herself to someone earning $90,000, the comparison is sustainable. It creates some tension, even a striving to do a bit better, to be more successful in a career. But when a reference group includes people who pull down six or even seven-figure incomes, that's trouble. When poet-waiters earning $18,000 a year, teachers earning $30,000, and editors and publishers earning six-figure incomes all aspire to be part of one urban literary referent group, which exerts pressure to drink the same brand of bottled water and wine, wear similar urban literary clothes, and appoint apartments with urban literary furniture, those at the lower economic end of the reference group find themselves in an untenable situation. Even if we choose not to emulate those who spend ostentatiously, consumer aspirations can be a serious reach.

Advertising and the media have played an important part in stretching out reference groups vertically. When twenty-somethings can't afford much more than a utilitarian studio but think they should have a New York apartment to match the ones they see on *Friends,* they are setting unattainable consumption goals for themselves, with dissatisfaction as a predictable result. When the children of affluent suburban and impoverished inner-city households both want the same Tommy Hilfiger logo emblazoned on their chests and the top-of-the-line Swoosh on their feet, it's a potential disaster. One solution to these problems emerged on the talk-show circuit recently, championed by a pair of young urban "entry-level" earners: live the *faux* life, consuming *as if* you had a big bank balance. Their strategies? Use your expense account for private entertainment, date bankers, and sneak into snazzy parties without an invitation. Haven't got the wardrobe for it? No matter. Charge expensive clothes, wear them with the tags on, and return them the morning after. Apparently the upscale life is now so worth living that deception, cheating, and theft are a small price to pay for it.

These are the more dramatic examples. Millions of us face less stark but problematic comparisons every day. People in one-earner families find themselves trying to live the lifestyle of their two-paycheck friends. Parents of modest means struggle to pay for the private schooling that others in their reference group have established as the right thing to do for their children.

Additional problems are created by the accelerating pace of product innovation. To gain broader distribution for the plethora of new products, manufacturers have gone to lifestyle marketing, targeting their pitches of upscale items at rich and nonrich alike. Gourmet cereal, a luxurious latte, or bathroom fixtures that make a statement, the right statement, are offered to people almost everywhere on the economic spectrum. In fact, through the magic of plastic, anyone can buy designer anything, at the trendiest retail shop. Or at outlet prices. That's the new consumerism. And its siren call is hard to resist.

The new consumerism is also built on a relentless ratcheting up of standards. If you move into a house with a fifties kitchen, the presumption is that you will eventually have it redone, because that's a standard that has now been established. If you didn't have air conditioning in your old car, the presumption is that when you replace it, the new one will have it. If you haven't been to Europe, the presumption is that you will get there, because you deserve to get there. And so on. In addition to the proliferation of new products (computers, cell phones, faxes, and other microelectronics), there is a continual upgrading of old ones—autos and appliances—and a shift to customized, more expensive versions, all leading to a general expansion of the list of things we have to have. The 1929 home I just moved into has a closet too shallow to fit a hanger. So the clothes face forward. The real estate agents suggested I solve the "problem" by turning the study off the bedroom into a walk-in. (Why read when you could be buying clothes?) What we want grows into what we *need*, at a sometimes dizzying rate. While politicians continue to tout the middle class as the heart and soul of American society, for far too many of us being solidly middle-class is no longer good enough.

Oddly, it doesn't seem as if we're spending wastefully, or even lavishly. Rather, many of us feel we're just making it, barely able to stay even. But what's remarkable is that this feeling is not restricted to families of limited income. It's a generalized feeling, one that exists at all levels. Twenty-seven percent of all households making more than $100,000 a year say they cannot afford to buy everything they really need. Nearly 20 percent say they "spend nearly all their income on the basic necessities of life." In the $50,000–100,000 range, 39 percent and one-third feel this way, respectively. Overall, half the population of the richest country in the world say they cannot afford everything they really need. And it's not just the poorer half.

This book is about why: About why so many middle-class Americans feel materially dissatisfied. Why they walk around with ever-present mental "wish lists" of things to buy or get. How even a six-figure income can seem inadequate, and why this country saves less than virtually any other nation in the world. It is about the ways in which, for America's middle classes, "spending becomes you," about how it flatters, enhances, and defines people in often wonderful ways, but also about how it takes over their lives. My analysis is based on new research showing that the need to spend whatever it takes to keep current within a chosen reference group—which may include members of widely disparate resources—drives much pur-

TABLE 1.1 How Much Is Enough?

Percentage Agreeing with Statement, by Income

STATEMENT	<$10,000	10,001–25,000	25,001–35,000	35,001–50,000	50,001–75,000	75,001–100,000	>100,000
I cannot afford to buy everything I really need	64	62	50	43	42	39	27
I spend nearly all of my money on the basic necessities of life	69	64	62	46	35	33	19

SOURCE: Author's calculations from Merck Family Fund poll (February 1995).

chasing behavior. It analyzes how standards of belonging socially have changed in recent decades, and how this change has introduced Americans to highly intensified spending pressures.

And finally, it is about a growing backlash to the consumption culture, a movement of people who are downshifting—by working less, earning less, and living their consumer lives much more deliberately.

Spending and Social Comparison

I am hardly the first person to have argued that consumption has a comparative, or even competitive character. Ideas of this sort have a long history within economics, sociology, and other disciplines. In *The Wealth of Nations,* Adam Smith observed that even a "creditable day-laborer would be ashamed to appear in publick without a linen shirt" and that leather shoes had become a "necessary of life" in eighteenth-century England. The most influential work on the subject, however, has been Thorstein Veblen's *Theory of the Leisure Class.* Veblen argued that in affluent societies, spending becomes the vehicle through which people establish social position. The conspicuous display of wealth and leisure is the marker that reveals a man's income to the outside world. (Wives, by the way, were seen by Veblen as largely ornamental, useful to display a man's finest purchases—clothes, furs, and jewels.) The rich spent conspicuously as a kind of personal advertisement, to secure a place in the social hierarchy. Everyone below stood watching and, to the extent possible, emulating those one notch higher. Consumption was a trickle-down process.

The phenomenon that Veblen identified and described, conspicuous consumption by the rich and the nouveaux riches, was not new even in his own time. Spending to establish a social position has a long history. Seventeenth- and eighteenth-century Italian nobles built opulent palaces with beautiful facades and, within those facades, placed tiles engraved with the words *Pro Invidia* (To Be Envied). For centuries, aristocrats passed laws to forbid the nouveaux riches from copying their clothing styles. At the turn of the century, the wealthy published the menus of their dinner parties in the newspapers. And fifty years ago, American social climbers bought fake "ancestor portraits" to hang in their libraries.

Veblen's story made a lot of sense for the upper-crust, turn-of-the-century urban world of his day. But by the 1920s, new developments were afoot. Because productivity and output were growing so rapidly, more and more people had entered the comfortable middle classes and begun to enjoy substantial discretionary spending. And this mass prosperity eventually engendered a new socioeconomic phenomenon—a mass keeping-up process that led to convergence among consumers' acquisition goals and purchasing patterns.

The advent of mass production in the 1920s made possible an outpouring of identical consumer goods that nearly everybody wanted—and were better able to afford, thanks to declining prices. By the fifties, the Smiths had to have the Joneses' fully automatic washing machine, vacuum cleaner, and, most of all, the shiny new Chevrolet parked in the driveway. The story of this period was that people looked to their own neighborhoods for their spending cues, and the neighbors grew more and more alike in what they had. Like compared with like and strove to become even more alike.

This phenomenon was chronicled by James Duesenberry, a Harvard economist writing just after the Second World War. Duesenberry updated Veblen's trickle-down perspective in his classic discussion of "keeping up with the Joneses." In contrast to Veblen's Vanderbilts, Duesenberry's 1950s Joneses were middle-class and they lived next door, in suburban USA. Rather than seeking to best their neighbors, Duesenberry's Smiths mainly wanted to be like them. Although the ad writers urged people to be the first on the block to own a product, the greater fear in most consumers' minds during this period was that if they didn't get cracking, they might be the last to get on board.

In addition to Veblen and Duesenberry, a number of distinguished economists have emphasized these social and comparative processes in their classic accounts of consumer culture—among them, John Kenneth Galbraith, Fred Hirsch, Tibor Scitovsky, Richard Easterlin, Amartya Sen, Clair Brown, and Robert Frank. Among the most important of their messages is that consumer satisfaction, and dissatisfaction, depend less on what a person has in an absolute sense than on socially formed aspirations and expectations. Indeed, the very term "standard of living" suggests the point: the standard is a social norm.

By the 1970s, social trends were once again altering the nature of comparative consumption. Most obvious was the entrance of large numbers of married women into the labor force. As the workplace replaced the coffee klatch and the backyard barbecue as locations of social contact, workplace conversation became a source for information on who went where for vacation, who was having a deck put on the house, and whether the kids were going to dance class, summer camp, or karate lessons. But in the workplace, most employees are exposed to the spending habits of people across a wider economic spectrum, particularly those employees who work in white-collar settings. They have meetings with people who wear expensive suits or "real" Swiss watches. They may work with their boss, or their boss's boss, every day and find out a lot about what they and their families have.

There were also ripple effects on women who didn't have jobs. When many people lived in one-earner households, incomes throughout the neighborhood tended to be close to each other. As many families earned two paychecks, however, mothers who stayed at home or worked part-time found themselves competing with neighbors who could much more easily afford pricey restaurants, piano lessons, and two new cars. Finally, as Robert Frank and Philip Cook have argued, there has been a shift to a "winner-take-all" society: rewards within occupations have become more unequally distributed. As a group of extremely high earners emerged within occupation after occupation, they provided a visible, and very elevated, point of comparison for those who weren't capturing a disproportionate share of the earnings of the group.

Daily exposure to an economically diverse set of people is one reason Americans began engaging in more upward comparison. A shift in advertising patterns is another. Traditionally advertisers had targeted their market by earnings, using one medium or another depending on the income group they were trying to reach. They still do this. But now the huge audiences delivered by television make it the best medium for reaching just about *every* financial group. While *Forbes* readers have a much higher median income than television viewers, it's possible to reach more wealthy people on television than in the pages of any magazine, no matter how targeted its readership. A major sports event or an *ER* episode is likely to deliver more millionaires *and* more laborers than a medium aimed solely at either group. That's why you'll find ads for Lincoln town cars, Mercedes-Benz sports cars, and $50,000 all-terrain vehicles on the Super Bowl telecast. In the process, painters who earn $25,000 a year are being exposed to buying pressures never intended for them, and middle-class housewives look at products once found only in the homes of the wealthy.

Beginning in the 1970s, expert observers were declaring the death of the "belonging" process that had driven much competitive consumption and arguing that the establishment of an individual identity— rather than staying current with the Joneses—was becoming the name of the game. The new trend was to consume in a personal style, with products that signaled your individuality, your personal sense of taste and distinction. But, of course, you had to be different in the right way. The trick was to create a unique image through what you had and wore—and what you did not have and would not be seen dead in.

While the observers had identified a new stage in consumer culture, they were right only to a point. People may no longer have wanted to be just like all others in their socioeconomic class, but their need to measure up within some idealized group survived. What emerged as the new standards of comparison, however, were groups that had no direct counterparts in previous times. Marketers call them clusters—groups of people who share values, orientations, and, most important, *lifestyles*. Clusters are much smaller than traditional horizontal economic strata or classes and can thereby satisfy the need for greater individuality in consumption patterns. "Yuppie" was only the most notorious of these lifestyle cluster groups. There are also middle Americans, twenty-somethings, upscale urban Asians, top one-percenters, and senior sun-seekers. We have radical feminists, comfortable capitalists, young market lions, environmentalists. Whatever.

Ironically, the shift to individuality produced its own brand of localized conformity. (In chapter 2, I discuss just how detailed a profile of spending habits marketers can now produce within a cluster.) Apparently lots of people began wanting the same "individual identity-creating" products. But this predictability, while perhaps a bit absurd, brought with it no *particular* financial problem. Seventies consumerism was manageable. The real problems started in the 1980s as an economic shift sent seismic shocks through the nation's consumer mentality. Competitive spending intensified. In a very big way.

The Intensification of Competitive Consumption: Feeling Poor When Spending Is Rising

Throughout the 1980s and 1990s, most middle-class Americans were acquiring at a greater rate than any previous generation of the middle class. And their buying was more upscale. By the end of the 1990s, the familiar elements of the American dream (a little suburban house with a white picket fence, two cars, and an annual vacation) have expanded greatly. The size of houses has doubled in less than fifty years, there are more second homes, automobiles have become increasingly option-packed, middle-income Americans are doing more pleasure and vacation travel, and expenditures on recreation have more than doubled since 1980. Over time new items have entered the middle-class lifestyle: a personal computer, education for the children at a private college, maybe even a private school, designer clothes, a microwave, restaurant meals, home and automobile air conditioning, and, of course, Michael Jordan's ubiquitous athletic shoes, about which children and adults both display near-obsession. At a minimum, the average person's spending increased 30 percent between 1979 and 1995. At a maximum, calculated by taking into account a possible bias in the consumer price index, the increase was more than twice that, or about 70 percent.

Yet, by the midnineties, America was decidedly anxious. Many households felt pessimistic, deprived, or stuck, apparently more concerned with what they could not afford than with what they already had. Definitions of the "good life" and even of "the necessities of life" continued to expand, even as people worried about how they could pay for them. What was going on? The economic trend was a diverging income distribution. The sociological trend was the upward shift in consumer aspirations and the vertical stretching out of reference groups. They collided to produce a period of consumer anxiety, frustration, and dissatisfaction.

The growth of inequality dates back to the 1970s, the beginning of a phenomenal rise in the earnings of the rich and very rich. Between 1979 and 1989, the top 1 percent of households increased their incomes from an average of about $280,000 a year to $525,000. (They got a big tax break from Reagan, benefited from trends in financial markets, and wrote themselves bigger paychecks.) In terms of wealth, they did even better comparatively, boosting their share of the nation's financial wealth to just under one-half.

The so-called decade of greed was off and running. The rich and super-rich took conspicuous consumption to new levels, buying Lexuses, Rolexes, Montblanc pens, designer outfits, and art collections. These visible public excesses reverberated through the upper part of the upper-middle class, which calibrates its success by the Newport set. To compensate for the growing chasm between their lifestyles and those of the rich and famous, these upper-middles also began conspicuously acquiring the luxury symbols of the 1980s— buying the high-prestige watches and pens, looking for "puro lino" labels, and leasing luxury vehicles they often couldn't afford. "Feeling poor on $100,000 a year" articles began appearing in the press.

That might have been that. But the upper-middle group is special. It became the new focal point. The new consumerism made it so, by orienting aspirations upward in ways I have already described.

By upper-middle-class I mean roughly the top 20 percent of households, with the exclusion of the top few percent. In 1994 the lower-income cutoff for this group was about $72,000 a year, and its midpoint $91,000. The top 5 percent of this group—which includes the super-rich—earned on average $254,000. The standard of living of this upper-middle is now widely watched and emulated. It is the group that defines material success, luxury, and comfort for nearly every category below it. It is the visible lifestyle to which most aspiring Americans aspire. Even people earning far less now look up to the lifestyle of the brother-in-law who's a VP and lives in a gated community, the friends with a center entrance colonial or, if their tastes run to the urban, a luxury apartment in a prewar doorman building in Manhattan or in Boston's Back Bay. The average American is now more likely to compare his or her income to the six-figure benchmark in the office down the corridor or displayed in Tuesday evening prime time. (Even in a relatively affordable town like Seattle, Frasier's apartment—and view—must cost a bundle.)

And these aspirations play themselves out in the retail sector: the furnishings, attire, and lifestyle accessories of the upper 20 percent are the prototypes for the less expensive versions found at Macy's, Sears, WalMart, and K-Mart. (That's what K-Mart's partnership with Martha Stewart is all about.) Pottery Barn is similar to Williams-Sonoma. Pier 1 looks a lot like Bloomingdale's. Ditto Land's End and Brooks Brothers. Designers create lower-priced lines that are still far more expensive than the no-names.

By 1991 almost everybody was gazing at the top of the pyramid. According to a study by marketing professor Susan Fournier, now of Harvard Business School, and her former colleague at the University of Florida, Michael Guiry, more than one-third (35 percent) of their sample of consumers reported that they would someday like to be a member of the "really made it" group, a category they identified as representing the top 6 percent of American society. (Average income for this top group is about $250,000 a year.) Half the sample (49 percent) identified the "doing very well" group as their aspirational standard, a designation that referred to the next 12 percent of households. Taken together, 85 percent aspired to be in the top 18 percent of American households. Only 15 percent would be satisfied by "living a comfortable life" or something less. Only 15 percent would be satisfied ending up as middle-class.

But keeping up with that top quintile is not easy, because they keep getting richer—considerably richer than the four-fifths of the country that watches them. Between 1979 and 1994, families in the top 20 percent increased their share of income from 42 percent to 46 percent. Excluding the top 5 percent of that group (in other words, looking only at families in the 80–95 percent range) the rise was from 26 percent to 27 percent. And the share of income for every group beneath them fell. So four-fifths of Americans were relegated to earning *even less* than the people they looked up to, who were now earning and spending more. And something similar happened within the bottom 80 percent. The top half did much better than the bottom half, whose comparative (and absolute) position went to hell in a handbasket. As the ordinary middle class got farther from that four-bedroom colonial or the designer loft in San Francisco, the lower-middle and working classes fell even farther behind, their dream of owning any kind of home fading into the far-distant future. As the middle classes started keeping their cars a bit longer, the working class started having theirs repossessed. All down the line, the gaps between the groups got larger and larger. And the hopes of many to participate in the new consumer economy were replaced by a daily struggle to survive.

By 1996 only one in four believed that the standard of living would rise in the next five years. Nearly half the population felt that their children's generation would not enjoy a higher standard of living than their own. The middle class was shrinking, companies were downsizing at a manic rate, economic pessimism and job anxiety abounded. Per capita consumption *was* rising. But consumers' expectations were rising even faster.

Unfortunately the government doesn't collect systematic data on "the American dream and its upscaling." But there is evidence of a sharp escalation over this period. In 1986 the Roper polling organization asked Americans how much income they would need to fulfill all their dreams. The answer was $50,000. *By 1994 the "dreams-fulfilling" level of income had doubled, from $50,000 to $102,000.* Upscaling had definitely taken hold. Of course, $102,000 is not everyone's dream. In a consumption system premised on differences, dreams will also differ. And predictably, the higher one's income, the more one must have to feel fulfilled. Those making more than $50,000 said they would need $200,000 for total fulfillment, while lower-income people calculated that they would need only about $88,000 a year.

Other surveys also indicate an expansion of desire and expectation. Asked what constitutes "the good life," people in 1991 focused far more on material goods and luxuries than they did in 1975. Items more likely to be part of the good life now than then include a vacation home, a swimming pool, a color TV, a second color TV, travel abroad, nice clothes, a car, a second car, a home of one's own, a job that pays much more than the average, and a lot of money. Less likely, or no more likely, to yield the good life, according to respondents, were a happy marriage, one or more children, an interesting job, and a job that contributes to the welfare of society. Not surprisingly, by 1991 far fewer Americans thought they had a "very good" chance of achieving the good life.

TABLE 1.2 Making Americans' Dreams Come True

Question: *How much income per year would you say you (and your family) need to fulfill all of your dreams?*

	MEDIAN RESPONSE
1987	$50,000
1989	$75,000
1991	$83,800
1994	$102,000
1996	$90,000

SOURCE: Roper Center, University of Connecticut. 1987–91 figures reported in *American Enterprise* (May–June 1993), p.86; 1994 figure from Crispell (1994); 1996 figure is directly from Roper.

Americans' concept of need has also clearly changed. Data from 1973, 1991, and 1996 reveal that a variety of consumer items are seen as necessities by an increasing number of people. About one-quarter of Americans consider home computers and answering machines to be necessities, one-third feel the same way about microwaves, more than 40 percent can't do without auto air conditioning, and just over half say home air conditioning is essential. VCRs and basic cable, which weren't included in the 1975 survey, are necessities to 13 and 17 percent of the nation's consumers. The list of things we absolutely have to have is growing. (Interestingly, one product Americans are less likely to see as necessary in the 1990s is television, perhaps because substitutes have emerged.)

Throughout the nineties, the moving target of the top 20 percent has continued to move. A mere car now carries a slightly downscale image, as people shift to sport utility vehicles. The trend includes urban spas, personal trainers, limousine rides, fancy computer equipment, "professional-quality" everything—from cookware to sports equipment—and, perhaps most strikingly of all, the "trophy" house, or McMansion. These showy dwellings, which range from four thousand to twenty-five thousand square feet, are proliferating around the country. In older suburbs, an existing house will be razed to make way for a larger one. Outside Boston, in affluent Wellesley, the median size of a new home rose from twenty-nine hundred to thirty-five hundred square feet between 1986 and 1996, and the number of *really* big houses (more than four thousand square feet) quadrupled. Inside McMansion? A range of amenities now considered de rigeur for affluent families—granite countertops in the kitchen, Jacuzzi, media room or fitness center, enlarged kitchen and family room areas, a three- or four-car garage, sometimes even a home office and au pair suite. And, of course, bathrooms. Lots of bathrooms.

TABLE 1.3   The Good Life Goes Upscale

Percentage Identifying Item As a Part of "The Good Life"

	1975	1991
Vacation home	19	35
Swimming pool	14	29
Color TV	46	55
Second color TV	10	28
Travel abroad	30	39
Really nice clothes	36	44
Car	71	75
Second car	30	41
Home you own	85	87
A lot of money	38	55
A job that pays much more than average	45	60
Happy marriage	84	77
One or more children	74	73
Interesting job	69	63
Job that contributes to the welfare of society	38	38
Percentage who think they have a very good chance of achieving the "good life"	35	23

SOURCE: Roper Center, University of Connecticut; published in *American Enterprise* (May–June 1993), p. 87.

It seems that "needs" have been upscaled disproportionately among those with more money. In my survey at "Telecom," among those who reported dissatisfaction with their incomes, the more they made, the greater the additional amount needed to reach satisfaction. In the $75,000+ household income category, nearly two-thirds said they'd need an increase of 50 to 100 percent in their annual incomes to reach satisfaction, while fewer than 20 percent of those making $30,000 or less would need that much.

Focus groups and interviews with consumers also reveal the upscaling process. Here's downshifter Jennifer Lawson: "In the fifties, grow-

Table 1.4 The Expanding Definition of "Necessities"

Percentage Indicating Item Is a Necessity

	1973	1991	1996
Second television	3	15	10
Dishwasher	10	24	13
VCR	— *	18	13
Basic cable service	—	26	17
Remote control for TV or VCR	—	23	—
Answering machine	—	20	26
Home computer	—	11	26
Microwave	—	44	32
Second automobile	20	27	37
Auto air conditioning	13	42	41
Home air conditioning	26	47	51
Television	57	74	59
Clothes dryer	54	74	62
Clothes washer	88	82	86
Automobile	90	85	93
Cellular phone	—	5	—
Housekeeper	—	4	—

*Item did not exist, was not widely in use, or was not asked about in 1973.
SOURCE: Roper Center, University of Connecticut; 1973 and 1991 data published in *American Enterprise* (May–June 1993), p. 89.

ing up in upstate New York, my parents were considered middle-class pillars of the community. My father was an accountant. It's a fairly poor rural area, and most people worked in a factory or waitressed or something. My dad was actually a professional person with a sign out in front. [My parents] had one car, and they drove it until it fell apart, and then they bought a new one, usually a station wagon. They had a fairly modest house. We took a vacation as a family for two weeks and rented a little cabin in Maine. And drove—nobody flew anywhere. I can't remember anyone who had a second car. Everyone walked everywhere; children certainly didn't have $100 sneakers. It amazes me now that my younger brother, who still lives there and who has a job that's roughly equal to the job my dad had when I was growing up . . . he has three teenage daughters. And since they were about nine, they've each had their own color TV, and they have their own CD players, they all have their own telephone lines, because they complain about calls not being able to get through."

A Merck Family Fund focus-group participant seems less judgmental: "I used to think of the American dream as the house with the little picket fence and the two-car garage, two kids, and a dog and a cat. If you look at the old *Beaver* or the old movies, the family movies, they didn't show these huge mansions." What's different now? "Just the whole thing of 'more.' I'm not saying that's bad, and I'm not saying I'm not in that category. I'm just saying that the American dream has . . . I think it's expanding."

Thus, the competitive upscale consumption that began in the 1980s, with the attendant expansion of the American dream, wasn't invented by Nancy Reagan and it wasn't a cultural accident. It was created by the escalating lifestyles of the most affluent and the need that many others felt to meet that standard, irrespective of their financial ability to maintain such a lifestyle. If you missed the upscaling in your own neighborhood and workplace or at the mall, you could watch it on TV. *Dallas, L.A. Law,* and *Beverly Hills 90210* ascended to the television norm, while the appeal of Roseanne's working-class life came out of its uniqueness on television. The story of the eighties and nineties is that millions of Americans ended the period having more but feeling poorer. Nearly all the pundits missed this dynamic, recognizing only the income trends *or* the spending increases.

But is consumption really a competitive process? If you're like many, you don't necessarily experience it in this way. (On the other hand, if you've organized a birthday party for middle- or upper-middle-class children lately, you probably do.) A full answer to this question awaits in chapters 2 through 4, but one point is worth making here. American consumers are often not conscious of being motivated by social status and are far more likely to attribute such motives to others than to themselves. We live with high levels of psychological denial about the connection between our buying habits and the social statements they make.

Most Americans would deny that, by their spending, they are seeking status, in the usual meaning of the word—looking to position themselves in a higher economic stratum. They might point out that they don't want everything in sight, that purchases are often highly selective. Indeed, what stands out about much of the recent spate of spending is its *defensive* character. Parents worry that their children need computers and degrees from good colleges to avoid being left behind in the global economy. Children, concerned about being left out in the here and now, demand shoes, clothes, and video games. (As Jennifer Lawson said of her teenage nieces, without the right sweatshirts and jeans they will be "ruined in school.") Increasingly overworked, adults need stress-busting weekends, microwaves, restaurant meals, and takeout to keep up with their daily lives. But the cost of each of these conveniences adds up.

The Quality-of-Life Squeeze

Not surprisingly, as upscale competitive consumption intensified, family finances deteriorated. One indicator is the rise of consumer borrowing and credit card spending: through the 1990s, households have been taking on debt at record levels. And the largest increases have been not among low-income households, but among those earning $50,000 to $100,000 a year. (Sixty-three percent of these households are now in credit card debt.) Debt service as a percentage of disposable income now stands at 18 percent, even higher than during the early 1990s recession. Another indicator is the rise in worktime: average hours of work have risen about 10 percent in the last twenty-five years. To finance their lifestyles, millions of families also sent a second earner into the workplace, but this created a squeeze on household work and family time. Despite working all these hours, somewhere between a quarter and 30 percent of households live paycheck to paycheck. With the margin of error so thin, it is not surprising that personal bankruptcies are at historic levels.

The national savings rate has also plummeted. The average American household is currently saving only 3.5 percent of its disposable income, about half the rate of a decade and a half ago, before spending pressures began to intensify. In 1995 only 55 percent of all American households indicated they had done any saving at all in the previous year. (This figure has fallen, despite the expansion of the economy.) The French, Germans, Japanese, and Italians save roughly three times what Americans do, and the British and Dutch more than twice. Even Indian and Chinese households, most of which are dirt poor, manage to save about a quarter of their paltry yearly incomes.

As a result of low household savings, a substantial fraction of Americans live without an adequate financial cushion. In 1995 the median value of household financial assets was a mere $9,950. By 1997, well into the stock market boom, nearly 40 percent of all baby boomers had less than $10,000 saved for retirement. Indeed, 60 percent of families have so little in the way of financial reserve that they can only sustain their lifestyles for about a month if they lose their jobs. The next richest 20 percent can only hold out for three and a half months.

What is perhaps most striking is the extent to which upscaling has undermined savings among the nation's *better-off* households. In 1995 one-third of families whose heads were college-educated did no saving. The vast majority of Americans say they *could* save more but report themselves unwilling to cut back on what one study calls "the new essentials." (This unwillingness also appears to be increasing over time.)

Thus, the new consumerism has led to a kind of mass "overspending" within the middle class. By this I mean that large numbers of Americans spend more than they say they would like to, and more than they have. That they spend more than they realize they are spending, and more than is fiscally prudent. And that they spend in ways that are collectively, if not individually, self-defeating. Over-spending is how ordinary Americans cope with the everyday pressures of the new consumerism.

The intensification of competitive spending has affected more than family finances. There is also a boomerang effect on the public purse and collective consumption. As the pressures on private spending have escalated, support for public goods, and for paying taxes, has eroded. Education, social services, public safety, recreation, and culture are being squeezed. The deterioration of public goods then adds even more pressure to spend privately. People respond to inadequate public services by enrolling their children in private schools, buying security systems, and spending time at Discovery Zone rather than the local playground. These personal financial pressures have also reduced many Americans' willingness to support transfer programs to the poor and near-poor. Coupled with dramatic declines in the earning power of these latter groups, the result has been a substantial increase in poverty, the deterioration of poor neighborhoods, and alarming levels of crime and drug use. People with money try to spend their way around these problems. But that is no solution for these social ills.

One problem with the national discourse is its focus on market exchanges, not quality of life, or social health. Gross domestic product is the god to which we pray. But GDP is an increasingly poor measure of well-being: it fails to factor in pollution, parental time with children, the strength of the nation's social fabric, or the chance of being mugged while walking down the street. The genuine progress indicator, an admittedly crude but relatively comprehensive measure of the quality of life, has increasingly diverged from GDP since 1973, and negatively. The index of social health, another alternative measure, has also declined dramatically since 1976, remaining at record lows through the 1990s. When we count not only our incomes but also trends in free time, public safety, environmental quality, income distribution, teen suicides, and child abuse, we find that things have been getting worse for more than twenty years, even though consumption has been rising.

Jumping off the Bandwagon: Voluntary Downshifters

Of course, not everyone is going along with the new consumerism. Or not forever. The pressures for upscale consumption, and the work schedules that go along with it, created millions of exhausted, stressed-out people who started wondering if the cycle of work and spend was really worth it. And some concluded that it wasn't. So they started downshifting, reducing their hours of work and, in the process, earning and spending less money.

Downshifters are opting out of excessive consumerism, choosing to have more leisure and balance in their schedules, a slower pace of life, more time with their kids, more meaningful work, and daily lives that line up squarely with their deepest values. These are not just fast-track yuppies leaving $200,000 jobs in Manhattan to settle in Montana, although there are plenty of those. Downshifters can be found at all income levels, from the comfortable suburbanites whose homes are paid for, to those who are counting every penny, resigned to the fact that they'll never own a home. Their jobs were leaving them drained, depressed, or wondering what life is all about. Now they may not have as much money, but they are spending every day answering that all-important question. And they are much happier. Other downshifters were compulsive shoppers, mired in credit card debt with little of value to show for it, or caught up in competitive consumption that had spiraled way above what their means could support. Some are kids, just out of college, farsighted enough to avoid the blind alleys taken by older siblings or parents.

Downshifters are making a wide variety of work-life changes to bring what they do into synch with who they are. Many are switching careers. Others are going to part-time work, starting home-based businesses, or stopping work altogether to raise their kids. The price for doing what they want: they earn less money. For downshifters from the middle class and below, this usually means big changes. They don't shop much, they make more of what they need themselves, and they spend less money in the world of commodified leisure. Their birthday parties don't have magicians or clowns; the kids play pin-the-tail-on-the-donkey and fish for coins in the bathtub. They go to an in-state camping site instead of Saint Maarten. They drive a seven-year-old car or maybe take the bus to work. Their patronage of restaurants drops off precipitously. They stop going to first-run movies. But for virtually all of them, these changes are worth it.

There's been a lot of media coverage of downshifting, ranging from the accurate to the hyperbolic, including a rash of stories about how women are rushing home in droves to be with kids. (I find that downshifters are no more likely to be women than men, by the way.) What most of the downshifting stories lack is data. Until this point, our knowledge of this trend has been mainly anecdotal. In chapter 5, I report on a nationwide survey of downshifters I have conducted.

Of course, this is not the first such movement in our history. We have had Quakers, Shakers, transcendentalists, and hippies. But these were small, ideologically coherent groups. And these movements have been much more self-consciously anticonsumerist than most of today's downshifters. What's different about downshifters is that they are not dropping out. They're not back-to-the-land types. They don't live together. And they don't share a religion. They don't proscribe all modern acquisitions as part of a system of belief. By job category, they're actually quite mainstream—nurses and salespeople, teachers and managers. They're urban and suburban. They may well be the next-door Joneses we've been keeping up with all these years. And they represent a striking countertrend to the ideology that has dominated America since European settlement—that of moving up, bettering oneself, rising in the social order.

Most important, downshifting brings one's lifestyle into correspondence with one's values. And downshifting is happening because millions of Americans are recognizing that in fact their lives are no longer in synch with their values, either because they have no time for what they care about most (their children, their families, their communities, or their personal development), because they can't believe in the work they are doing, or because the money and the consumption-identity link has started to seem meaningless. For these reasons, downshifting often involves soul-searching and a coming to consciousness about a life that may well have been on automatic pilot.

Beyond the Culture of Consumerism

There is accumulating evidence that Americans are growing uneasy with the new consumerism. Surveys show that many believe materialism is ruining the country, perverting our values, and damaging our children. We yearn for what we see as a simpler time, when people cared less about money and more about each other. After drugs and crime, people see materialism as the most serious problem affecting American families. In a recent book, the Princeton sociologist Robert Wuthnow argues that we are ambivalent about money. On the one hand, we want it, are strongly committed to success and achievement (it has been said that it is how America keeps score), and believe in hard work. At the same time, we hold the contradictory view that money is profane, polluted, even evil. Talking about how much we have, or make, is taboo. Doing something for money seems dirty in a way that doing it for love, personal fulfillment, or social commitment is not.

Yet our discomfort with money and materialism is hard to pin down, in part because consumerism as a way of life is so ingrained it's hard to recognize within us and around us. It is, in the now-famous words of George Orwell, "the air we breathe." Like air, it's everywhere, we're dependent on it, and perhaps most important, until it's really dirty, it cannot be seen. We experience consumer society as something natural. But it's not. As a growing number of historians have shown, the culture we live in today was *created*. Consumer capitalism did not triumph without opposition, but triumph it did. One measure is that by the 1990s, college students reportedly relate far more to commercials and advertising culture than they do to history, literature, or probably anything else. As James Twitchell of the University of Florida argues, "adcult" now *is* our culture.

I do not raise this point to suggest that change is not possible. Certainly it is. But the first step toward transforming America's consumer culture is to understand it better. I wrote this book in part as a reflection on the thousand and one ways our daily lives, and indeed our very identities, are structured and regulated by acts of spending. Because that, more than anything, is the first step to understanding why so many of us have become overspent Americans.

Communicating with Commodities: How What We Buy Speaks Volumes

"If you're a certain income, you're supposed to look a certain way, you're supposed to be a certain way. You're supposed to be in a class system based on your income."

SUSAN ANDREWS, A STRUGGLING DOWNSHIFTER

To understand consumer desire, we need to start with what attracts. And what repels. No matter how upscale our desires, a tour through a Newport mansion does not lead most of us to covet a twenty-five-thousand-square-foot home, with marble floors and gilt-edged mirrors. Nor does a museum visit cause us to want to buy a Van Gogh or a Rothko, no matter how beautiful we may find them. At the other extreme, when an upscale housewife drops in to K-Mart to pick up a mop and paper towels, she is unlikely to be tempted by the clothes, furniture, and home furnishings she finds on display. *Lack* of desire, like desire, is also a social construct.

What, then, compels us to consume? Traditionally, consumer desires have been prompted by exposure to the possessions and lifestyles of a reference group—a comparison group located nearby in the social hierarchy. In a now-classic treatment, Leon Festinger makes the point: we gravitate to "situations where others are close [in] both abilities and opinions," and we are less attracted to "situations where others are very divergent." The salience of proximity in making comparisons is important for understanding the new consumerism precisely because it is breaking down. But that gets us ahead of the story.

Reference groups exist because we are social beings. Each of us has a gender, race, and ethnicity, an economic class and occupation, an age, a religion. We are members of a type of family, and we hold political views and cultural values. We construct our personal identity in relation to these social groups, thereby creating a social identity. Even those of us who shun our associations with these identities can be fitted into a category of similar individualists. At the broadest level, the related variables of class, education, income, occupation, and gender matter most in determining a reference group. Of course, the reference group is a mental category, a comparison concept a person carries around in his or her head, not something we can measure directly. What we *can* measure is the extent to which individuals conform to the consumer patterns of the objectively defined groups they belong to. And by this measure, variables such as social class, occupation, education, and income tell us a great deal. This is a central feature of American consumer life: what people spend both reflects social inequalities and helps to reproduce and even create those distinctions. In a very basic sense, we are what we wear, drive, and live in.

The Social Patterning of Consumption: Creating Distinctions

In his pathbreaking book *Distinction: A Social Critique of the Judgement of Taste*, the French sociologist Pierre Bourdieu found striking regularity in French consumer patterns in the 1960s and 1970s. Not only could one predict the obvious, like the prevalence of consumer durables by economic class, but Bourdieu discovered that a person's educational level and father's occupation revealed much about that individual's taste in music and art, what kinds of shops they patronized, and the type of cooking they did. Working-class people were far more likely to prefer light classical, such as Strauss's "Blue Danube Waltz"; the middle classes went for "Rhapsody in Blue," and the rich chose "Art of the Fugue" and "The Well-Tempered Clavier." In painting, only the wealthy appreciated Brueghel and Goya; the middle went for Buffet; and popular taste preferred Raphael. Working-class people bought their furniture at department stores or furniture shops, while social climbers scoured flea markets and the upper classes frequented "antique" shops and auctions. Modes of decoration also differed—from cozy and warm for workers to imaginative, sober, and discreet, moving up the social scale. The rich cooked exotic, the middle class inclined to "simple, but well presented," and potluck was most common among working-class families.

What accounts for these regularities? While we would expect patterns of product ownership to be partly, even largely, determined by income, money itself cannot account for the fact that preferences in music or furniture style vary by class. Something else is going on. Part of that something else is a quest for social position. Bourdieu contends that we should think of consumption as a "field" (of battle perhaps) and that "taste" is a weapon. Thus, contrary to our conscious experience of consumer preferences and tastes as something that's just *us,* what we like (and dislike) is socially produced, in part by inequalities of class. (See, for example, Bourdieu's chapter 4, "The Dynamics of the Fields.")

In the consumption field, taste is created through what Bourdieu calls cultural capital (measured by education and the family socialization process). People from families rich in cultural capital assimilate knowledge of what good and bad taste is. They are trained to appreciate fine art and music, to like certain foods, to understand complicated art forms. In this way, a systematic hierarchy of tastes has emerged, associated with cultural capital and status. Legitimate, or highbrow, taste is what those rich in cultural capital prefer; the great middling classes are associated with middlebrow culture (knock-offs of the high stuff); and the masses are into popular culture. While not everyone aspires to the tastes of the highbrows, nearly everyone accepts the basic ordering: few claim that sitcoms are great art or that Neil Diamond produces brilliant music. While Bourdieu identifies the objective economic and social variables that predict taste, he also believes that individual tastes vary depending on personal experience, or what he calls *habitus.* The habitus is a habitual condition, set of social conditionings, or "open set of dispositions." It is the mental schema that individuals use to process subjectively the objective world around them. Through the habitus, socially produced tastes become what we experience as natural, personal, and individualized (just what we are). (See Bourdieu, page 101, on habitus.)

Taste therefore ceases to be a personally and socially innocent category. Almost everyone who has interacted with persons rich in cultural capital has had at least one distressing experience that revealed their own deficiencies in taste: serving the wrong foods, dressing improperly, not knowing an artist or an author, expressing a poor opinion. Taste also has economic ramifications. You can blow a job interview by exhibiting improper table manners at lunch, wearing the wrong outfit, or using language inappropriate to the station to which you are aspiring. Cultural capital can be used by those on the higher rungs of the ladder to devalue those below.

Of course, we cannot simply assume that Bourdieu's findings from 1960s and 1970s France are relevant to America in the 1990s. The France of that period was a far more homogeneous nation, with a finely tracked education system and less fluidity across economic classes. Furthermore, research on some categories of American consumption (for example, art) suggests that class differences are not as great as one might expect from Bourdieu's perspective. On the other hand, it will surprise no one that the sociologist Michèle Lamont and her coauthors found that higher-income Americans are still more likely to watch PBS, to go to art museums, and to attend classical music concerts. Richard Peterson and Albert Simkus found that a prestige index of musical tastes still correlates well with an index of occupational prestige, as does attendance at concerts, museums, plays, shows, dance, and opera. (They also found, by the way, pure status effects—groups low in cultural capital attend prestige concerts even though they do not particularly *like* that type of music.) Studies of museums have found that both attendance and how museum-goers "do" a museum are heavily skewed by social class.

But even conceding the real differences between France of the 1960s and 1970s and the United States of today, a wide range of data suggests the continuing relevance of a central tenet of Bourdieu's story: consumption patterns and tastes are stratified by socioeconomic categories such as class, education, and occupation. They are a source, as well as an indicator, of social differentiation. If you doubt the point, perform the following thought experiment. If you're upper-middle-class, imagine having to entertain your boss, or an old college friend, in Roseanne's living room. If your social background would lead you to feel comfortable in Roseanne's house, picture having your cousins over to Ann Kelsey and Stewart Markowitz's spacious Tudor. (If you've never heard of Roseanne, Ann Kelsey, or Stewart Markowitz, pat yourself on the back.)

Unfortunately there are no recent, comprehensive, quantitative analyses of U.S. consumption patterns and tastes by social class. At one time, the relationship between consumption and social class was an important scholarly topic, for example, in the classic sociological accounts, such as the Lynds' Middletown studies or W. Lloyd Warner's ethnographies. (Warner found, for example, that the "right kind of house," the "right" neighborhood, and the "right" furniture were among the most important expressions of status position in a community.) But this research is decades old and was often conducted in small-town settings, where face-to-face contact and strong social ties predominated. We know that in the nineteenth century a solid middle-class home could be identified by the presence of a parlor organ, and that in the early twentieth century car ownership was a sure sign of status. In the late 1950s, Vance Packard's witty book *The Status Seekers* was a guide to the ways in which Americans were trying to create "distinction" in the postwar era. Packard describes real estate developers selling snob appeal: to raise sales, write the ad in French, even if it's just a ranch you're selling: "C'est magnifique! Une maison Ranch très originale avec 8 rooms, 2½ baths . . . 2-Cadillac garage . . . $21,990." Packard reports on antique dealers whose clients would "buy a pair of ancestor portraits and, after a few years, find themselves telling people that those ancient people in the portraits are their own great-grandparents." And lest anyone feel too smug about having gone beyond such crude snob appeal, consider the trend toward "gentrification." How many think that they "just love" the details, the turrets, the elegance of Victorian houses? How many stop to think about what gentrification literally means? Namely, creating a gentry—asserting upper-class credentials through ostentation and superfluity. Inside these houses, the fashion is to obliterate the ("tacky") working-class influence (hence, the popularity of internal gutting).

What about now, when the majority have (or can afford) the status symbols of the past? Have new prestige items emerged? Is there still a "right" way to consume in our more anonymous, urbanized, mass media–dominated culture?

In the 1970s, many researchers began concluding that the answer was no. Two influential, but flawed, studies made such a claim, arguing that Chicago-area consumers could no longer even identify the high-status cars, clothing stores, and suburbs. One widely cited article proclaimed "the decline and fall of the status symbol" in our "post-industrial society." Ironically, by the beginning of the 1980s, with its intensification of status consumption, researchers had given up on the idea that social class structured spending. So when Bourdieu's book was translated into English in 1984, no one responded with a comparable study for this country.

While academics had given up on this research, for-profit companies were busy making a bundle using similar concepts. Their surveys told them that class-based consumption was very much alive. But their analyses also showed that, within social classes, members did not all want precisely the same things and certainly did not all favor the same brands, despite the lore of a "standard package" of goods that defined the middle-class dream. So they began to get even more detailed information about each of us, information precise enough to develop highly individualized consumer profiles. Thus, for example, the middle-aged, heterosexual, divorced, Democratic female professional with two children and a degree from an Ivy League college who we find in the personals ads has a particular consumption profile. (She is a likely consumer of this book, for example.) In time, such profiles became so sophisticated that they enabled marketers to predict with a fair amount of accuracy which Americans within each social class would be more likely to buy certain products and even what brands they would favor. (In the process, these marketers also became privy to intimate details of our material lives.)

One market research model that has proved particularly revealing of consumer buying patterns within social classes is based on geographic, or residential, clustering. Why housing? It is far and away the largest expenditure for most American households. If consumption varies systematically by social class, it should certainly show up in housing. Furthermore, if this model is correct, housing-related patterns should be correlated with expenditures for other items—food, clothing, vehicles, consumer durables, and travel. This is exactly what the market researchers have found. Because residential patterns are so segregated by socioeconomic categories, zip codes and even census blocks have proven to be excellent tools for predicting consumer behavior. Within a given zip code or census block, households have a high degree of commonality in educational background, social position, income, and the like. Another way to think about it is that reference groups tend to live together, not so much because people take their neighbors as their standard of comparison anymore, but because they choose homes that fit their incomes, social aspirations, and tastes. (One study found that most people matched their housing choices with who they hoped to be socially, what the author dubbed their "ideal social selves.")

The close connection between housing and social class is revealed by the efforts of homeowner associations to maintain appearances. As Evan McKenzie describes them in *Privatopia: Homeowner Associations and the Rise of Residential Private Government*, these groups regulate minor details of people's lives in order to maintain property values and impart the proper class image to subdivisions and condo developments. Trucks or campers in the driveway, window air-conditioning units, putting out the laundry, loud noise, TV antennas, and rabbit hutches? Forget it. Outlawed by the association. Why? They reek of the lower classes. At the Chartwell homes outside Philadelphia, which sold for $225,000 in the late 1980s, a couple was banned from putting a metal swing set in their yard. It would have to be wood, said the association, because this was the "proper image" for the "overall community." When the parents objected to tasteful wood because of the poisonous chemicals used in the pressure treatment, they were fined.

For marketers, housing patterns have proved so valuable that they are able to use this information to predict how many credit cards you have, which appliances fill your kitchen, where you buy your clothes, and the magazines you read. Here's the broad-brush version of one census-block classification system: "successful suburbanites" drive minivans, own PCs, and spend a lot on home furnishings. "Prosperous baby boomers" have camcorders and four-by-four vehicles, play racquetball or tennis, like making home improvements, and spend a lot on insurance. "Upper-income empty nesters" belong to country clubs, buy "metropolitan" magazines, spend on furniture, and dine out. "Thriving immigrants" have two-door sedans and belong to HMOs. "Low-income city dwellers" spend money on shoes and video rentals. And "middle Americans" (the "megamarket" of all consumer markets) drive pickup trucks and go bowling. (Didn't we know that already. . .)

One of the central tenets of lifestyle cluster systems is that symbolism, as much as function, determines choices. So, for example, two researchers found that what they (rather liberally) defined as a yuppie consumer was more likely than the average person to consume a symbolic constellation of products (Häagen-Dazs ice cream, imported wine, and porcelain cookware), to use an American Express card, to read certain magazines (*Esquire* and *Gourmet*), and to watch certain TV shows (at that time, *Newhart* and *Hill Street Blues*). Recent research by Douglas Holt of the University of Illinois also suggests that it's not only what but *how* we consume that differs by class and social capital. Those with low cultural capital experience a movie emotionally, and those with high cultural capital analyze the screenwriting and directing. The latter are also much more likely to become connoisseurs of products or to participate in national consumer markets.

Of course, the public is well aware of all this effort to find out about them, both from the dinner-hour phone calls and a growing national self-consciousness about "lifestyles." We know the researchers are watching. We've heard of zip-code marketing. Indeed, the codes themselves have become consumption symbols, as in the "02138" T-shirts that dot Harvard Square or the name of the popular television show *Beverly Hills 90210*. Both neighborhoods convey affluent lifestyles and prestige.

Decoding Consumer Meanings

Marketers have developed sophisticated models to interpret the social messages in consumer buying patterns, but what about the rest of us? Can we intuit the social messages underpinning the spending of others? Do we recognize lifestyles as a kind of pseudo-language of social communication, telling us where other people have put or are trying to put themselves on the social map? The broad answer is yes. Research suggests that material goods (and to a lesser extent consumer experiences) are a bit like words: they can be "read" by observers in a process known as decoding.

But first we must ask another question. Who created the code, determining which items would carry what kinds of status? The usual answer looks at deliberate acts of encoding—advertisers' and marketers' attempts to invest social meaning in goods. Sidney Levy's classic article "Symbols for Sale" makes the now-commonplace point that marketers are selling "symbols" as well as products, and that to be successful a businessman must attach the right symbol to his product. A huge literature on brand image is devoted to helping sellers figure out how to position (or symbolize) their product. But symbolic meanings long predate the efforts of contemporary advertisers. In the eighteenth and nineteenth centuries, the meanings of different kinds of carriages were widely understood: people knew how expensive they were, and therefore the status that could be ascribed to their owners. In the twentieth century, the automobile has played a similar role. The structure of use and ownership of products is therefore the underlying foundation of social meaning; class (and other) inequalities are at the foundation of the code. It is difficult (although not impossible) for advertisers to buck our deeply ingrained associations.

This point is controversial. Some observers argue that advertising has become sufficiently powerful to create its own, deep associations, creating, in combination with growing numbers of products, a crowded and chaotic symbolic field, a status "pandemonium." While I believe that's an overstatement, the new view does raise a number of questions. Can Americans decode more than what the advertisers encode? And perhaps most important for our purposes, are they "reading" the class structure of consumption that undergirds the more democratic symbolism of much of American advertising? As with most questions about class and consumption, there's not much contemporary evidence. But the evidence that does exist supports the idea that Americans have historically and still can extract the social messages coded in our product choices.

The data on decoding stretch back to the 1920s, when Stuart Chapin found that social class could be accurately inferred from an inventory of products found in the living room. The Harvard sociologist James Davis found in the 1950s that subjects could clearly distinguish class differences on the basis of photographs of living room interiors. A follow-up on Chapin's work thirty years later found that living rooms continued to vary systematically by social class, attesting to the continuing importance of the front region of the house in "impression management." (This study also confirmed fluidity in the social consumption map and a distinctive style of decor—trendy, modern—among the upwardly mobile groups.) A 1986 study found that respondents could look at a person depicted in front of a house and tell his or her occupational status by the type of house. And a 1997 study of living room interiors also found correlations between style and perceived class and status.

In a series of studies in the 1980s, Russell Belk and his associates looked at houses and automobiles and found that a range of people were able to connect Chevrolet models and sizes and styles of homes with how much money the owner had, his occupation, and how successful he was. Belk also found that observers could predict reasonably well a person's family income and occupation by investigating the contents of his or her purse or wallet. And he found that students could consistently rate a wide variety of products (ranging from clothes to food to electronics equipment) on their connection to social class.

Not surprisingly, children learn the language of symbolic consumption at an early age. Belk and his colleagues found that by second grade, boys and girls could associate different houses and Chevrolet models with owners. In finishing the question "Which of these two cars (houses) is most likely to be owned by a man who . . . ," their strongest social association was ". . . has a lot of money." The children could also differentiate by occupation (doctor versus mailman). Furthermore, children of a higher social class were more conscious of status issues than those from lower classes. The psychologist Helga Dittmar's study of more than one hundred British adolescents from a variety of backgrounds had similar results: the teenagers were able to decode the well-to-do and lower-middle-class settings they were shown in a video and were uniform in their assessments of the socioeconomic status and wealth of the persons shown. (They also reported that the richer persons were more intelligent, successful, educated, and in control.)

While housing is probably the most important symbolic communicator, we are probably more conscious of the role that clothing plays in this regard. Georg Simmel's classic contribution depicts fashion as an ever-shifting process in which high-status individuals attempt to keep a step ahead of low-prestige imitators. Alison Lurie's popular account, *The Language of Clothes*, reminds us of the long history of clothing as an indicator of social position. In ancient Egypt, only those in high positions could wear sandals; in Greece and Rome, even the number of garments a person could wear was prescribed. Throughout the Middle Ages, all manner of dress was regulated. By the eighteenth century, these sumptuary laws were in decline and social position had come to be inferred from the cost of garments, indicated by the type of materials, the extent of unnecessary ornamentation, and the quality of the cut. Such differences persist today, as do other class-based sartorial habits: for instance, wealthier people still tend to wear more garments at a time, be they vests, silk scarves, wraps, or bathing-suit cover-ups.

The infrequency with which people repeat wardrobe choices is another class marker—at a special occasion, to have one's dress remarked on as a repeat is an embarrassment among the better-heeled (note the term, by the way). To wear the same clothes to the office too often is a taboo. Income is also correlated with the possession of special-event clothes, such as formal wear, semiformal wear, and outfits for particular sports or activities, all of which mark the wearer as a high-status person. Lurie illustrates the continuing importance of clothes as social communicators with an anecdote about a journalist friend whose clothes change with the story. When interviewing rich easterners, he chooses the dark-gray Savile Row suit (never new) and an exclusive Cartier watch; among the nouveaux riches, he wears a new suit with flashier accessories, like Italian tassel loafers and monogrammed shirts; in the Washington power corridor, his suit is a few years out of fashion, and his haircut a bit shorter; and in California, he puts a turtleneck under a tweed sport jacket. If his interviewee is rich, he adds the expensive watch. Clearly, this man has learned the lesson that clothes demarcate social groups.

While most of us are not as attuned to clothing differences as Alison Lurie's friend, there is recent evidence that ordinary people can "read" the ways in which clothes reflect social status. The anthropologist Grant McCracken found that experimental subjects readily decoded conventional clothing ensembles, connecting occupation and socioeconomic indicators with the clothes.

The ability to make social interpretations of products continues in the 1990s. In 1993 my student Tracy Tefertiller surveyed a group of middle-class teenagers. Her subjects showed a high degree of knowledge about the fashionableness of brands of clothes, athletic shoes, jeans, and makeup—particularly the more prestigious brands. For example, majorities in the range of 90 percent or more reported that

Levis and clothing from the Gap were "in." Similarly, more than 90 percent of the boys knew LA Gear shoes were "out." With makeup, 78 percent of girls labeled Clinique as "in." Tefertiller also found that these preferences were not locally specific; similar results were found with a national group and a midwestern one. While this research is not a test of decoding per se, it does validate one condition for a system of status markers: common attitudes about the fashionableness of products—a condition that some researchers think has broken down. Teens not only knew what the popular brands were but preferred them. Among the girls, the brand ordering of clothing by how popular they believed it to be (Gap, J. Crew, Limited/Express, Esprit, and Ups and Downs) correlated perfectly with the fraction choosing that brand as their favorite. For boys, Tefertiller found a high degree of consensus about athletic shoes.

Finally, a 1995 study using the PRIZM cluster system supports the idea that people perceive the lifestyle clusters accurately. Bruce Englis and Michael Solomon gave incomplete product profiles of four cluster groups and asked a sample of business students to name products that members of each cluster group would have. They found that the students were relatively accurate and rich in product details about the group they aspired to join; they were accurate, but not detailed, about groups they wanted to avoid or didn't care about; and finally, they allocated products exclusively to one group or another, indicating clear "distinctiveness" between the clusters. Thus, research supports what is probably the commonsense view, expressed well by one social psychologist: "Fine feathers make fine birds ... the *placement* and *evaluation* of other people in terms of their possessions fulfills the important function of orienting us in our social worlds, so that we can form impressions of others and anticipate just how to interact with them."

After encoding and decoding comes social interaction. Researchers have found that what you wear, drive, and own affects how people treat you. In the past, researchers have found that if you delay at a green light, you are less likely to be honked at if you are in a prestige automobile. They have found that if your dress conveys high status, people are more willing to return the dime you "accidentally" left in a phone booth. In experiments, subjects characterize more favorably people pictured in front of upper-middle-class homes than those in front of lower-class homes. And studies have demonstrated what most people know already: the way you dress affects how salespeople treat you, even the price you are asked to pay in some contexts. While some of these studies are dated, there are good reasons to believe that products still affect interpersonal behavior.

Positioned at the Bottom

While spending is certainly a reflection of social distinctions, it does have at least one profoundly egalitarian aspect: just about *everyone* wants in. Desire for Nikes, Evian water, or a BMW can be found at all income levels. Expensive branded goods and designer logos are popular with nearly everyone. In late-twentieth-century America, the culture of desire is pervasive.

In many ways this universality is new. Despite the fact that there have always been individuals who strived for upward mobility, working-class cultures have also historically opposed bourgeois ideals and affirmed nonconsumerist values such as solidarity. At the same time, when class distinctions were more rigidly marked, lower-income groups were less free to consume ostentatiously. (Indeed, this was the premise of centuries of sumptuary laws used by aristocrats to keep the lower orders in their places.) But with more social openness, conspicuous consumption is more acceptable at all income levels. That, of course, is a very good thing. But it has its downside. For many low-income individuals, the lure of consumerism is hard to resist. When the money isn't there, however, feelings of deprivation, personal failure, and deep psychic pain result. In a culture where consuming means so much, not having money is a profound social disability. For parents, faced with the desires of their children, the failure can feel overwhelming.

This is most visible in the poorest neighborhoods. In his ethnographic study of inner-city children in Philadelphia, the historian Carl Husemoller Nightingale describes their need to participate in mainstream consumer culture. The kids Nightingale studied were really poor—they often lived without proper heat, clothes, or even enough food. The status and prestige of consumer products helped them to compensate for their racial and economic exclusion. But unlike middle-class kids, neither they nor their parents had the money for the $100 athletic shoes, Nike sweats, or gold jewelry necessary to be respected socially. On a daily basis, they suffered from having only "bummy rags" to wear to school or from unmet parental promises of Nintendos or sneakers. Dealing drugs was one of the few ways to get the money to buy the stuff. As one young subject of Nightingale's research explained, after he left school and began selling: "I just feel so proud. Out on the corner with your nice clothes, a decent rope around your neck. Nobody can't buss on you or nothing no more."

While television, print, and billboard advertising have played a role in the growth of conspicuous consumption in inner cities, companies have also invaded these neighborhoods with sophisticated street-level marketing, helping to create a social dynamic whose power goes far beyond the ads. Converse began its sneaker promotions in the late 1960s, and by the 1980s Nike had it down to a science, distributing complimentary sportswear and shoes to trend-setting members of the community. By the 1990s, inner-city tastes had become an important driver of middle-class fashion, as reps from hip companies cruised poor neighborhoods looking for "cool" youth and what they were into. In the process, the companies accelerated the fashion cycle and widened the gap between what people feel they have to have and what is affordable. (The street life of a trendy athletic shoe has fallen in some cases to a month and even fifteen days.)

By the 1980s, desperation for various consumer items had become intense, and criminal modes of acquisition had increased. Reported shoplifting offenses rose, from 773,000 in 1980 to 1.2 million in 1994, a 50 percent increase. (While shoplifting is most prevalent among those of limited incomes, police recently apprehended a wealthy Minnesota dentist and his family who had hired a personal shoplifter to filch $250,000 worth of Baccarat, Chanel, and other brand names. The scheme came to light when the family sent him back to the store for the right brand of suits—only Armani would do.) Robbery and even killing for products became commonplace. A rash of "sneaker murders" were committed in major cities. The list of must-have products grew: eyeglasses, leather jackets, gold chains, even Eddie Bauer coats became coveted objects worth stealing and killing for. In some places, the streets became a battleground for a game of "consumer's chicken": only the bravest (or most fool-hardy) dared to flaunt, or even wear desirable possessions.

Meanwhile, outside the inner cities, legal but costly routes to product acquisition also flourished among those with limited incomes. Overtime hours increased, as did rates of second-job hold-ing and credit card usage. Suburban high school students took on jobs and worked longer hours. Never mind falling asleep in class, doing poorly academically, or missing out on extracurriculars. Hav-ing money to spend at the mall had become more important. By the 1990s, the fashion shows enacted daily in school hallways had become so worrisome that calls for uniforms emanated from bully pulpits around the country, including the presidential one. Adults were genuinely stumped about how to get the kids' minds off clothes and into books.

The Complexity of Symbols

To say that a symbolic system exists and that consumers can read it does not imply that it is simple, static, or one-dimensional. It is complex, fluid, and polysemic (or many-meaninged). A key point to keep in mind is that consumers are not passive recipients of sym-bolic associations. They can appropriate the meanings that advertis-ers hope to connect to products, changing them to fit their own lifestyles. It is unlikely that the Bavarian Motor Works intended to have its cars known as Black Man's Wheels, but what consumers do with symbols is not something that Madison Avenue can control. Not only are consumers creative, but advertising is hardly the only source of symbolic meaning. As I noted earlier, a far more important source is the basic structure of tastes and social inequality onto which any ad is projected.

Second, it is important to remember that the symbolic system operates in a more complex fashion than as a trickle from rich down to poor. While most products *do* travel the established path from the top to the bottom, this is not always the case. Products also trickle up or across. Even from the eighteenth century we have examples of workers' clothes providing inspiration for upper-class fashion. Jeans and Doc Marten work boots have followed the same trajectory. Yves St. Laurent went peasant in the 1970s; Chanel has made tons of money selling leather jackets with chains; and thousands of people have paid extra money for shirts with holes in them. Go figure.

We also should not overstate the consumption-as-communication metaphor. As a variety of researchers have pointed out, there are important ways in which material goods are unlike language: they are less flexible, more ambiguous, and context-dependent for their meaning. In semiotic terms, material culture is "undercoded." And as the sociologist Colin Campbell has reminded us, even though products carry well-recognized levels of prestige, are associated with particular kinds of people, or convey widely accepted messages, we cannot automatically infer the motivations of the consumers who buy them. That requires further research.

Finally, I have focused exclusively on the ways in which consumer goods connect to social inequalities, but there are other sources of meaning. Gender, ethnicity, personal predispositions, and many other factors help structure the meanings and motivations attached to consuming. I have taken a rather single-minded focus because the social comparison aspect is salient for the escalation of norms (which we get to in chapter 4), and because it has been relatively neglected in recent research. We need reminding of it.

The Visible Lifestyle:
American Symbols of Status

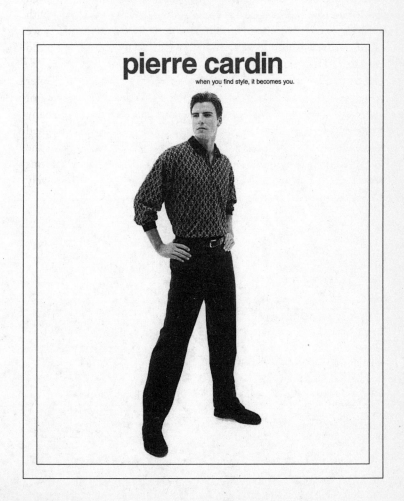

Clothes, cars, wristwatches, living room furniture, and lipsticks are well-known purveyors of social position. Furnaces, mattresses, bedroom curtains, foundation powders, and bank accounts, on the other hand, are not. What separates the items in the first list from those in the second? Where we use them. Competitive spending revolves around a group of socially visible products.

You probably know the type of car a friend drives, whether she wears designer clothes (perhaps even which designers), and how large her house is. What you probably do not know is the kind of furnace in her basement, the brand of mattress she sleeps on, and how much life insurance she has. You're aware of the visible status items, but not the invisibles. Visible products become status goods for an obvious reason: their ownership can be easily verified. What you drive, wear, or have on your wrist is almost instantaneously known by observers. This is not to say that products hidden from view cannot become status items. They can, but we must work to make them so. We need to let others know, either directly or indirectly, what's in the basement, where we ate, or that we went to particular destinations. However, there is always an element of doubt involved: it is far easier for someone to exaggerate the size of his bank account or life insurance policy than to claim to have a Jaguar in the garage, especially if he's usually seen driving a Tercel. We do relay information about our consumption, and this is increasingly important as certain invisibles become new status symbols, a point I return to later. But doing so always carries risks. It must be believable. And it must be subtle. If you tell the people in your office about your fabulous trip to the South of France, you'll need to be careful about that fine line between casually conveying information and boasting; crossing over to the point where you are obviously trying to gain status can undermine the object. One of the features of status games is that trying too hard doesn't work. "Brand name–dropping" carries its own opprobrium.

Of course, social visibility is not something that is purely inherent in goods. Companies expend enormous effort to *make* products identifiable, through branding, packaging, marketing, and advertising. Twenty years ago, who would have thought that Americans would be drinking designer water or wearing underwear with Calvin Klein's name on it. But once people started undressing in front of each other more often (courtesy of the sexual revolution and the popularity of health clubs) and carrying water around in public (courtesy of growing informality in the social space), these products became fair game. The desire to turn invisibles into visibles can also explain why many computers bear a sticker on the outside reading "Pentium inside," or why automobile companies now advertise on the back of the car what's going on under the hood. Ever notice those metal logos indicating that it's a four-wheel drive? Who needs to know? One wonders whether all this free advertising has contributed to the rage for four-wheel-drive vehicles, even in parts of the country that hardly ever get snow. Or consider the large letters printed across the back of Volvos—"Side Impact Protection System." Arguably a visual impediment themselves, they're there because Volvo is trying to "sell" safety. Advertising on the outside of the car can both increase awareness and turn something inside the door into a visible commodity.

The importance of visibility can be seen in the rise of designer logos. In the era when only the rich bought from designers, logos were unnecessary. The number of people involved in the market was small, and participants could not only tell what clothes were designer but identify individual styles. As a larger, middle-class market developed, the fashion industry gained millions of buyers and observers, but ones with little knowledge of the different designer lines and their relative standing. To get her money's worth in terms of status, the middle-class purchaser needed to make sure that others knew what she had bought—hence, the visible logo. By the 1990s, the logo had become essential. According to the designer Tommy Hilfiger: "I can't sell a shirt without a logo. If I put a shirt without a logo on my selling floor next to a shirt with a logo—same shirt, same color, same price—the one with the logo will blow it out. It will sell 10 times over the one without the logo. It's a status thing as well. It really is." And what does a Tommy Hilfiger logo symbolize? Interpreters of the Hilfiger craze have this to say: "These clothes, traditionally associated with a white, upper middle class sporting set, lend kids from backgrounds other than that an air of traditional prestige." "Upper income fashion is about success and that's what people are buying into." The clothes, quite simply, say, "We aspire." By contrast, the most expensive designer clothes carry far fewer outside labels. In haute couture, we never see them. Why should we? These bizarre outfits are immediately recognized as expensive, cutting-edge, and outside the range of ordinary incomes. They are dazzling status markers without the labels.

Research on youth preferences also supports the importance of public visibility. When asked how important a brand name is for a variety of products, teenagers ranked socially visible items, such as sneakers, radios, and CD players, two to three times as important as underwear, shampoo, and stationery. According to Marla Grossberg, director of tracking studies for Teenage Research Unlimited, "The coolest brands are often fashion brands or 'badge items' that kids can wear and relay a message about themselves." And it turns out that many of us are like youth in at least one way—we care a lot about what our peers think of our visible consumption choices. Terry Childers and Akshay Rao found that peer group influence is always higher for visibly consumed products than for those we consume in private. We seek social approval from our friends and coworkers when choosing brands of golf clubs, wristwatches, cars, dresses, and skis, far more than when we choose refrigerators, blankets, or video games.

A whole group of consumer goods that were once neutral symbolically are now highly recognizable—athletic shoes (and athletic equipment more generally), T-shirts (on account of those Gap ads?), bicycles, sunglasses, even a cup of coffee. In the old days, all the coffee shops used the same generic cup. Today everyone in the elevator knows we bought it at Starbucks. Or consider bottled water, for which Americans now spend $2.5 billion a year. It didn't turn designer by accident. As an ad agency executive noted of one aspiring brand, "We wanted to make this the Nike of bottled water." The hallmark of all these products is their history at one time of being mere background, outside the system of fashion and prestige. Now they're in, and noticeable. As a Los Angeles resident recalled about the old days, "You could pretty much fake a coat from K-Mart; usually there's nothing on it." Today, he notes wistfully, the kids "are so aware of what's cool." The extension of brands, and hence visibility, is an important counterweight to other forces that have made decoding more complex and may have arisen partly for just those reasons. The growth of branded middle-class consumption can also be interpreted as evidence that status competition in certain classes of products has become more widespread, with more people participating, around ever more products. So too can the explosion in fake designer goods, the number of which has reportedly more than tripled since 1985. (Of course, brand logos have been around for a long time, even showing up on Chinese pottery during the Han dynasty.)

The expansion to new products has begun to encompass formerly nonvisible expenditures, such as dining out, leisure activities, and tourism. The last (where you went, where you stayed, the restaurants you ate at, what you saw) is increasingly a positional good, thanks in part to the efforts of resort owners, travel agents, and tour operators, but also to consumers' own willingness to get into the game. How to overcome tourism's liability as a status good, the fact that it's an activity performed out of view? Acquire a marker of having been there: a piece of art, a T-shirt, a poster for the wall, pictures, or a video documentary. Souvenirs, high-class or low-, are part of how we make visible the latest not-too-visible status items. The importance of these markers can become almost comical, as research on museums shows. Watching buses pull up to museums, Robert Kelly reports that one-third of the visitors, "upon being discharged from a tour bus . . . entered the museum foyer; searched for and found the museum shop; purchased some object in the museum shop representative of (usually labeled by) the museum or its best-known objects; and then returned to their bus without ever entering the museum galleries." The shop *is* the experience.

A Test of Status Consumption: Women's Cosmetics

A few years ago, a student and I designed a test that can differentiate between consuming with and without a "status" element. We look at buying patterns across products that are similar in most respects but differ in their social visibility. We test to see whether people pay more for products with higher social visibility. The reason: visible goods give status that invisibles do not. For example, we predict that people will spend more money on furnishings for the living room than for the bedroom. Or that they will buy a notch above their usual price range for a coat (the most visible apparel item), or that they are more likely to wear underwear than shirts from WalMart. In tests of this sort, it is important to control for differences in quality and functional requirements. So, in looking at home furnishings, we would compare purchasing patterns for two functionally similar items, such as living room and bedroom curtains. (When discussing this project with a colleague, he reported that he decided not to buy curtains for the bedroom at all, because no one would know they were missing!)

Our test is from women's cosmetics, a multibillion-dollar business. This industry provides a fascinating look into the workings of appearance, illusion, and status. In many ways, the cosmetics companies are not too different from the snake oil peddlers of the nineteenth century. Despite the white coats of the salespeople (to make them look scientific), the hype about company "laboratories," and the promises made in the advertising, it's hard to take the effectiveness claims too seriously. Names like "Eye Repair Diffusion Zone," "Ceramide Time Complex Capsules," and "Extrait Vital, Multi-Active Revitalizer with Apple Alpha-Acids" don't help the products' credibility either.

But despite its dubious effectiveness, women keep on buying the stuff. They shell out hundreds, even thousands, for wrinkle cream, moisturizers, eye shadows and powders, lipsticks, and facial makeup. And why? One explanation is that they are looking for affordable luxury, the thrill of buying at the expensive department store, indulging in a fantasy of beauty and sexiness, buying "hope in a bottle." Cosmetics are an escape from an otherwise all too drab everyday existence.

While there is undoubtedly truth in this explanation, it is by no means the whole story. Even in cosmetics—which is hardly the first product line that comes to mind as a status symbol—there's a structure of "one-up-womanship." It turns out that women *are* looking for prestige in their makeup case. Why do they pay twenty dollars for a Chanel lipstick when they could buy the same product for a fraction of the cost? They want the name. As *Mademoiselle*'s publisher, Catherine Viscardi Johnston, explains, "If they can't afford a Chanel suit, they'll buy a Chanel lipstick or nail polish and move up later." Crude as it may sound, many women want or need to be seen with an acceptable brand. A caption describing a Chanel lipstick in a recent newspaper article puts it bluntly: "A classic shade of scarlet, scented with essential oil of roses, in Chanel's signature black and gold case. *Perfect for preening in public.*" One of my downshifters has less expensive taste (and less money than the typical Chanel buyer), but she conforms to the same principle: "I have a fifteen dollar lipstick I only take out in company," she tells me.

The status component in cosmetics purchasing comes out clearly in our research. We have looked at brand purchasing patterns for four cosmetics products: lipsticks, eye shadows, mascaras, and facial cleansers. Facial cleansers are the least socially visible of the four because they are almost always used at home in the bathroom. After a woman applies makeup in the morning, she doesn't clean her face again until she takes the makeup off. Eye shadows and mascaras are in an intermediate category. Women do reapply them during the day, typically in semipublic "powder rooms" (note the name). Lipsticks are the most visible of the four products. They are applied not only in the semipublic rooms but in public itself, at the end of a meal, in an elevator, on an airplane. The visibility difference can also be seen in the packaging strategies of the companies. Lipstick containers are quite distinctive and recognizable from across a table, while containers for mascara and facial cleansers are less so. (Eye shadows are often packaged to match lipsticks.) If you are skeptical, try this experiment, possible only with upscale women, and most naturally done over dinner. When the lipsticks start appearing after the dessert, ask each person how many of the brands they can recognize from across the table. When I tried this, the level of recognition was impressive.

To test our assumptions about the relative visibilities of the four products, my former Harvard student and coauthor Angela Chao conducted an informal survey among Harvard students, who reproduced our rankings nearly to a woman. Lipsticks are most visible, facial cleansers are least visible, and eye shadows and mascaras are intermediate. Having established the differences in social visibility across this group of cosmetics products, we then tested two propositions. The first was that socially visible products deliver less quality for a given price. And the second was that people buy top-end brands of visible products far more than high-quality invisible ones. Both these propositions are strongly supported by the data.

Independent quality tests conducted by *Consumer Reports* reveal that among a range of brand lipsticks consumers did not find systematic quality differences. Of course, there are different types of lipsticks. But within types, the lipsticks tend to be chemically similar, and users rated none of them better than any other in terms of quality, despite prices ranging from a few dollars to twenty-five dollars. (See figure 3.1.) By contrast, users *can* distinguish between the qualities of facial cleansers, thereby supporting our prediction that with visible products price is less connected to quality. The fraction of expensive brands purchased also varies systematically with visibility, as shown in figure 3.2. Women are far more likely to buy expensive lipsticks than they are to buy expensive facial cleansers. In fact, with lipsticks, the higher the price, the *more* consumers tend to purchase them. This finding flies in the face of the received wisdom that a higher price discourages buyers. (Regression analyses contained in Chao and Schor [1998] make these points in more detail.)

This perverse relation between price and demand has been called the snob effect, to highlight the role of social status in such purchasing. How else can we explain the results of the cosmetics study? If women were merely in search of quality, attractive packaging, the chance to buy something at a swanky department store, the illusion that they could look like a model, or any of the many other explanations that have been offered for the success of this industry, we would not have found the patterns of purchasing across these four products that we did. Women would be buying expensive facial cleansers at the same rate that they buy expensive lipsticks. They would be getting all their cosmetics in the department store and not picking up the facial cleanser at the local druggist. Buying patterns across the four products would not differ.

Of course, this test does not explain what is going on in consumers' heads, that is, whether they desire social status or are trying to avoid social humiliation. We cannot say whether they are even conscious of the buying pattern we have found, and we can infer nothing concerning their feelings—for example, whether they enjoy consuming status goods or feel oppressed by a perceived need to do so. However, the absence of direct information on the inner life of the consumer should not detract from these findings. Unlike other approaches, this is a decisive test. There is no other plausible expla-

FIGURE 3.1   Price vs. Quality

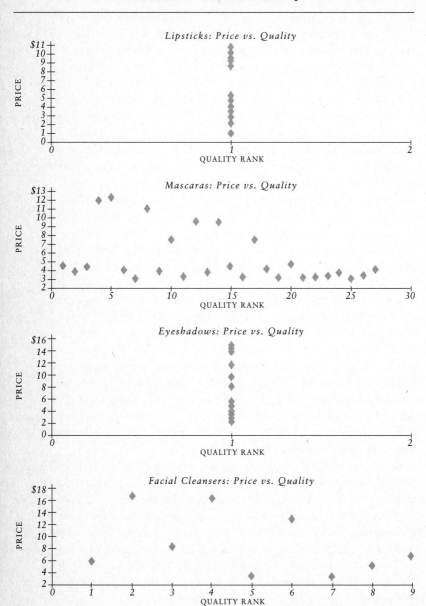

FIGURE 3.2   Product Distribution Graphs

Lipstick Distribution Among Brands

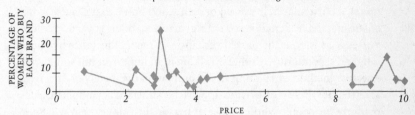

Mascara Distribution Among Brands

Eyeshadow Distribution Among Brands

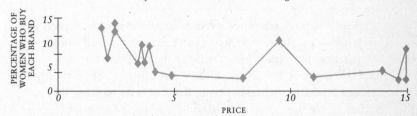

Facial Cleanser Distribution Among Brands

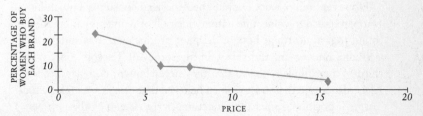

nation for the marked differences in brand buying by the public-ness of the product.

Of course, there is more to status than visibility. As I argued earlier, nonvisible commodities do become status symbols—foreign travel, a particular hairdresser, or a vacation home that none of your colleagues have actually seen. Information about your nonvisible possessions is typically passed verbally—in the first instance by yourself, and secondarily by others. Talking is an imperfect but somewhat effective method of creating desire and emulative behavior. There is also the possibility of private approaches to status symbolism, particularly for people whose values or personality make them reluctant to participate publicly. These people can join in by purchasing less conspicuous products or refraining from advertising what they have. A woman can derive inner satisfaction from buying unknown but expensive designer clothes, knowing they are luxury items that would confer status if others knew about them. At the same time, she does not have to contend with the negative psychic consequences associated with flaunting wealth, besting others, or trying to impress. But these exceptions aside, visibility and status do go together.

Who Cares?

Of course, there are plenty of Americans who refuse to spend for labels, who purchase their lipsticks in drugstores, and who shun brand names altogether. Many will pay the premium for some commodities and not for others. Others attempt to achieve a certain consumer position without paying full price, frequenting discount houses that sell designer merchandise. Although my research confirms the presence of status buying, it does not lead to the conclusion that everyone engages in it.

However, millions do. Despite the American consumer's much-ballyhooed return to value, one nationwide poll of women by Ethel Klein found that almost half bought designer products such as sunglasses, perfume, underwear, and shoes. In my survey at Telecom, only one-third of the sample reported that they never bought designer clothes. Klein also found that most women believed that others are looking for image or position, rather than function. In the case of clothes, 77 percent of respondents believed that consumers are paying for the label and only 13 percent believed that consumers are seeking quality. This mentality is thought to dominate other decisions, such as the choice of college. More than half of those polled believed that it's the name that attracts parents to Ivy League colleges, compared to 33 percent who thought it was the high quality of the schools.

There are, as a Bourdieu-style analysis predicts, statistically significant socioeconomic and demographic differences between those who spend for status and those who do not. In the cosmetics study, we found that women with higher education levels and higher incomes did more status purchasing. We found that urban and suburban women did much more status buying than those from rural areas. And we found that Caucasian women were much more likely to engage in status purchasing than African American or non-Caucasian Hispanics. This finding accords with Duesenberry's research, which found that, controlling for income, African Americans saved more, presumably on account of their lower economic position and a resulting tendency to drop out of status competitions. In the Telecom survey, I found that the likelihood of buying designer clothes increased with income and education.

Other studies have highlighted the impact of psychological traits, such as insecurity. Peter Gollwitzer and Robert Wicklund found that business majors with lower grades and poorer job prospects were more likely to buy expensive briefcases, pens, and wristwatches. In a second study, Ottmar Braun and Wicklund found that both insecurity and a commitment to a particular personal identity figured in vacation and leisure activities. If I care about being a golfer but not a tennis player, and I am not good at either, I will buy fancy clubs but not an expensive racket. That is, we are not indiscriminate status seekers. Another study found that self-consciousness is connected to certain behaviors, such as being fashionable or consuming conspicuous products. We also know that compulsive buyers are more status-oriented, and that people who are more materialistic (as measured by a materialism scale) value their more visible possessions more highly.

The proliferation of imitation status goods is powerful testimony to our ongoing concern with making an impression. Counterfeiting has quadrupled over the last decade and is now estimated as a $200 billion a year business. Today at least 5 percent of *all* products sold worldwide are estimated to be fakes. Fakes make up a large segment of the market in visible commodities such as jeans, watches, sunglasses, designer apparel, and leather goods. (In the mid-1980s, it was estimated that the share of fakes on the U.S. market was 25 percent for designer sunglasses, more than 25 percent for watches, and 10 percent for jeans.) There are also fake colognes, baby foods, videos, and software. And you can buy these products at fake Tupperware parties. The buyer almost certainly knows the product is not real (on account of its low price) and prefers (or can only afford) the status component, not the full quality. Whether the "audience" can tell is another story. Only those really in the game will recognize a fake Rolex by its jumpy (rather than smooth) second hand.

Fakes are, of course, a big headache for the designers. Louis Vuitton withdrew from the luggage business temporarily in the late 1970s because it could not compete with fakes. At one point, Cartier estimated that there were nearly as many Tank imitations circulating as real ones. Other legitimate designers have decided that if you can't beat them, join them: they now produce the T-shirts sold on street corners ostensibly as copies. The fakes are reals. Whatever we mean by that.

And then, it's always worth remembering the principle of faker beware. Donning a fraud can backfire. Having stocked up at the counterfeit designer market in Seoul, an economist acquaintance of mine unwittingly exposed his daughter to ridicule at school: classmates knew her three-legged Polo horse wasn't real. Can you take the heat on the cocktail party circuit? A student reports that her mother has been known to gossip indignantly after social events: "That wasn't a *real* St. John that woman was wearing."

Consumption and the Construction of Identity

The possibility of private status seeking immediately raises the issue of identity, and the connection between what you consume and who you are. The attempt to tie individual personal characteristics to consumer choice was once very popular in marketing research. Tremendous efforts have been made to figure out what kind of woman buys instant coffee rather than regular grind, who's behind the wheel of a Ford instead of a Chevy, and what Marlboro men are really like.

It is now widely believed that consumer goods provide an opportunity for people to express themselves, display their identities, or create a public persona. The chairman of one of the world's largest consumer products multinationals well understands that "the brand defines the consumer. We are what we wear, what we eat, what we drive. Each of us in this room is a walking compendium of brands. The collection of brands we choose to assemble around us have become amongst the most direct expressions of our individuality—or more precisely, our deep psychological need to identify ourselves with others." As the popular culture would have it, "I shop, therefore I am."

Through the strong personal connections people come to feel toward products, our possessions become, in the words of Russell Belk, our "extended" selves. "That we are what we have is perhaps the most basic and powerful fact of consumer behavior." One consumer survey found that nearly half of car owners saw their car as a reflection of who they are either "a lot" or "some." Only 26 percent said their car is "not at all" a reflection of themselves. Car owners could also readily say what kind of car they would want to be if they *were* a car. For certain "sacred" goods, like wedding attire, the identification can be intense. ("When I found that dress, I mean, I put it on . . . I started crying, 'cause I was like, 'Lisa, this is my dress!' ")

In fact, the identity-consumption relationship is a two-way street. Who we are not only affects what we buy. What we buy also affects who we become. Recent research suggests that the more we have, the more powerful, confident, and socially validated we feel. Clothes do make the man. John Schouten's work on cosmetic surgery suggests that it transforms people, not only literally but also psychologically. His subsequent research with James McAlexander on the subculture of Harley-Davidson bikers shows how important consumption can be in establishing group identity. (It also turned the researchers themselves into obsessive bikers, as if to prove the point.)

Identity and the New Consumerism

As I noted in chapter 1, there's a new game in town—individuality. In the words of one advertising magazine, "Lifestyle advertising is about differentiating oneself from the Joneses, not as in previous decades, keeping up with them." In the so-called new middle (and upper-middle) classes, individuality and differentiation are essential. Why? Because mass-produced goods are too homogeneous, too common. Everybody has them. This makes them incapable of conferring distinction. These groups prefer items with a customized dimension.

This is nowhere so evident as in home furnishings. The upper- and even middle-class home has become a refuge from the flatness and unaesthetic quality of the mass-produced world. As Robert Wuthnow has argued, it is now a haven of authenticity, in which individuals express themselves. Handmade goods are preferred, and a card bearing the artist's name is a bonus on a craft item. So too with wearables—a one-of-a-kind wedding ring, unique clothing. As a saleswoman in an upscale craft-oriented store explained to me about an exquisite, handmade, $1,000 sweater, "We have clients who come especially for this collection. They work hard for their money and feel they deserve and are entitled to these things."

Some individuals may also seek distinction through collecting. Antiques are perfect, although expensive. Where one shops also matters. The new middle class likes boutiques and tends to dislike national chains. Some better-off individuals may even buy products that are sold privately, by appointment, or in relatively obscure shops. The ostensible reasons for these preferences: quality, craftsmanship, individuality. The less obvious symbolic message: social distance. For those who are creating for themselves the new upper-middle-class lifestyle, it's important to avoid being too mass-market. IKEA was great when it had one or two stores and was an innovating Scandinavian importer; now it's on the verge of becoming McCouch. It's no fun to walk into someone else's living room and see your sofa. (Or, as one interior decorator explained to me, when the pieces start appearing in the department stores, forget it. Couldn't possibly buy them.)

Similar considerations inform this group's strong preference for solid wood, or cotton. Ever wonder—as you search rack after rack in frustration because only a 100 percent cotton outfit will do for the baby shower—why natural fabrics are so important? Many consumers cite their aesthetics and quality, but it's more than that. Natural fibers and materials symbolically obliterate the connection to assembly lines and factories. By being "natural," they are symbolically *not* man-made. Never mind that the same factories that churn out the polyesters also make the cottons. With packaging and marketing, a different symbolic association can be created. Of course, the quest for individuality through products pertains to a certain (large) segment of the consumer market—highly educated, higher-class individuals. People low in Bourdieu's cultural capital remain enthusiastic about mass goods. They want the best of them, the prestige products that higher-class people *used* to like. Not everyone has shifted from Cadillacs to foreign cars or disdains cruises, the Hilton, and wall-to-wall carpeting.

The irony of the "new differentiation" is that it too has become common. Upmarket tastes, just like downmarket ones, are predictable. Even the really differentiated symbol, like the Caribbean island you get to first, the newest high-performance sport, or art clothing, is just the latest status item. While most people *experience* these tastes as just being themselves, they are actually being a lot like everyone else. As one advertiser put it: "Although people may claim that they are striving for individuality, they all end up looking more or less predictably the same." At the end of the day, gaining status by being *different* from Mr. Jones has become the latest twist in a continuing social ritual.

While the literature typically classifies identity and status as alternative sources of consumer motivation, they should not be seen as two independent processes. The self is not public or private, it is always both. Personal identity does not exist prior to the social world, it comes into being within it. For example, research on self-image (a common psychological category) has found that the higher the status of the brand, the more closely people associated their self-image with it. Competitive spending may be increasingly experienced by individuals as an affirmation of personal identity, but it is competitive all the same. Indeed, as some have argued, it is precisely when traditional markers of identity and position, such as birth and occupation, begin to break down that spending comes to the fore as a more powerful determinant of social status.

The downshifter Doris Shepley is a classic example. In discussing her "before" patterns, the importance of the visible triad (house, auto, and wardrobe) emerged. Moreover, she was unusually conscious about her status motives and the desirability of being different. I met Doris, recently married, in her large and obviously expensive home in Bellevue, an exclusive Seattle suburb. The combination of two incomes had allowed the Shepleys to take a giant step up. Ostensibly looking for more space to keep their combined possessions, they ended up in what Doris described as a "perfect, classic example of trying to impress friends." When she first saw the house, she "thought of people at work; we could have parties, we would entertain. I did like to have dinner parties. And I just thought of Bellevue as being kind of a nice address; you know, you could tell people you live in Bellevue. It was not lined up with other houses, it had more spaciousness around it. I remember the real estate agent said, 'This is a real executive home.'" That gave her a thrill, "because it made me think that it was a prestigious home, more than just a home like in a tract where they're all the same; this was different. So that got to me." As far as her automobile went, she "got a used Mercedes, because I heard that it was a good car and I think I thought I'd impress my friends." And clothes? They were "to impress clients as well as to impress friends, to make them think I was more successful than I was in sales, because I would never tell anybody what I made, so everybody assumed that I was really doing extremely well, and I kept up that image." Unfortunately for Doris, a few months after she moved in she decided to downsize her spending radically. Now the house is an albatross, and the wardrobe a painful reminder of money wasted.

The Costs of Status

Doris Shepley has paid dearly for her status seeking. It kept her from saving enough to be financially secure, led her to buy an excessively large house, and for years kept her tied to a job she didn't really like. But what about society as a whole? How does status seeking affect our quality of life and well-being? What does status consumption *cost*?

There are a variety of ways to think about this question. One way is to calculate the price differential between a generic and a branded version of a product, controlling for quality. With lipsticks, the differential would be any excess in price above the $4 or $5 drugstore brand. Taking the price differential for each lipstick and multiplying by the total number sold would give us an overall figure for the amount spent on status in the lipstick market.

With such a method, the key is to control for quality. But doing so is difficult with many products, because status and quality are often intertwined. How do you separate the functional and status components of houses and their furnishings, or restaurant meals, or vacations? It's especially difficult in today's world, where quality has become a status item for upscale consumers. But the difficulties of measurement should not lead us to ignore the thousands of four-wheel-drive vehicles sold to people who almost never use the feature or the extra fee paid to flash a gold (or platinum) credit card (above and beyond the value of whatever services it comes with). With a wide variety of visible commodities, we are shelling out billions for status.

Another way to think about the costs of status is to consider products we do not purchase, for status reasons. Aluminum siding is an excellent insulator, never needs painting, and is extremely durable, thereby saving homeowners many thousands of dollars. Why don't more people use it? A common explanation is that it's "unaesthetic." But what does this mean? Our sense of the "aesthetic" is drenched in class associations. How about the warehouse, which went from being "unaesthetic" to a fashionable dwelling? The real problem with aluminum siding is not that it's objectively ugly, but that it has a decidedly low-class image. As a consequence, millions of people won't use it, saying they think it's ugly. Indeed, it is proscribed in many middle- and upper-middle-income communities, a testament to the need to keep up the class image. The proliferation of such "taste codes" and restrictions indicates a whole realm of social costs paid to the god of positional consumption.

We can also think about the costs of status by considering the money that companies spend to turn identical or virtually identical products into differentiated goods. Savants in advertising know this is what the game is about, although we consumers are often resistant to the idea. Nike buys $150 million of ads annually to convince us to don the Swoosh, but in many ways its shoes are no different from those of archrival Reebok or plenty of no-name brands. Drug companies spend huge sums promoting branded drugs that are the same as generics. Cosmetics companies market identical products under different lines that vary only in their packaging, positioning, and, of course, price. (Insiders know that Bourjois—owned by Chanel—markets last-season Chanel products, in plain cases, at a fraction of the price.) Kellogg's shells out millions to convince us that its corn flakes are better than the other guy's, and we pay through the nose for them. (Ever wonder why cereal is so expensive?) Many of the nation's vitamins come from a single company but are sold in different bottles at a wide range of prices. Fashion companies spend more than $1 billion a year on advertising, trying to keep us from noticing that a hefty segment of that market is also for identical or similar goods at different prices. (For example, a large worldwide manufacturer reports selling jeans with essentially the same manufacturing costs to mass-market chains such as Wal-Mart, mid-market outlets like JC Penney, and high-end designers and department stores, such as Calvin Klein, at retail prices ranging from about $15 to $65.) Not only jeans but many other virtually indistinguishable items of clothing are sold in different retail outlets with wide price differentials. (Designer hosiery is another good example.) Let's not forget that these stores are doing business with the same overseas suppliers, whose products often vary only or mainly by the label. An educated shopper can find bargains this way. But many consumers don't know what they're looking for.

These claims may be hard to digest. It just doesn't seem possible that so many (most?) branded goods are not actually different from other branded goods. Or that their differences are sufficiently small that most consumers don't know which is which, or which they like better, when the labels are removed. Our daily experience tells us something else, often leading us to be fiercely loyal to brands or fashion labels. Tide really *is* better. But don't forget the classic studies, one of which tells us that beer drinkers rated all beer identically without the labels and weren't even able to pick out their favorite brew. Or the lipstick test I reported earlier. I grew up believing that Royal Crown Cola was actually the drink of choice over Pepsi and Coke in blind taste tests. (Can that really be true?) And by the way, remember that local bottling means these soft drinks aren't even identical in different parts of the country. Have you ever done a taste test with bottled water? (I have, and I still can't believe that I didn't choose Evian, to which I have a classic brand attachment.) In the next chapter, I report on similar research on clothing preferences: consumers rank identical garments differently depending on which label the researchers sew on the inside. And so on and so on. For a whole host of symbolic reasons, status-related identity among them, American consumers continue to buy into a brand-oriented market in which they are paying not only a large sum for advertising but also higher prices for products that are only symbolically, but not functionally, different from lower-priced products.

I do not mean to imply, by the way, that there are *no* quality differences between goods. There certainly are. Colleagues report that IKEA's veneer bookshelves apparently do not last too long, but solid wood will. Toyotas have better repair records than Hyundais. Rather, my point is twofold: first, for a significant number of branded and highly advertised products, there are no quality differences discernible to consumers when the labels are removed; and second, variation in prices typically exceeds variation in quality, with the difference being in part a status premium.

While a numerical estimate is difficult to settle on, it is clear that the costs of status consumption in the U.S. economy are considerable. In most of the major expenditure categories—housing, furnishings, automobiles, apparel, cosmetics, footwear, travel, and an increasing large group of food items—some fraction of our consumption is addressed to positional concerns. The extra money we spend could arguably be better used in other ways—improving our public schools, boosting retirement savings, or providing drug treatment for the millions of people the country is locking up in an effort to protect the commodities others have acquired. But unless we find a way to dissociate what we buy from who we think we are, redirecting those dollars will prove difficult indeed.

When Spending Becomes You

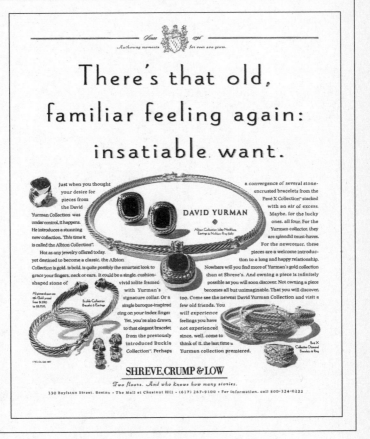

The most striking feature of household spending in modern America is its sheer volume. The typical middle- to upper-middle-class household occupies more than two thousand square feet of floor space, owns at least two cars, a couple of couches, numerous chairs, beds, and tables, a washer and dryer, more than two televisions, a VCR, and has cable. The kitchen contains a conventional oven, a microwave, a frost-free refrigerator, a blender, a coffee maker, a tea kettle, a food processor, and so many pots, pans, dishes, cups and glasses, storage containers, kitchen utensils, and pieces of flatware that they aren't even counted. Elsewhere in the house are a personal computer and printer, telephones, an answering machine, a calculator, a stereo or CD player, musical instruments, and many pieces of art—in addition to paintings and reproductions, there are decorative items such as vases, plates, and statuettes, photographs in frames, and knickknacks. In the bathroom are a hair dryer, a scale, perhaps an electric toothbrush or shaver, and cabinets overflowing with towels, shampoos, conditioners, face creams, and other cosmetics. The closets are stuffed with clothes and shoes of all types: dresses, suits, pants, shirts, sweaters, coats, hats, boots, sneakers, flats, pumps, walking shoes, patent leathers, and loafers. And don't forget the jewelry. In addition to watches, the diamond ring, and other high-value items, there's usually a large collection of costume jewelry: bead necklaces, bracelets, and earrings, earrings, earrings. The family room is filled with books, videos, tapes, CDs, magazines, and more photos and knickknacks. The floors are covered with rugs or carpet, and throughout the house are scattered other pieces of furniture, accented perhaps with dried or silk flowers. Stored in the garage or basement is all the sports equipment, such as bicycles and skis, as well as luggage and totes, lawn and garden tools, and broken appliances. (Some developers now routinely build three-car garages—two spaces for the cars, one for the junk.) In addition to all these durable products (of which this is a very incomplete inventory), households spend heavily on services such as child care, movies, restaurants and bars, hotel stays, airplane trips, haircuts, massages, visits to Disney

World, lawyer bills, insurance premiums, interest payments, and, sometimes, rental on the storage space where even more stuff resides.

If you are a typical American consumer, you did not always have so much. There was probably a time in your adult life when you could fit everything you owned into your car and drive off into the sunset. Now you need professionals to transport your possessions. You spend hundreds, perhaps thousands of dollars a year to insure or protect them. As you survey your material landscape, you may wonder how this state of affairs came to be. You certainly didn't intend to imitate those medieval armies that became sitting ducks—unable to move on account of the creature comforts they started lugging around. Each purchase made sense at the time. Many were truly necessary. Some were captivating, giving you that "I just have to have this" feeling. But added together, they raise the possibility that yours is a lifestyle of excess.

How does it happen? And so quickly? To understand how your possessions came to fill a full-size moving van, or why you never seem to have enough closet space, we need to begin with the acquisition process. The sequence of events starts with a social act—being exposed to consumer goods. It proceeds through the mental stages of fantasizing, wishing, and rationalizing. Borrowing may be the next step before the process culminates with a purchase. See, want, borrow, buy.

Seeing: The Many Sites of Exposure

"My little girl had a friend visit her who was really into Guess jeans. My nine-year-old didn't even know what Guess jeans were. Well, after that kid left, that was all she talked about. She had to have a pair of Guess jeans."

"Every time they see kids with something new, other kids on the block go home and say they want it. Or something they see on TV, they think they should get it."

"Sue, who went with me to submit the application, just fell in love with the place because it's on top, by Mulholland, with beautiful rolling lawns, a brand-new gorgeous facility, and she hasn't stopped talking about how she wants to go to Stephen Weiss for school. So even a four-year-old can discern the differences. She was very impressed with the lawns and the playgrounds."

Inner desires are prompted first and foremost by exposure. The seeds are "planted" by seeing what people at work wear or drive; by visiting others' homes and observing their private spaces; by hearing about a coworker's new purchase; by window and in-store shopping; by looking at mail-order catalogs; and by viewing (or to a lesser extent, hearing about) consumer items in advertisements and films or on television. As the North American president of Montblanc Pen put it, referring to the Euro Classique, the company's entry-level ($90) pen, "They will see their friend with one and go out and get the same." While most critics of consumer society focus on ads and the media, it's important to remember that the more powerful stimulator of desire is what friends and family have.

For Lauren Vandermeer, work was the place where her desires were stimulated. After graduating from a Seven Sisters college, Lauren wanted only three things: a camera, a stereo, and a bike. In her sales job at a large corporation, she quickly acquired them. "Then I became aware of people going on vacation, and then I wanted to go on vacation. I went to Mexico for a week. I really liked it." The townhouse came next. "Very quickly after [the vacation], several of my colleagues started buying houses and townhouses. And all these people were moving to York and Yardley and Newtown, Pennsylvania. It's a great little yuppie area, and it's all very beautiful. It was like one started and then everybody else followed suit. Everybody was looking, everybody was putting down payments down. And so I jumped on board too. But I will admit, the only reason I did it is because everybody else was doing it. And I felt not so much keeping up with the Joneses as their logic. I bought into the logic of not wanting to pay rent, and that it was worth it to have a mortgage and the deductions for your taxes and all of that."

Being single, Lauren opted for an urban rather than suburban area. While the "Joneses'" financial logic got her started, once she started looking, the aesthetic and symbolic motivations "became the thrill, because then I saw what was available. It wasn't just to get a brownstone in Chambersburg; it was to get the brownstone with the leaded windows and the hardwood floors, and the nice brick pointing on the outside. Then I realized how important light was to me. I wanted to own something really nice."

Wanting: The Inner World of Desire

Between seeing and buying lies the inner world of desire. Recent literature has focused on fantasy, imagination, and vicarious experience as key aspects of modern consumer behavior. Spending fantasies are prevalent, indeed commonplace. People anticipate, they daydream, and they plan their participation in the "enchanted domain" of consumer culture. In their study of inner desire, Susan Fournier and Michael Guiry found that 61 percent of respondents "*always* have something in mind that [they] look forward to buying." Twenty-seven percent of the sample said that they "dream about things they do not own" very often.

In fact, these desires were rather structured; many respondents had well-articulated "wish lists." Defined as "things that you would like to own or do someday," these lists contained an average of 6.3 items and were heavily dominated by material possessions. (Consumption wishes outnumbered idealistic ones by three to one.) The most popular item (on 67 percent of all lists) was an exotic vacation. Then came the everyday-life items. Forty-seven percent of people wanted a "better, bigger, or more beautifully situated home." Another 28 percent wanted a vacation house. Forty-two percent wanted new cars, mainly luxury models. (As the title to Fournier and Guiry's article suggests, what Americans dream about is "An Emerald Green Jaguar, a House on Nantucket, and an African Safari.") Of course, respondents wanted other things beyond the house, car, and travel trio. About one-quarter cited household electronics—big-screen TVs, home computers, VCRs. Fifteen percent wanted a boat, 10 percent yearned for nice clothes, and 16 percent just asked for the money—enough to buy anything they could possibly want. These wish lists did not vary by sex, income, education, or standard of living. Apparently consumerism is an equal opportunity ideology.

John Caughey's ethnographic study of four hundred subjects' imaginary social worlds supports the existence of these standard fantasies. "Americans regularly fantasize the same American dreams. . . . Fantasy descriptions of ideal houses often sound like commercials, and many can be traced directly to particular media productions." Here is one dream, characterized by Caughey as "restrained":

A common daydream of mine involves my first "real" apartment. I enjoy walking through furniture stores, which is somewhat inconsistent, considering my allegedly liberal, antimaterialistic values, and picking out the furniture I would like to have. I particularly like Roche-Bobois and Scan, so the daydream usually begins with me walking into such a place with nary a care about such mundane details as cost or money. I wander through the store, in and out of all the model rooms, and I just point. "I'll take that . . . and that . . . and two of those. . . . " I have all the rooms planned, and the floor plan is perfect. There is a beautiful old fireplace and a huge window filled with plants in the living room. The kitchen is fantastically modern, with wooden cabinets, with all the newest gadgets. It is sunny, bright, and enormous. The apartment is, of course, a duplex, so up the spiral stairs, in the bedroom, you can look down over the living and dining rooms. The bathroom has a huge sunken bathtub and a phone. There is a balcony with a small greenhouse and a glorious view.

The decorations throughout the apartment are magnificent. There is a mixture of modern and antique furniture. I would have an oak dresser and desk and a satin quilt. The living room furniture would be modern with brass lamps and glass tables. The chrome and glass dining room set would sit on deep, plush carpet. There would be beautiful paintings and pieces of art all around, and it would all be paid for.

Our fantasies also reveal the centrality of gaining others' esteem. The ideal house fantasy is not complete without "showing the house to admiring others." In the words of one dreamer, "The awe and respect and wonder of my guest are basic to every daydream about my house." This is also true of the luxury goods featured in the standard "material wealth" fantasy. Displaying goods and gaining respect for them are crucial to our preoccupation with things.

While fantasy and imagination are important, we should not lose sight of the fact that much of this wishing is really wanting—wanting that turns into buying. In the wish list study, people had very high expectations of actually attaining the items on their list, but not without effort. Sixty percent of respondents reported that advertisements for prestige items motivated them to "earn more money so that I can afford the things they show." Students reported that the ads inspired them to study more. In the words of one: "I'd better get a good grade so that I can get out and make a lot of money."

Borrowing: The Role of Plastic in Consumer Spending

Not everyone earns before buying. Most of what we purchase we finance through borrowing. The earning comes later. Nearly all Americans borrow to buy their homes, and most automobiles are bought on time. Add to this the credit card balances, finance company loans, department store debts, and debts to individuals, and you begin to get an idea of the pervasiveness of household debt (about $5.5 trillion in late 1997). We "sign and travel" for vacations, charge the wife's birthday present, and put the health club membership on plastic. About one-third of the nation's population describe themselves as either heavily or moderately in financial debt, one-third report being slightly in debt, and only one-third report no financial (that is, excluding home mortgage) debts at all. As I write these words, the fraction of Americans' disposable income that goes toward debt servicing continues to rise; it has now reached 18 percent. The total amount of debt held by the average household has increased relentlessly for decades, and it now equals just about what that household makes in any given year.

The rise in indebtedness is in large part due to credit cards. Between 1990 and 1996, credit card debt doubled. Credit cards, with interest rates reaching nearly 20 percent, are a remarkably lucrative part of the loan business. Debtors pay an average of $1,000 a year in interest and fees alone. And the companies look increasingly like "credit pushers," soliciting heavily and beyond their traditional creditworthy base. Using subtle tactics to encourage borrowing, the recent onslaught has led consumers to hold more cards, to borrow more, and to fork over an increasing fraction of their incomes to the companies. If you don't borrow, the company may cancel your card, since it isn't making money on you.

A significant number of spending downshifters are ex-credit card debtors. Donna Schudson began accumulating her balances while she was in college, entering what she calls a debt cycle. "I wanted to drive a nice car, and so I went into debt for one. Then I got a credit card to 'establish credit' when I was twenty. Since my wages mainly went to my car and related expenses, I used my credit card for expenditures." Originally she thought that after graduation she would make a lot of money and pay everything off. But "once I got my job after college I needed a newer car, my own apartment, furnishings for the apartment, etc. I never stopped to pay off past debt. Little by little it kept piling up." Working her way up in a financial services company, she was eventually earning $47,000 a year but had accumulated credit card debts of $19,000 plus a $10,000 loan on her car.

The credit card–spending link has become almost Pavlovian. Researcher Richard Feinberg placed some Mastercard signs and logos in the corner of his lab, with instructions to subjects that they were for another experiment and should be ignored. Apparently that's no longer possible. In comparison to a control group, those who saw the red and yellow logo spent more during the experiment. Credit card tips tend to be higher than with cash, and people report feeling looser with their money when they use plastic. The painlessness of spending with plastic makes it hard for many people to control.

Rich Moroni, a downshifter who eventually exchanged his job as a bad-debt collector for a more satisfying one as a consumer credit counselor, believes there's an underlying structural problem. "The bottom line for most people is they just simply don't think about what kind of money they make and what kind of lifestyle they're living. And they do want to be richer. They want to look richer than they are. If you have five credit cards, that actually makes it very easy to look richer than you are. And then add merchandisers and advertisers to that, and it's a formula for disaster for a lot of people."

At Telecom, debt emerged as a prominent feature of life. Only 11 percent of employees reported having no consumer debt, excluding mortgages. The average level of nonmortgage consumer debt was $13,700. About two-thirds of these respondents carry persistent credit card balances, and 14 percent pay only the minimum due each month. They identified debt as the single most important factor keeping their noses to the grindstone. Of the 68 percent of the sample who said, "I would like to reduce my working hours but feel that I just cannot afford it at this time," more than half named debt as the reason. Among those who said they would like to live a simpler life, debt outpaced all other reasons as the main barrier to doing so.

Buying: Looking to the Corner Office

See-want-borrow-and-buy is a comparative process; desire is structured by what we see around us. Even as we differentiate ourselves through fashion or culture, we are located within, and look for validation to, a particular social space.

For most of us, that social space begins with relatives, friends, and coworkers. These are the people whose spending patterns we know and care most about. They are the people against whom we judge our own material lifestyles, and with whom we try to keep up. They are the groups that spur our consumer desires. This perspective is supported by answers from the Telecom survey. Among the primary reference groups offered (celebrities, television families, and media referents were not included), friends were the most commonly chosen option. They were followed by coworkers, relatives, others of the same religion, and others in the same occupation.

On the other hand, we're no longer keeping up with the neighbors. They were chosen by only 2 percent of the sample as the primary reference group. In fact, Telecom employees said they didn't know too much about the spending habits of the folks next door. Nearly half the sample said they were "not at all aware" of the spending patterns and lifestyles of their neighbors. (However, this does not mean that *no* neighborhood comparison is going on. Virtually all respondents were able to rank how much money they had compared to others in their neighborhood.)

What is perhaps more important than *who* makes up these reference groups is how powerful they are in perpetuating a

Table 4.1 Social Comparison at Telecom

Question: *What is your most important reference group?*

Friends	28.2%
Coworkers	22.1%
Relatives	12.1%
Others of same religion	11.4%
Others in same occupation	8.9%
Neighbors	2.2%
All others	14.9%

dynamic of rising consumer norms. These comparisons matter deeply to us. And we act upon that deep feeling. According to the research I have done, how Telecom employees stack up financially against their chosen reference group has an enormous impact on their overall spending. Despite the widespread view that comparative spending went out with bouffant hairdos and semiautomatic washers, my research shows that it is alive and well in middle America. When some innovate, the rest of us emulate.

After asking all the respondents in my sample to identify their primary reference group, I then asked them, "How does your financial status compare to that of most of the members of the reference group you have chosen?" Is it just about the same? Are you better off? Much better off? Are you worse off than the people you compare yourself to?

I elicited this information in order to figure out whether Americans really do keep up with others. I reasoned that a person who is trying to associate or identify with a group above himself or herself will spend more, all other things being equal, than someone who has chosen a comparison group of people with less money. If a university professor tries to keep up with her college friends who have all gone into investment banking, according to my theory there's a decent chance she'll be sinking into consumer debt (or at least not saving much). On the other hand, the theory predicts that the senior vice president who hangs on to his old buddies from middle management is likely to build a tidy bank balance. The idea is that where you stand relative to those with whom you compare yourself has a significant impact on your spending.

Just asking people about this doesn't yield much information. As I explain later in the chapter, Americans have a lot of psychological resistance to recognizing and admitting the extent to which they follow the lead of others. People say they don't do it—but my evidence shows they do.

What is that evidence? I estimated statistical equations that explained the amount of saving and spending each person did in the year of the survey. (Here I report only the savings equations, but the estimates for spending are virtually identical.) I included a wide range of factors likely to affect spending, such as the respondent's age, number of dependents, household income in that year, long-term expected income (or what economists call permanent income), age, and so on. These are the standard variables that economists typically use to explain variations in spending propensities across the population. Then I added my own comparative variable—how the respondent stacked up financially compared to his or her reference group.

As it turns out, this variable has a very large impact. In the savings equation, each step a respondent moved down the scale (from much better off than the reference group to better off) reduced the amount saved by $2,953 a year. Moving down two steps reduced saving by twice that. The sheer magnitude of this effect can be appreciated when we remember that the average Telecom employee saved only $10,450 per year, including retirement savings. According to these estimates, disaster ensues as a person slides down the reference group scale. Moving from the top to the bottom would lead you to save $15,000 less each year—or more likely, to take on some of that amount in debt.

Now we can understand why the millionaires next door—in contrast to most Americans—save so much. They never change their reference groups. They don't move into the most upscale neighborhoods. They don't start emulating Bill Gates or Malcolm Forbes, and they don't change their friends. They keep on drinking Budweiser. And there's something else. The millionaires next door tend not to have too much formal education. According to my results, that's good for the bank balance. Controlling for other factors, it appears that the more education a person has, *the less he or she saves*. Each additional level of education (going from a high school diploma to some college, for instance, or from a college degree to a postgraduate credential) reduces annual savings by $1,448 (see table 4.2). More education also leads to more shopping, particularly for women. Women with graduate degrees spend more time shopping than individuals in any other category. (Women with college degrees are a close second.) Apparently people with more education are more status-oriented, more tuned in to identity and positional consumption, and more concerned about keeping up with the upscale groups to which they aspire and belong. It's hard to say why. Maybe the more status-conscious among us are more likely to stay in school. Or maybe status orientation is a value system that we *learn* in school. But whatever the causality, the outcome seems clear: the highly educated are more immersed in the culture of upscale acquisition.

It is important to remember that the reference group variable is not a measure of income. The equation already accounts for the commonsense notions that having a higher income leads people to save more, that having more dependents leads people to save less, and that saving varies over the life cycle. Rather, these results tell us that whatever your level of income, your *comparative* position has a major effect on your saving.

How relevant are these findings to Americans as a whole? We must

---

Table 4.2   Multiple Regression Analysis of Factors Influencing Saving among Telecom employees

INDEPENDENT VARIABLE*	COEFFICIENT	T-STATISTIC**
Constant term	$19,995.00	(2.18)
Household income	.112	(6.16)
Permanent household income	.025	(0.69)
Household net worth	.016	(1.04)
Sex	-3,763.00	(-2.68)
Age	-9,916.00	(-2.13)
Age-squared	1,140.00	(1.67)
Race	-204.00	(-0.15)
Occupation	-174.00	(-0.47)
Educational level	-1,448.00	(-1.89)
Number of dependents	-1,232.00	(-2.58)
Satisfaction with income	629.00	(0.86)
Hours per week watching TV	-208.00	(-3.30)
Financial status compared to Reference Group	2,953.00	(3.60)

*Adj-R^2: .275. Dependent variable is annual household saving (mean: $10,450).

**White's t-statistics, which correct for heteroskedasticity, are reported in appendix B.

How to read this table: Coefficients represent impact of one unit change in independent variable on spending. For example, one additional dollar of household income leads to 11 cents of savings. One additional hour of television watching results in a $208 reduction in savings. Each additional step of education results in a $1,448 reduction in savings. Each additional dependent reduces annual saving by $1,232 per year.

For variable definitions, see table B.3

remember that the Telecom sample is not a sample of the whole U.S. population. (See Appendix table B.1 for sample demographics.) It is made up of middle- and upper-middle-class people who work full-time in a large corporation. Their median income is between $60,000 and $75,000 a year. They own their own homes, and they all reside in the southeastern United States. (The South has not been known for being a particularly status-oriented area, by the way.) But while they are not representative of the entire population, they do represent their own group—middle and upper-middle America. There is every reason to believe that, for the issues I am investigating, their behavior is typical for their group.

The Telecom data provide a statistical case for the role of social comparison in spending. From downshifter interviews, we can also get a sense of how some individuals experience the upscaling of desires. Lauren Vandermeer, a rational woman raised with a strong sense of thriftiness, found herself deeply influenced by the social processes of consumption. "You get sucked in, and you start to buy things—from a sociological standpoint, to be in the mainstream with your peers and all of that."

For Rich Moroni, the experience was decidedly frustrating: he had inadvertently slipped into a situation in which the people in his reference group had a lot more money than he did. As my theory predicts, this had a profoundly negative impact on his ability to save. With only a B.A. degree and fairly modest jobs, Rich had never been a high roller. He found himself struggling to "keep up with these [very

---

Table 4.3   Summary of Factors Influencing Saving by Telecom Employees

---

SOCIAL COMPARISON

Each step up in financial status compared to respondent's reference group raises annual saving by $2,953. Each step down reduces savings by an equivalent amount.

TELEVISION WATCHING

Each additional hour of television watched per week reduces annual saving by $208.

upscale] Joneses" at his expensive health club, where he was a pas-sionate squash player. At the time, he was working as a cook at a nice restaurant next to the club, making only about $20,000 a year. His wife had a higher-paying job, but even their combined incomes did not match those of other club members, who tended to be lawyers or company executives, people with "very nice homes," high salaries, and fancy cars. "They were very nice people," but, Rich concedes, "I was definitely out of my league." The money for lessons, rackets, tournaments, and the restaurant after the games was a real stretch for him, yet he found the scene compelling. Even without children, the Moronis found they were spending nearly everything they made.

The scene at the club also led Rich into a lot of mental comparison, enough to provoke an "identity crisis." "Here I am around a lot of very motivated upper-middle-class people, and I was thinking, am I ever going to get there or not? So a lot of my frustrations financially were about that, thinking, am I ever going to be rich? There's a lot to be said for somebody who says, 'I'm going up to the San Juan Islands this weekend to a cabin of a friend,' or who takes a sailboat up to Van-couver Island. You hear things like that, and you know you're not going to be doing them anytime soon. And I thought, well, maybe I should go back to graduate school and get a higher degree and I'll make more money. Not that I even wanted one, and I don't care about them, but driving the BMWs and the Saabs and the Mercedes and liv-ing a lifestyle like that, it really is kind of enticing." While Rich never got into debt, some of his friends at the club did. They were "having financial problems because they were trying to play that game—not 'play that game,' that sounds kind of derogatory, but literally they were spending out of their means, trying to keep up with those folks." For the Moronis, it took quitting the club to begin to build up a bank balance and some control over their finances.

Keeping an Eye on the Fresh Prince: The Role of TV in Consumer Upscaling

In one way, Rich Moroni's story is typical of the new con-sumerism. Despite his low-level job, he had affiliated with a refer-ence group far above his financial station. He aspired to upscale consuming but couldn't afford it. That's one hallmark of the new situation. But in another way, Rich is not typical. His desires were clearly instigated by his real-life friends. For many Americans, it's imaginary buddies who provide the prompts. They're looking to the Fresh Prince of Bel Air.

While television has long been suspected as a promoter of consumer desire, there has been little hard evidence to support that view, at least for adult spending. After all, there's not an obvious connection. Many of the products advertised on television are everyday low-cost items such as aspirin, laundry detergent, and deodorant. Those TV ads are hardly a spur to excessive consumerism. Leaving aside other kinds of ads for the moment (for cars, diamonds, perfume), there's another counter to the argument that television causes consumerism: TV is a *substitute* for spending. One of the few remaining free activities, TV is a popular alternative to costly recreational spending such as movies, concerts, and restaurants. If it causes us to spend, that effect must be powerful enough to overcome its propensity to save us money.

Apparently it is. My research shows that the more TV a person watches, the more he or she spends. The likely explanation for the link between television and spending is that what we see on TV inflates our sense of what's normal. The lifestyles depicted on television are far different from the average American's: with a few exceptions, TV characters are upper-middle-class, or even rich.

Studies by the consumer researchers Thomas O'Guinn and L. J. Shrum confirm this upward distortion. The more people watch television, the more they think American households have tennis courts, private planes, convertibles, car telephones, maids, and swimming pools. Heavy watchers also overestimate the portion of the population who are millionaires, have had cosmetic surgery, and belong to a private gym, as well as those suffering from dandruff, bladder control problems, gingivitis, athlete's foot, and hemorrhoids (the effect of all those ads for everyday products). What one watches also matters. Dramatic shows—both daytime soap operas and prime-time drama series—have a stronger impact on viewer perceptions than other kinds of programs (say news, sports, or weather).

Heavy watchers are not the only ones, however, who tend to overestimate standards of living. Almost everyone does. (And almost everyone watches TV.) In one study, ownership rates for twenty-two of twenty-seven consumer products were generally overstated. Your own financial position also matters. Television inflates standards for lower-, average-, and above-average-income students, but it does the reverse for really wealthy ones. (Among those raised in a financially rarefied atmosphere, TV is almost a reality check.) Social theories of consumption hold that the inflated sense of consumer norms promulgated by the media raises people's aspirations and leads them to buy more. In the words of one Los Angeles resident, commenting on this media tendency, "They try to portray that an upper-class lifestyle is normal and typical and that we should all have it."

Television also affects norms by giving us real information about how other people live and what they have. It allows us to be voyeurs, opening the door to the "private world" inside the homes and lives of others. There was a time when we didn't need television to get such information. In the past, homes, possessions, and habits were much more open to view and fully part of what Erving Goffman has called the system of "impression management." But as we have gotten richer, we have become more private. Much more private. We may not surface between the garage and the house. We rarely linger on the street. We build a deck instead of a front porch. We almost never hang out in our front yards. Indeed, as I unpacked a box in my front yard the other day, so I could keep an eye on the kids, a drive-by shopper stopped for my "yard sale." (Apparently the only thing we use our front yards for now is to sell the junk we can't fit inside.) As O'Guinn and Shrum note, television has replaced personal contact as our source of information about "what members of other social classes have and how they consume, even behind their closed doors."

Another piece of evidence for the TV-spending link is the apparent correlation between debt and excessive TV viewing. In the Merck Family Fund poll, the fraction responding that they "watch too much TV" rose steadily with indebtedness. More than half (56 percent) of all those who reported themselves "heavily" in debt also said they watched too much TV.

It is partly because of television that the top 20 percent of the income distribution, and even the top 5 percent within it, has become so important in setting and escalating consumption standards for more than just the people immediately below them. Television lets *everyone* see what these folks have and allows viewers to want it in concrete, product-specific ways. Let's not forget that television programming and movies are increasingly filled with product placements—the use of identifiable brands by characters. TV shows and movies are more and more like long-running ads. We've become so inured to this practice that it's hard to remember that a can of soda in a TV show was once labeled "soda" rather than "Coke" or "Pepsi."

One research study about television and consumer desires found that as television was introduced in America, it led to a significant increase in crime. Looking across different locales, before and after the introduction of television in the 1950s, Karen Hennigan and her colleagues found that one type of crime jumped up significantly. Not violence, not rape, not murder, but larceny. Larceny is a crime of property, mostly committed by lower-income people. Seeing all those products on television made people who didn't have them, and couldn't afford to buy them, really want them. Want them enough to steal them.

Of course, stealing is something most people don't do. Most of us use money we have (or borrow) to purchase the stuff we see and want. But the impact of television is also powerful for the law-abiding. Television viewing results in an upscaling of desire, and that in turn leads people to buy—quite a bit more than they would if they didn't watch. In the Telecom sample, I found that each additional hour of television watched in a week led to an additional $208 of annual spending. To my knowledge, this is the first statistical evidence tying television to spending. Sitting in front of the television five extra hours a week (two sitcoms a night during the week) raises your yearly spending by about $1,000. Just watching *ER* can set you back a couple of hundred bucks.

Telecom employees watch quite a bit of TV. They estimate their average viewing at eleven and a half hours a week. While that's a lot less than the fifteen hours for the average American estimated from time diary studies, or the twenty-eight hours found by the Neilson people meters, it's still substantial. Even excluding the price of the set, the cable, and the electricity, Telecom employees watched enough TV to cost them more than $2,200 a year.

Of course, the TV effect is hard to prove. My results do not unravel what is undoubtedly a complex link between watching a program and ending up at the cash register. One difficulty with pinning down the impact of television is that almost everyone watches TV, and most people watch a lot. So it's difficult to find individuals who are not affected by it. However, the fact that different types of programming have different effects provides one piece of evidence, as do the Telecom results I report on later in this chapter: TV and social pressure in one's daily life are interchangeable sources of consumer upscaling.

Living in Denial

Part of what keeps the see-want-borrow-and-buy sequence going is lack of attention. Americans live with high levels of denial about their spending patterns. We spend more than we realize, hold more debt than we admit to, and ignore many of the moral conflicts surrounding our acquisitions. The importance of denial for dysfunctional consumers has been well documented. We've all heard the stories about people who drive around in cars full of unpaid credit card bills, who sneak into the guest room at 2:00 A.M. to make a QVC purchase, or who quietly slip off at lunchtime for a quick trip to the mall. What is not well understood is that the spending of many normal consumers is also predicated on denial. (How many times have you heard someone say, "Oh, I'm not materialistc, I'm just into books and CDs—and travel"?)

At Telecom respondents fit these patterns. Sixty-five percent agreed (and 18 percent of those strongly agreed) that "in looking back on my spending, I often wonder where the money goes." Eighty percent felt they should be saving more. Forty percent said they'd like a simpler life. But while 70 percent of the sample described "the average American" as "very materialistic," only 8 percent felt they were materialistic themselves.

Nowhere is denial so evident as with credit cards. Contrary to economists' usual portrayal of credit card debtors as fully rational consumers who use the cards to smooth out temporary shortfalls in income, the finding of the University of Maryland economist Larry Ausubel was that people greatly underestimate the amount of debt they hold on their cards—1992's actual $182 billion in debt was thought to be a mere $70 billion. Furthermore, most people do not expect to use their cards to borrow, but, of course, they do. Eighty percent end up paying finance charges within any given year, with just under half (47 percent) always holding unpaid balances.

Not paying attention to what we spend is also very common. How many of us really keep track of where the cash from the ATM goes? Most Americans don't budget. And they don't watch. Many "fritter," as this downshifter recalled: "All I know is at the end of the month I never had anything left. And so I have to say I spent it all. I don't know what I frittered away. I certainly could have cut my frittering in half, whatever that means. I really don't know what I spent the money on." Doris Shepley recalls her shopping pattern: "Mine was more of a mindless thing." Rich Moroni found himself "not paying any attention. We spent $10,000 on our credit cards last year, and then really never kept track of what it was we were spending on there, going to the mall, buying some things. And that adds up. We had to really examine where all of our money was going. And I would submit to you that most of it was the little stuff that added up over a period of time."

Finally, denial also helps us navigate the moral conflicts associated with consumption. Most of our cherished religious and ethical teachings condemn excessive spending, but we don't really know what that means. We have a sense that money is dirty and a nagging feeling that there must be something better to do with our hard-earned dollars than give them to Bloomingdale's. As our salaries and creature comforts expand, many of us keep alive our youthful fantasies of doing humanitarian work, continuing the inner dialogue between God and Mammon. Not looking *too* hard helps keep that inner conflict tolerable. Squarely facing the fact that you spent $6,000 on your wardrobe last year and gave less than one-third of that sum to charity is a lot harder than living with a vague sense that you need to start spending less on clothes and giving away more money. (Does $6,000 sound like a lot? It is. But Elysa Lazar, queen of New York's bargain hunters who also teaches shopping classes, says that when she asks her mostly professional attendees to calculate their yearly spending on clothes and jewelry, the total is typically two or three times what they had thought—$6,000 instead of their original guess of $2,000.)

Keeping up for the Kids

For parents, the pressure to emulate is often experienced through their children. This comes through loud and clear in focus groups, discussions with downshifter parents, and other scholars' research. The one place where keeping-up behavior is paramount and conscious is where the kids are concerned. Whatever doubts the average American parents may have about the importance of the Joneses' new kitchen, there's little doubt that they are worried about whether their children are maintaining the pace with the Joneses' offspring.

John and Louise Mattson are making do on one income so that Louise can take care of their son. She insists that the externals don't matter to her. "It doesn't bother me if other kids are wearing Osh-Kosh and my kid is wearing K-Mart." However, in the same breath, she makes sure I know that Adam *doesn't* wear K-Mart. "I pride myself on the fact that I find Osh-Kosh for pennies on the dollar at garage sales, looking brand-new." John and Louise's greatest anxiety is in the area of education. "Mostly I worry about, should he have a computer to be keeping up education-wise? Should he have computer access by the age of five, online? What will he need to consume to stay ahead, to stay educationally on par so that even if I can keep the trends and the Ninja Turtles out of the scene . . . what will he need educationally?" For Louise, the perils of the global economy loom large. Succeeding economically is the key to future options. "So, if what it takes for him to have an enjoyable family life is landing a Boeing job, he has a choice. If he doesn't want to and he wants to be a park ranger, or whatever, he can do that." John agrees. Despite the fact that Adam, gurgling away in his high chair, is only two, John is worried they've *already* fallen behind. "I already think that we should have a computer at home. I don't have a lot of rationale, but I do think he needs to be exposed to it, just to get the interest going." As conscious, thoughtful, and values-driven as she is, Louise Mattson finds herself bedeviled by that nagging question, "What are people in Bellevue doing?"

The Mattsons won't have the money to send Adam to private school. But increasing numbers of parents are spending large sums for a private education for the same kinds of reasons the Mattsons articulate. They are worried about their children's chances in a competitive global economy; they want the "best" for them. Sometimes these expenditures entail serious financial sacrifices and may even may make it difficult or impossible to save for college. For other, wealthier families, the substantial tuitions preclude aspects of the good life to which they feel entitled. A small study of upper-class

Los Angeles women on the "path to power kindergarten" explores these issues. Says one mother: "We've had more fights this year than in the ten years we've known each other. It becomes a real battle over how we're going to meet everybody's priorities if all of our discretionary income is going to go for elementary school. And it's been *very* difficult for my husband, as a forty-seven-year-old physician, to have all that delayed gratification."

While fears about economic success are part of what's going on, the motivational issues are complex. In many places, private school is becoming a part of the upper-middle- (and even middle-) class standard of living—a requisite element in the basic package. Parents worry that without it their children will fall behind. Fears about education become magnified because they tap into larger, more deep-seated anxieties. Class position seems to be at stake. And, of course, as the middle and upper-middle classes abandon the public schools, the class divisions widen. Public school becomes tainted with a lower-class image. As another mother in the Los Angeles study explained, the public schools work well for her "housekeeper's child," who will have language problems, but not for her children, who have no special needs. Race and class concerns come together. "Our concern with the public schools is really the safety issue. I have blond-haired, blue-eyed children who are not very physical and not very aggressive, and I worry about interactions on playgrounds."

At the same time, these parents have to deal with the complications of schooling alongside the super-wealthy. The same woman who is afraid of the public school playgrounds also worries about her children being at the bottom of the economic ladder in their private school. "The wealth of these kids is just mind-boggling. You put them in an environment in which we cannot compete, nor do we *want* them to compete and have those kinds of values. I don't want them to come home and say, 'Why don't we live in a ten-bedroom house?'"

Education is only the most expensive of the "goods" that make American parents feel a need to keep up. There are also costly extracurricular activities, such as lessons and sports teams. The standard for birthday parties is escalating. Americans give their kids more in pocket money than the world's half-billion poorest adults earn each year. However sensitive a parent may be to these dynamics, as children get older they weigh in with their own consumer desires. They don't want to be left out. In focus groups organized by the Merck Family Fund, athletic shoes (partly as a metaphor) figured prominently: "Somebody down the block got the new Jordans, and my kids want the Jordans too, and I want them to have them." "If you don't provide your child with Reeboks, or whatever the current fad is, then you're not a good parent." And if you can't swing the $100? "I'm not being a good parent. He wants those new Jordans, and all I can afford was a tennis shoe that Payless was selling."

We also feel that young people are raising the stakes. Robert Wuthnow argues that many Americans now experience their children as "agents of materialism," insinuating consumerist values into the home. This is a widespread complaint. The downshifter Jennifer Lawson describes her nieces, whom we have already met: "These aren't bad kids, they're just kind of limited. They watch MTV a lot, and they're very consumer-oriented. You'd think it was the patriotic thing to do. You know, they spend their Saturdays at the mall. If you ask them what they want for Christmas, they don't have to stop and think about it. They have pages of shopping lists. And they started being this way when they were seven or eight years old—only Barbie's Dream House would do for Christmas. They're just amazing."

The adult critique of youth is remarkably widespread. In the Merck Family Fund poll, 86 percent of respondents agreed that today's youth are too focused on buying and consuming things. In the Telecom survey, 84 percent agreed that "today's youth are too oriented toward money and material success." Maybe so, but are they really any different from earlier generations? Apparently. Survey data show marked increases in materialist values among young people. This finding accords with popular perception, such as Jennifer Lawson's: "When you get to be about forty, I think you always start saying, 'When I was your age,' and there's always something that you can look back to nostalgically. But I really do think kids are different than they were twenty or thirty years ago, because I grew up in a middle-class family, and I don't remember ever even paying attention to what I wore until I was in high school. At least you waited until you were a teenager to get into that. And now, I know seven- and eight-year-old kids who are very, very picky about the brands of things that they will consume."

Many grown-ups blame television, marketing, and advertising for the excessive consumerism of young people. Probably fewer recognize how much we are also teaching by example. Lawson again: "They're definitely learning it at home. I mean, what they see is that both of their parents work like dogs, sixty hours a week, to have not only two cars but two new cars. And a better house than they had three years ago, and a swimming pool that has to be put in out back, and vacations where you fly to the Caribbean twice a year. And I think they figure, if you're willing to work that hard for it, it must be worth it." Even in families not nearly so upscale as this one, children pick up the vibes. They *know* their parents are anxious about whether they are keeping up with other children. At least one focus-group participant recognized that we grown-ups want the Jordans too. "You can afford to go to Thom McCann's and buy your shoes, but you want to go to Bergman [*sic*] Goodman and buy the $150 sneakers because that's what everybody has."

Meanwhile, What's Going on Under the Tree?

Part of what keeps the consumer escalator moving ever upward is the significant fraction of our buying that takes the form of gifts. Retail stores report that they do almost 25 percent of their total volume during the Christmas season. Even pets are in on the action, with 75 percent receiving Christmas gifts, and 40 percent getting a present for their birthday.

Psychologically, it can be harder to hold the line on gift buying than on purchases for oneself. One reason is that within social classes, or lifestyle groups, there are real norms about gift giving. If the customary outlay for wedding gifts in your circle is $150, it may not be acceptable to spend $75. One of my acquaintances reports that she lost a friend by doing just that. Whether it's for a birthday, holiday, wedding, or baby shower, gift norms escalate along with general spending. And even between friends, one person can inadvertently ratchet up the spending level just by splurging once. You feel compelled to reciprocate with something a bit nicer. Somehow you're then spending $50 or $100 or more on a holiday gift exchange with a friend.

Generous gift giving is also one reason couples end up spending more than they should. One partner begins by giving something really nice (and expensive), something he wouldn't get for himself but feels his partner deserves. That act creates the license for a return gift of equal or greater luxuriousness. An upward spiral ensues. Because the partners are spending for gifts, the usual restraints of prudence, guilt, and cash flow are far less effective. It feels okay to splurge on someone else. They begin to let each other know what they want. Eventually gifts become a way for each of them to upscale, working their way down the "wish list" without actually having to take responsibility for making the purchases.

Gifts have also become a way that parents cope with shortages of time with their children. In her undergraduate thesis at Harvard University, my student Karen Greve found that the more time parents worked, and the less time they spent with their children, the more they bought them gifts—discretionary items such as toys, videos, and books. Parents who were with their kids more spent less. Greve found this result both in the official data on consumer expenditures and in her own survey of upper-middle-class and rich families in the Boston suburbs.

Of course, in consumerist America we buy not only gifts for other people but also what researchers call "self-gifts," presents for ourselves—as a reward, to achieve a certain deserved image, to lift our spirits, or to prolong a good feeling. Shopping becomes "retail therapy." One woman explained: "I bought a diamond ring for myself. It made me feel worthwhile, loved, secure. My husband doesn't believe in giving diamond rings, so I had to accept the fact that I had to buy one for myself if I wanted to get all those good feelings."

Gifts are fundamental elements of any culture and society, a form of social glue that creates and cements relationships. But as we survey the landscape of contemporary American gift giving, we have to wonder whether age-old social gift-giving rituals haven't been sucked into the larger vortex of consumerism. Many of us are looking back longingly to an era when gifts were not obligations but expressions of our generosity, when couples didn't use bridal registries as shopping lists, and when kids didn't hand out must-have Christmas lists. The commercialization of gift giving, with all its social pressures, seems to have taken some of the meaning out of the exchange. And the irony is that it has also taken away some of the value. According to a study by the economist Joel Waldfogel, much of what we give each other as gifts is not what we want anyway. Of the roughly $38 billion that Americans spent on gifts in the 1992 Christmas season, Waldfogel estimates that between $4 billion and $13 billion was absolutely wasted—money spent that gave no value to the receiver whatsoever.

The Psychology of Competitive Spending

Rich Moroni has an unusual degree of self-awareness about the forces that led him to spend. But this awareness has come from reading and thinking about the issue, carefully tracking his spending, and experiencing an identity crisis related to the mismatch between what he aspired to and what he could earn. For many people, the pressures to keep up are not well articulated, not always well understood, and often denied. Middle- and upper-middle-class Americans find it much easier to see others doing the keeping up.

We have no problem acknowledging the "conspicuous consumption" of the early twentieth century that Veblen wrote about. Middle class Americans shake their heads at what inner-city youths do to obtain expensive sneakers or gold chains. We can even get passionate about the dangers of status symbols in the Third World. Many Americans boycotted Nestle for promoting infant formula, the often deadly status alternative to breast milk. (Nestle and other companies had women in "modern" white uniforms doling out free supplies of formula in hospitals, leading to sickness, malnutrition, and even death among "bottle babies.") Many Americans deplore the entry of soft drinks and fast-food outlets into poor countries because they contribute to comerciogenic malnutrition: the poor spend their few pesos on soft drinks or French fries, forgoing nutritious food and becoming sick in the process. On the lighter side, we can chuckle at Peruvian Indians carrying rocks painted like transistor radios, Chinese who keep the brand tags on their designer sunglasses, Brazilian shanty-town dwellers with television antennae but no TVs, or the Papua New Guineans who substitute Pentel pens for boars' nose pieces. Third World status consumption seems straightforward, unambiguous in motive.

We have more trouble seeing the counterparts of these behaviors in the American middle class, and in ourselves. Telecomers certainly did. They emphatically rejected the importance of "keeping up with the

Joneses" in their lives. Sixty-two percent of the sample said that in the past two years they personally had felt no pressure at all to keep up. Another 28 percent rated the level of pressure at 2 on a 1–4 scale. Only 10 percent of the sample rated the amount of pressure to keep up at 3 or 4 (4 being "a great deal" of pressure). And yet, when I probed more deeply, I found that even those who said they didn't feel pressure, really did. They kept up with different people, however—with their TV buddies rather than their real friends. On the other hand, the people who consciously felt the Joneses breathing down their necks *were* more affected by them. It stands to reason.

In order to investigate differences in competitive consumption among Telecomers, I divided the sample into two groups: those who said they felt the need to keep up and those who didn't. Among the former, the pressure was intense, in the sense that reference groups mattered more than for the average Telecomer. Each downward step on the reference group scale (say, from being just about the same to being worse off financially than one's group) caused a reduction in savings of $3,451 a year—or more than 10 percent more than for the "I don't feel it" types. On the other hand, those who felt such social pressures remained mercifully free of pressure from the tube. Their viewing hours had no impact on their spending patterns, as the low t-statistic (.16) reveals. They were too busy watching their real friends to notice what Cybill was wearing or to covet her spectacular terrace view.

By contrast, the majority of Telecomers didn't think they felt the pressure, but they seemed to. They had a strong reference group effect ($2,938) *and* a strong TV effect (-$225). They are exemplars of how the new consumerism has taken hold: they keep up with both real and fictitious people in a dynamic of upscale consuming.

The finding that individuals relate differently to consumption norms is no surprise. We would expect considerable variation across the population in the extent to which individuals are psychically tied into consuming, how sensitive they are to comparisons with others, and how well they exercise self-control. What *is* surprising is that 90 percent of the Telecom sample denied that they personally felt pressure to keep up with the Joneses, and that more than two-thirds denied it categorically, claiming to feel no pressure at all. Only 10 people from this group of 834 admitted to feeling a great deal of pressure. So why do people say they don't try to "keep up" when they do?

One explanation is that people sincerely believe they feel no pressure to keep up. Maybe they don't consciously measure their own spending by what others have, don't care if they are below the norm for their social circle, and don't covet goods for their socially sym-

---

Table 4.4   Multiple Regression Analysis of Low or High Pressure on Telecom Employees to "Keep Up with the Joneses"

INDEPENDENT VARIABLE COEFFICIENT*	LOW PRESSURE COEFFICIENT	HIGH PRESSURE COEFFICIENT
	(t-statistics in parentheses)**	
Constant term	$25,094.00 (2.57)	$16,451.00 (-.056)
Household income	.106 (5.56)	.226 (3.85)
Permanent household income	.037 (0.97)	-.130 (-0.29)
Household net worth	.013 (0.76)	.76 (1.11)
Sex	-4,513.00 (-3.03)	4,379.00 (0.89)
Age	-12,168.00 (-2.45)	572.00 (0.04)
Age-squared	1,465.00 (2.02)	-266.00 (-0.12)
Race	-589.00 (-0.41)	2,075.00 (0.36)
Occupation	-200.00 (-0.51)	-205.00 (-0.17)
Educational level	-1,595.00 (-2.00)	733.00 (0.23)
Number of dependents	-1,326.00 (-2.63)	-431.00 (-0.29)
Satisfaction with income	523.00 (0.66)	2,387.00 (1.08)
Hours per week watching TV	-225.00 (-3.36)	28.00 (0.16)
Financial status compared to reference group	2,938.00 (3.31)	3,451.00 (1.70)

*Adj-R^2: .269 (low pressure); .444 (high pressure). Dependent variable is annual household saving mean: $10,292 (low); $11,973 (high).

**White's t-statistics, which correct for heteroskedasticity, are reported in Appendix table B.4 for the low pressure group. Sample is too small for heteroskedasticity correction for high pressure group.

For variable definitions, see Appendix B.3.

bolic values. But if that's the case, we need an alternative account of other aspects of their behavior and attitudes. Why do they spend so much more than they would like to? Why do two-thirds of them buy designer clothes? And why do 40 percent feel that their coworkers are very materialistic? Furthermore, we need an alternative account of my finding that they *do* spend to a group norm.

Alternatively, they may simply not be comfortable admitting to feeling the pressure, either to a researcher or even to themselves. Or they may not experience it as "keeping up with the Joneses," those showy, obnoxious neighbors two doors down. When it's just a relative or coworker who sets the standard, there's a whole different feel to it. (The one major exception to this type of denial is around the need to keep our children up with the Jones kids.)

The sociologist Patricia Berhau found this resistance in her in-depth interviews with Philadelphia-area families. As the subject of others came up, her interviewees were quick to deny feelings of competitiveness or envy. They adamantly maintained that they did not begrudge what their friends or relatives had. But at the same time, the strong influence of others' possessions on their own desires, the need to attain a certain level, and the social bases of comparison were salient themes in the conversations.

In *Choosing the Right Pond*, the economist Robert Frank offers an explanation for our resistance to the keeping-up metaphor. From

---

Table 4.5 Summary of Factors Influencing Saving by Low- and High-Pressure Groups of Telecom Employees

---

SOCIAL COMPARISON

If pressure to keep up is **low**: each step up in financial status compared to respondent's reference group raised annual saving by $2,938.

If pressure to keep up is **high**: each step up in financial status compared to respondent's reference group raised annual saving by $3,451.

TELEVISION WATCHING

If pressure to keep up is **low**: each additional hour of television watched per week reduced annual saving by $225.

If pressure to keep up is **high**: no statistically significant effect on savings.

an early age, he argues, we are taught to repress feelings of jealousy, envy, and one-upmanship. We are encouraged to share with our siblings and friends, to be generous to others, and to deny our feelings of revenge and rage when others do better, get more, or defeat us. This is not to say that we are not also taught to be competitive, to achieve, and to accumulate for ourselves. There is no doubt that we are. But the overall cultural message we receive is complex, contradictory, and subtle. The contrast between the behavior of children and adults is instructive, as Frank points out. Children are open and un-self-conscious in their insistence on a favorable comparative position. Try giving one child a smaller portion of ice cream than you serve to the other children at the table. He or she will react instantaneously and forcefully, stressing not the absolute quantity of ice cream but the fact that he or she has been shortchanged. Perform a similar experiment with adults. Most will be too polite to mention it, as serving size is not a subject for public discussion. But the shortfall will be noticed. As adults, we have not ceased to care about where we rank, but we are socialized not to talk about it.

Scholars have argued that in modern consumer societies traditional taboos against envy, competition, and unlimited accumulation have been reduced. In traditional cultures, having too much, or showing it too readily, has been discouraged in order to maintain harmony. A greedy or ostentatious person is thought to risk the wrath of the ubiquitous "evil eye," which exacts revenge by causing misfortune. By contrast, conspicuousness has long been more acceptable in the West. But we should not overstate this difference. For all its focus on getting rich, our culture still has an ambivalent view of consumption excess, one-upmanship, and showing off. The "primitive" taboos have not disappeared, explaining perhaps why luxury products are so often advertised with a message designed to assuage guilt—go ahead, you've earned it, it's okay to flaunt it.

Taboos surrounding envy or comparison also explain why we often think "function" when our subconscious is screaming "status." Our directed thoughts center on the usefulness of the purchase—how it will save us money or time, how it will satisfy a real need. We tell ourselves that our four-year-old car is on the verge of needing repairs. That if we get a pair of really nice gold earrings, we can wear them every day and stop buying so many pairs of inexpensive ones. That with a remodeled kitchen we'll be more likely to eat in, so we'll save money on restaurants. While these rationalizations may be true, what's driving us emotionally is the craving for the new model, the classy look of gold earrings, or the image conjured up by *Gourmet* magazine.

Take the choice of a place to live. Who among the middle or upper-middle class have told themselves (and others) that their first criterion is safety and quickly gravitated to high-end neighborhoods? But who actually looks at the crime statistics for different areas? Very few, because although people genuinely want safety, many also want class, charm, proximity to an exciting retail district, and an address to which they feel comfortable inviting colleagues. Saying that you chose a certain neighborhood because it has a "certain class of people" feels less socially acceptable than saying it is safe or has good schools. Safety, good schools, better quality, saving money—these are all acceptable consumer motives in a way that status is not. Telling yourself (and then your husband) that you want a shearling coat because you've been freezing all winter is a far "better" reason than because your best friend just got one.

Indeed, research shows that consumers conflate status (as measured by brand names) and quality. One study found that women rated an identical shirt differently on the basis of the label it carried and the store it supposedly came from. When the shirt carried a designer label or a Nordstrom's tag, it was rated as more stylish than when it bore K-Mart's private label. A similar study asked men to evaluate three nearly identical pairs of Haggar slacks, two of which had been relabeled as Ralph Lauren and Hart Schafner and Marx. Among men who were familiar with the brand names, the two prestige brands rated higher on quality and on willingness to purchase. Studies showing that consumers often cannot discern brand differences without labels provide further evidence of the widespread conflation of status and quality.

One question remains: how *does* that part of social comparison that is consciously experienced take place? In going upscale, what are American consumers trying to achieve? Are we looking for superiority? Trying to fit in? Hoping to avoid being humiliated? Or just trying to be ourselves? Apparently the answer is, all of the above. Some of us are like the Dallas businessman whose boss had a $10,000 Rolex. He went out and bought the $20,000 model. It was unattractive, he conceded, but bigger—and that was the point. Or consider the plight of a woman from suburban Washington whose house was one of two large ones on the block. When a new family moved in between the two, tore down the existing house and proceeded to build a much larger one, she was distraught, because her formerly fine house would now look *so small*. She did what she could to stop the construction, from lobbying neighbors not to sign variances to attending county meetings to oppose the issuance of permits. Others are like an acquaintance of mine, a successful New York professional and a socially conscious, self-aware woman who saves money and is not interested in the consumerism around her. Hearing about my lipstick research, she confesses that, no, she would not feel comfortable pulling out a drugstore no-name in a work situation. There's a "professional undoing" about it she is unwilling to risk.

Professional or social undoing is one important motive. Fifty years ago, most people just wanted to secure their place in the American middle class, doing whatever it took to stay there. At one time, that was acquiring a houseful of "decencies," the status symbols of the middle class, situated between the necessities of the poor and the luxuries of the rich. Today, in a world where being middle-class is not good enough for many people and indeed that social category seems like an endangered species, securing a place means going upscale. But when everyone's doing it, upscaling can mean simply keeping up. Even when we are aiming high, there's a strong defensive component to our comparisons. We don't want to fall behind or lose the place we've carved out for ourselves. We don't want to get stuck in the "wrong" lifestyle cluster. How we spend has become a crucial part of our self-image, personal identity, and social network.

The historical record highlights the fact that beneath—indeed driving—our system of competitive consumption are deep class inequalities. The classless-society and end-of-ideology literature of twenty-five years ago turns out to have been wishful thinking. Ironically, inequality began to arise soon after these ideas appeared. The dirty little secret of American society is that not everyone did become middle-class. We still have rich and poor and gradations in between. Class background and income level affect not only the obvious—if and where you go to college, the quality of your children's elementary school, the kind of job you get—but also your likelihood of getting heart disease, the way you talk, and how respectfully you're treated by others. At all levels of the class structure, we are motivated, as Barbara Ehrenreich put it some years ago, by "fear of falling." Accounts of downsizing captured the nation's imagination in the 1990s: the laid-off plant manager who clung to his aging Mercedes, suspenders, and sprawling suburban home, depleting his retirement fund in the process; the divorced engraving company employee clutching the remnants of her middle-class existence but reduced to burying her food in the snow in the yard because she could not afford a new refrigerator; unemployed aerospace workers waging a daily battle not to lose their homes and slip into the scary world of poverty. They found themselves driving around without a spare tire, giving up their health insurance, and waiting between haircuts as long as possible. At all levels, a structure of inequality injects insecurity and fear into our psyches. The penalties of dropping down are perhaps the most powerful psychological hooks that keep us keeping up, even as the heights get dizzying.

Neither market researchers nor their academic counterparts have done much direct analysis of the psychology of consumer emulation. So no one knows too much about how consumer reference groups are chosen or about the different psychological attitudes people bring to the process. Research on positional consumption is rare. However, one famous segmentation typology does shed some light on these issues. Excluding the bottom segment of economically struggling individuals, the Values and Life Styles (VALS) schema of the 1970s and 1980s defined nearly 80 percent of the remaining consumers as outer-directed, or positionally oriented, in their consumption. These in turn were divided into "belongers" (43 percent), "emulators" (11 percent), and "achievers" (24 percent). As their names suggest, belongers "are more interested in fitting in than standing out," emulators aspire to climbing up the ladder of social class, and achievers have made it. (These groups reflect the income distribution to a significant degree—belongers are more likely to be lower-middle-class, and achievers have higher incomes.)

In the revamped 1990s VALS typology, the categories have changed significantly, but achievers and "strivers" still comprise 30 percent, as do "fulfilleds" and "believers." The lifestyles of "actualizers" (the 13 percent who have reached the pinnacle of the VALS pyramid—and incidentally, the pinnacle of success) "reflect a cultivated taste for the finer things in life," but they are reportedly interested in image as evidence of taste, independence, and character, not status. (Yeah, right. Apparently these researchers have forgotten that taste *is* an important part of status.)

The Consumer Escalator

The fact that people pay extra money for status, or replicate the lifestyles of their friends, is not in itself an insurmountable problem. If we aped the guy in the corner office once and that was the end of it, it would be a relatively minor issue. The difficulty is the dynamic aspect of keeping up: the emulation process never ends. Growth is built into the very structure of our economy. Manufacturers strive for continuous productivity improvements. Retailers count on higher sales volume each year. Investors demand that their capital increase each quarter. The market imperative is bigger, better, more. Consumers have not escaped this escalation mentality. We expect our standard of living to rise annually, and throughout our working lives. Indeed, the rising standard is a national icon, firmly rooted in the political discourse. It is progress.

The commitment to rising incomes can be seen in a variety of public opinion polls. The standard answer to the amount of money a family of four needs to live in "reasonable comfort" has been $1,000 to $2,000 more than whatever the median family income happens to be. In 1978, $19,600, or $1,960 more than the national median, was thought to be necessary for "reasonable comfort." In 1985 reasonable comfort cost $30,600 (compared to median income of $27,734). By 1994 the reasonable-comfort level had risen to $40,000. Rising standards are also evident in our changing attitudes to necessities and luxuries. A wide range of consumer products considered luxuries in the 1970s are deemed necessities today. The luxuries of 1998 will be the necessities of the early twenty-first century.

The Merck Family Fund poll revealed another way in which having more is hardwired into our psyches. We are not satisfied with whatever level we have. When asked to define their own economic situation on a scale of 1–10 (with 10 representing the wealthiest people in the country), respondents on average chose 5.1, almost smack in the middle, as we would expect. Asked to define the *lowest* number at which they would feel satisfied with their economic situation, the average response was higher—5.4. Apparently, we still don't feel we have enough. In the high-earning Telecom sample (almost no one earned below $25,000 annually, and 35 percent earned above $55,000), 28 percent of those surveyed expressed dissatisfaction with their incomes, and 54 percent said they were only "somewhat satisfied." Of those, about one-third said they'd need 20 percent more income to be satisfied, and one-quarter said they'd need twice as much or more to reach satisfaction.

What drives the escalation of standards? Why do we never seem to have enough? There are cultural reasons, of course. But the economic structure itself is also to blame. As I argued in *The Overworked American*, the nation has become enmeshed in a cycle of work and spend. Employers, rather than employees, choose hours of work, and they typically choose long hours. Firms' annual productivity increases—courtesy of technological change or a better-educated workforce—cannot be used by employees to reduce hours of work but is passed on as income (if it *is* passed on).

Once they have it, employees spend their additional income. The

---

Table 4.6 The Upgrading of a "Comfortable Life"

Question: *In order to live in reasonable comfort around here, how much income per year do you think a family of four needs today?*

	MEDIAN RESPONSE	MEDIAN INCOME
1978	$19,600	$17,640
1981	$24,800	$22,388
1983	$28,400	$24,673
1985	$30,600	$27,734
1987	$32,500	$30,970
1990	$36,800	$35,353
1992	$38,000	$35,939
1994	$40,000	$38,782

SOURCE: Reasonable Comfort from Roper Center, University of Connecticut; Median Income from Council of Economic Advisers 1996. Table B-29, p. 314.

imperatives to spend in consumer society are numerous, and the incentives to save are weak. But there is another reason, unique to the work-and-spend dynamic. Rising incomes create social pressures to spend. A more leisured, lower-spending lifestyle does not emerge. Instead, people get more money and put in long hours on the job. As long as a few fashion-minded or highly consumerist households take on the role of innovators, spending their increased income on new, better, or more consumer items, the impact of their consumption ripples through the system. Marketing and advertising accelerate the process. Smiths emulate Joneses, and in turn are emulated by Bernsteins, Vitellis, and O'Rourkes. When the Chens don't want to go along, they are relatively alone—not only alone, but left behind.

There is an important irrationality in the system, and it is not hard to see: if we measure our satisfaction by how well we are doing compared to others, general increases in affluence do not raise our personal satisfaction (as mounting evidence shows). Then why do we participate? Why don't we learn after a few rounds of keeping up? Because, besides psychological factors, other powerful forces, both social and economic, keep us in the system.

Practical Reasons to Keep on Keeping Up

For professionals, managers, salespeople, and many of the self-employed—people whose stock in trade is their "human capital"—maintaining a certain standard is important for success in the market. Consumption is taken as a signal of their skills and talents. They have to dress, drive, even eat the part. The lawyer in a cheesy suit, the psychiatrist with a seedy office, and the salesman in a twelve-year-old car all project failure.

In some jobs, image can be all-important. A wardrobe is as necessary as a diploma, as my interviewees repeatedly stressed. Makeup, accessories, and jewelry are de rigueur. Indeed, attractiveness itself affects market success. Economists have found that people who are more physically attractive gain better jobs and higher wages. Advertising firms with better-looking executives have higher revenues. And physical attractiveness is often created with the help of consumer products—cosmetics, beauty shops, tanning salons, health clubs, exercise equipment. Even male executives, downsized, or downsizable, are getting blepharoplasty (to reduce droopy skin around the eyes) and other cosmetic surgeries to make themselves more marketable in a world where youth counts for everything. For Lauren Vandermeer, moving up the corporate ladder necessitated more spending, on clothes and other accessories. "Now, maybe not to the extent of a Rolex watch. We're in the nineties, and the Rolex is no longer cool. But definitely, a Tissot watch from Switzerland. I got this in the Cayman Islands on vacation. It was important to have. Because when I would extend my hand to present something, they would see that, and that meant I was somebody to reckon with." While we need not go all the way with the claim of Oxxford Clothes (purveyor of $1,500 suits) that "business is war—never underestimate the importance of your uniform," the clothier does have a point. Keeping up is good business.

Of course, business is not the only area where success entails spending. Nicole Brown Simpson and her three sisters, members of a well-off Orange County family, all had breast implants. One suspects the purpose was to get and hold desirable (rich?) men in the "marriage market." Some of the female downshifters I interviewed were quite explicit on this point. "Single women . . . well, we tend to spend more money on making ourselves look attractive, be it staying in shape or getting your hair done, waxing, all that kind of stuff. It's just the cost of doing business."

This is not just an issue for women. For everyone, socializing costs money. If coworkers routinely eat at the corner luncheonette, bringing a sandwich means you'll be eating alone. If a beer after the softball game is the usual practice, forgoing it means you'll miss half the fun. Within circles of friends or relatives, spending for social rituals such as long-distance phone calls and birthday or Christmas gifts is not always optional. To buck the tide requires explanation and does not always elicit understanding.

People who try to live on less become very aware of these social costs. In a free-spending society, a downshifter notes, there are few ways of socializing "that don't have expenses tied to it. If you're really into sports, you can do some of that, that could be free up to a point, but you've got to have the equipment." A woman who had to "pick and choose" her social encounters after her income dropped, missed the company, not the restaurant meals. She felt that being gay made it even more difficult. "There are not many resources in terms of meeting other women in the community that don't have expenses tied to them. While that barrier still exists in the straight community, I think it's probably a higher barrier for us. It's almost like a gay tax, because you always have to pay a cover charge."

The social dimensions of technological change also keep us on the consumer escalator. When the telephone was introduced, life without one posed no problems. But as phones became widely disseminated throughout the population, practical difficulties arose. Alternative forms of interpersonal communication declined. (Remember the private couriers so common in nineteenth- and early-twentieth-century novels?) Paying a social visit without an advance phone call became less acceptable among the middle classes. Today rotary phones, already inadequate for accessing certain services, have become nearly obsolete. Callers get annoyed if you don't have an answering machine. In business, voice mail, faxes, and mobile phones are standard, and they are becoming so in private life. As more and more people buy these items, substitutes disappear and life without them becomes more vexing.

Of course, technology also raises a host of daily paradoxes for us, as David Mick and Susan Fournier have argued. New products promise freedom but often feel enslaving. They promise to save us time but may not. And, of course, they come with their own keeping-up dynamic. As one of their informants noted about the laptop computer he had purchased just six weeks before, it "is not outmoded [yet], but in another six months it will be. I know I'm going to be envious of what's out there."

Getting along without a car—or, for many people, a second car—presents a similar challenge. In much of the country, public transport is minimal and shared transport among neighbors is rare. There are no bicycle lanes, and many suburbs don't have sidewalks. Workplaces are located far from housing. In suburbs, exurbs, and small towns, shops and malls are not within walking distance. The "built environment" virtually demands autos, which are expensive to buy, repair, and maintain. Houses in suburban and small-town neighborhoods also have lawns, which need lawn mowers, lots of water, fertilizer, flowers, and shrubs, all of which cost money. In

1995 alone, Americans spent $7.6 billion on residential lawn care, much of it environmentally destructive. But lawn upkeep (notice the term) has become an important realm of aesthetic standards (that is, taste), enforced by the fear of social disapproval or, increasingly, community regulations. The same can be said for exterior maintenance and having a reasonable-looking vehicle in the driveway. As one focus group participant explained, there's a constant pressure: "'The Joneses' is killing me."

More than practical considerations may be at stake. Some people experience a basic social alienation from being left out of the ongoing national shopping spree. As one stay-at-home mother remarked, "It's hard, though, because you see other people who have that new car or go out and they can buy their clothes at Jacobson's instead of Target. And you got to keep saying, 'But you're staying at home with your kids.' I mean, you have to keep saying it to yourself."

These examples remind us that "consumer choice" is subject in important ways to social, infrastructural, and market constraints. Our interactions with others are almost always mediated through things. The built environment mandates particular choices. Even the availability of consumer goods depends on the purchasing patterns of others. Time-consuming, high-stress jobs create another set of consumer pressures. Long hours at work put a premium on time and convenience. Those who can afford it buy prepared foods, restaurant meals, and takeout. They hire baby-sitters, accountants, and house cleaners. Their friends are busy too, so instead of asking for a ride to the airport (like they did when they were young), they take a taxi. They relieve stress with three-day weekends at hotels, entertainment, massages, and vacations to get away from it all. Earning to buy turns into buying to keep earning.

Unhappiness at work can also cause spending, as some downshifters attest. "When I think of the money I threw away to compensate for all the emptiness and all the stuff that wasn't being satisfied in the work I was doing ... I just spent it to kind of keep myself going." Lauren Vandermeer, whose relentless rise up the marketing ladder kept her traveling all the time, also spent to recover. "I would go on vacation because I was so stressed out from having traveled ... but I didn't go camping. I went to the Cayman Islands, and I stayed in the Marriott."

Upscaling transforms the consumer market itself. Once new products are diffused throughout the population, the items they replaced disappear. Where are the manual typewriters, houses without closets, and monochrome computer monitors? When the old appliances break, parts are no longer available. Indeed, there is a general bias in our economy against repair and in favor of buying new. (One reason this bias can prevail is that new products do not pay their true environmental costs.) For those who don't want to change what they have and are comfortable with a static lifestyle, the market offers limited choices. It is geared to newer and more expensive products. It is perpetually upshifting.

While these practical dimensions of consumer conformity are important, I do not believe they are the major explanation of why Americans spend as much as they do. They represent the logistical difficulties of a nonconsumerist way of living, but until recently, such difficulties mattered to relatively few Americans. Few had even been contemplating alternatives to consumerism. Upscaling has become the default option in a world where we have been trained not to think about these questions.

See-Want-Borrow-and-Buy—Then Give Away?

Of course, all this spending raises another question. What to do once we get the stuff home? Do we use it? Does it live up to its promises? Do we have *room* for it? The sociologist Colin Campbell has argued that one of the distinctive aspects of modern consuming is that we have strong desires for products before we have them, but once acquired they mean very little to us. Judging by consumer surveys of "post-purchase" regret, Campbell overstates the case, but he *does* have a point. Even leaving aside mistakes and faulty products, American consumers seem to accumulate large numbers of things in which they subsequently lose interest.

It's difficult to quantify how much spending falls into this category. We don't keep official statistics on items redistributed through secondhand markets, garage sales, giveaways, flea markets, charity bazaars, classified ads, or the garbage. But the volume of stuff eventually discarded is considerable. Of course, many perfectly good reasons for product divestment have nothing to do with impulse buying or loss of interest. Your children grow up, your bad knee prevents skiing, you can't be blamed for not liking a gift. But scouring the yard sales, we can also see the telltale impulse items of particular eras (the Salton yogurt maker of the 1970s, the cappuccino machine of the 1980s), as well as the perennial throwaways: kitchenware, sporting equipment, knickknacks, books, and—the most common impulse purchase—clothes. Mountains and mountains of clothes. (This raises a disturbing point of similarity between the purchasing habits of compulsive and ordinary buyers, by the way.)

Stymied in the search for a quantitative estimate, my research assistants spent a few days at the town dump in a prosperous Boston suburb. They came back with lovely gifts for everyone in the office. I got a three-volume color-plated *Treasury of Children's Literature* in perfect condition. Here's what else they found:

In the dumpster (in usable condition) were a charcoal grill, a headboard, a sawhorse, ancient downhill skis and poles, a beret, a stroller, lots of mattresses, box springs, two lawn mowers, a step stool, a table, and a children's plastic playhouse (about four feet by four feet). Unfortunately, they visited the dump just after the swap area was cleaned out, so the pickings there were slim: a lawn mower, a lamp, a folding chair, cushions, a desk chair with rolling wheels, a tire, storm windows, a beach chair, pie tins, a sofa with cushions, window shades, a weed whacker, a baby car seat, a mattress and box spring, a fireplace screen, a pot, old audio equipment, baby bassinets, a duffel bag, two cardboard shoe shelves for closets, a chest of drawers, a clothes drying rack, a baby bath chair, another sofa, rugs, carpeting, an adult bike, a child's bike, a large glass window pane, a mailbox, a toilet bowl brush, and a rocking chair and desk that were taken while my assistants watched. The local dump lore has it that a woman once left a Volkswagen, complete with keys, for someone to take. At the book swap, they found a great variety of stuff in "pretty good shape," including *National Geographic*s, old textbooks, SAT/AP test prep books, medical journals, old encyclopedia sets, several dictionaries, cookbooks, law books, travel guides, children's books, and novels. Next to the collection box for the Salvation Army, they found numerous baby and toddler clothes, a crib quilt, a pacifier, children's sweaters and pants, Playskool toys, water shoes for an adult, a bonnet, baby rattles, baby booties, and a functioning solar TI scientific calculator. All of these items appeared to be of pretty good quality and were clean, almost like new. (They couldn't see inside the box.) At the Goodwill shack, they found a child's dirt bike (almost new), a child's scooter, a rotary telephone, an iron, a bathroom scale, two leather suitcases, worn wicker bathroom shelves, as well as sheets, a wall-to-wall bath mat, a duffel bag, many, many clothes, many comforters, a bike rack, an afghan, a neck brace, a nightgown and matching robe (chiffon), a small "Oriental" rug, a leather briefcase (nice), a leather purse, wire coat hangers, dress shoes (outdated style), hiking boots, ski boots on a boot rack, running shoes, cowboy boots, an electric pencil sharpener, a plastic plate-and-cup set (for a beach house or picnic), a washcloth, a stuffed bunny, and a silk bow tie.

Part of the reason Americans are selling and giving away so much is that it's getting harder to find room for it all. Downshifters frequently describe a kind of material overload, or what is known in those circles as "clutter." As Beth Church noted, "Over the years people 'collect, collect, collect,' and although some of the things may be lovely, there's only so much space—and emotion—that you can put into things." One result has been an explosion of self-storage facilities. And the amount of stuff being transported around the country has also increased dramatically: over the last thirty-five years, freight tonnage per capita has risen 40 percent.

What's most impressive is that we are complaining about too much junk even as housing space per person has risen substantially, new homes increasingly boast walk-in closets, and garages are often used as extra storage areas. But then again, maybe that's part of the problem. Why is it that all those closets that were such an attraction when you moved in don't seem all that spacious now? Like new highways, which just lead to more driving, or household appliances that create extra work, storage space increases the propensity to acquire—yet another variant of Parkinson's Law. Not to worry. If things get tight, you can hire one of a thriving new industry of closet consultants, who will teach you how to cram ever more junk into the hole in your bedroom wall.

The Social Irrationality of Upscaling

However rational it may be for individuals to keep up with the upscaling of consumer standards, it can be deeply irrational for society as a whole. Or, as one Chicago woman put it, "We'd all be better off if we cared less about what someone's wearing and what kind of a car they're driving or where they're living." Like standing up in a crowd to get a better view, it stops working once others do it too. In the end, the view is the same, but everyone's legs are tired. The more our consumer satisfaction is tied into social comparisons— whether upscaling, just keeping up, or not falling too far behind— the less we achieve when consumption grows, because the people we compare ourselves to are also experiencing rising consumption. Our relative position does not change. Jones's delight at being able to afford the Honda Accord is dampened when he sees Smith's new Camry. Both must put in long hours to make the payments, suffer with congested highways and dirty air, and have less in the bank at the end of the day. And both remain frustrated when they think about the Land Cruiser down the street.

Of course, relative positions do change. Some people get promotions or pay raises that place them higher up in the hierarchy. Others fall behind. But these random changes cancel each other out. Of more interest is how the broad social groupings that make up the major comparison groups fare. From the end of the Second World War until the mid-1970s, growth was relatively equally distributed. The rough doubling in living standards was experienced by most Americans, including the poor. In fact, the income distribution was even compressed, as people at the bottom gained some ground relative to those at the top. Since then, however, and particularly since the 1980s, the income groups have diverged, as I noted in the introduction.

Middle-class Americans began to experience themselves falling behind as their slow-growing wages and salaries lagged behind those of the groups above them. Their anxiety grew, and it became a commonplace that it was no longer possible to achieve a middle-class standard of living on one salary. At the same time, increasing numbers began to lose completely the respectability that defined their class. Below them, a segment of downwardly mobile working people found that their reduced job prospects and declining wages had placed them in the ranks of the working poor. And the nonemployed poor fell even further as their numbers grew and their average income fell.

Thus, relative position has worsened for most people, making it increasingly difficult to keep up. The excitement, convenience, or joy that households may have experienced through the billions in additional spending between 1979 and the present seems to have been overshadowed by feelings of deprivation. Among the upper echelons, all those personal computers, steam showers, Caribbean vacations, and piano lessons have not been sufficient to offset the anxieties inherent in a rapidly upscaling society.

The current mood has led to nostalgia about the older, simpler version of the American dream. There is a palpable sense of unease, a yearning for the less expansive, and less expensive, aspirations of our parents. In the words of one young man, "My dream is to build my own house. When my parents grew up, they weren't so much 'I want this, I've got to have that.' They just wanted to be comfortable. Now we're more—I know I am—'I need this.' And it's not really a need."

The greater the weight people place on the social comparison aspect of their consumption, relative to other aspects like function, aesthetics, or convenience, the greater the social irrationality of upscaling. If, as some have argued, these social aspects become more important as basic needs are met and we grow more affluent, then the system takes on an increasingly perverse character. The problem is not just that more consumption doesn't yield more satisfaction (as in the extreme case where all satisfaction comes from relative position), but that it always has a cost. The extra hours we have to work to earn the money cut into personal and family time. *Whatever* we consume has an ecological impact, whether it's the rain forests cleared to graze the cattle which become Big Macs, the toxins collecting in our bodies from the plastics that now dominate our material environment, or the pesticides used to grow the cotton for our T-shirts. Americans increasingly resent paying taxes to buy public goods like parks, schools, the arts, or support for the poor because taxes are perceived as subtracting from the private consumption they deem absolutely necessary. We find ourselves skimping on invisibles such as insurance, college funds, and retirement savings as the visible commodities somehow become indispensable. In the process, we are threatening our temporal, social, and biological infrastructures. We are impoverishing ourselves in pursuit of a consumption goal that is inherently unachievable. In the words of one focus-group participant, we "just don't know when to stop and draw the line."

5

The Downshifter Next Door

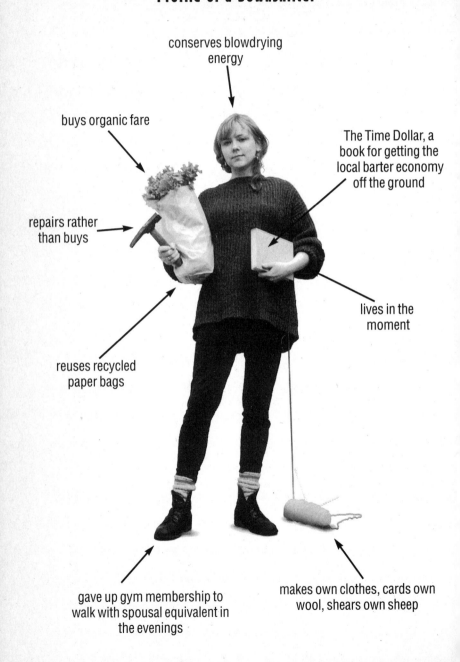

Profile of a Downshifter

conserves blowdrying energy

buys organic fare

The Time Dollar, a book for getting the local barter economy off the ground

repairs rather than buys

lives in the moment

reuses recycled paper bags

gave up gym membership to walk with spousal equivalent in the evenings

makes own clothes, cards own wool, shears own sheep

By the mid-1990s, consumerism was beginning to worry people. In surveys, 75 to 80 percent of the public was agreeing that the country had become too materialistic, even too greedy. They felt that Americans had become addicted to shopping, were spending wastefully, and had lost the values of thrift and prudence. They worried about how the ascendance of materialist values was affecting young people. Of course, we need to take these sentiments with a grain of salt. People often romanticize the past as a golden age of better values. And consumerism is an easy target when it's somebody else's disease. (These surveys show that people are more likely to attribute materialism to others than to themselves.) But that having been said, there's little doubt the nation's consumerist turn has generated considerable unease.

For some, dissatisfaction with the work-and-spend culture has become palpable enough to spur them to action. They have begun "downshifting." In the years from 1990 through 1996, nearly one-fifth (19 percent) of all adult Americans made a voluntary lifestyle change, excluding a regularly scheduled retirement, that entailed earning less money. Just over half of these people, or 55 percent, consider their lifestyle change to be permanent. And nearly all of them (85 percent) are happy about the change they made. Surprisingly, given the popular perception, downshifters are no more likely to be women than men. And they are hardly wealthy; almost half made $35,000 or less before their change.

Another 12 percent of Americans were involuntarily downshifted, that is, through no choice of their own their incomes were reduced. They lost a job, had their hours reduced, or suffered a pay cut. But even among this group, one-quarter (24 percent) consider the change "a blessing in disguise." So just about one-fifth of the adult American population is happily living on less.

Why is this happening? Primarily because people have had it with demanding jobs and stressed-out lives. One-third of Americans say they always feel rushed, just over one-third say that their lives are out of control, two-thirds say they want more balance, and about 60 percent would like to simplify their lives. Downshifting is a response to these daily realities. The most common reason cited for downshifting, by a wide margin, is "wanting more time, less stress, and more balance in life." Downshifters also articulate the need to do something more meaningful with their lives and to spend more time with their children. They accomplish these goals by working less—much less. Before changing their lives, about half of all downshifters worked more than forty hours a week, and more than half of those worked in excess of fifty. Afterward, half (48 percent) logged in fewer than thirty hours. Of course, their incomes and spending were also reduced.

In this chapter, I profile a variety of downshifters. For most, the change has been voluntary, but some began the process with a lay-off. These profiles are not in any strict sense representative. My sample was not random, and it did not reflect the full diversity of downshifters. I deliberately chose individuals who had gone through major lifestyle changes. (This is one reason I have included only one couple with young children.) I have also not included people who

---

TABLE 5.1 Prevalence of Voluntary Downshifting

Question: *In the last five years, have you voluntarily made a long term change in your life which has resulted in your making less money—other than taking a regularly scheduled retirement? (For example: switching to a lower-paying job, reducing your work hours, making a career change, or quitting work to stay at home.)*

Yes	19%
No	81

TABLE 5.2 Prevalence of Involuntary Downshifting

Question: *In the last five years, have you undergone a lifestyle change which has resulted in your making less money—but was not of your own choosing? (For example: losing your job, having to take a lower-paying job, being unable to find full-time work, or being forced to change occupations?)*

Yes	12%
No	88

are spending downshifters but not income downshifters, that is, those who continue to earn at a certain level but have reduced their spending in order to save more. Eventually many of these also reduce their hours or stop working. (The thrust of the following chapter is this downsizing of spending.)

There are many historical antecedents to today's downshifters. David Shi's *The Simple Life* is still probably the classic work on the recurring waves of people who have opted for intentionally simple living. What makes today's trend different is that downshifters are not dropping out of society, few are living communally, and most are not ideologically motivated. They are smack in the middle of the American mainstream. But they are swimming against a long-standing current of "economic progress."

TABLE 5.3 Voluntary Downshifters by Type of Downshift

Question: *Which of the following* best *describes the lifestyle change you made?*

Changed to a lower-paying job	29%
Reduced work hours	12
Quit working outside the home	16
Changed careers and/or went back to school	17
Started own business	10
Reduced the number of jobs held	2
Refused a promotion	1
Other	12

TABLE 5.4 Hours Reductions Among Voluntary Downshifters

Weekly Hours	Pre-Downshift	Post-Downshift
< 30	7%	48%
31–40	40	31
41–50	24	14
50+	28	7

The Path to "Freedom": Alice Kline

There is no typical downshifter profile, but Alice Kline's mentality (although not her income level) is just about as representative as any that I encountered. Alice, along with her husband (a chemical engi-

TABLE 5.5 Demographic Characteristics of Voluntary Downshifters

SEX	Male	48%
	Female	52
EDUCATION LEVEL	Some high school	8
	High school diploma	21
	Some college	30
	Four-year college degree	25
	Postgraduate degree	14
CHILDREN UNDER 18	None	53
	One	17
	Two	20
	Three	8
	Four or more	3
RACIAL/ETHNIC BACKGROUND	White Caucasian	85
	African American	9
	Hispanic	4
	Asian	0
	Other	2
MARITAL STATUS	Married	54
	Single, never married	24
	Divoced, separated, or widowed	19
	Living with partner	3
AGE	18–19	3
	20–29	18
	30–39	34
	40–49	27
	50–64	15
	64+	4

neer) and two children, lives in a well-to-do Boston suburb. In her midfifties, she is an attractive, articulate professional in the advertising business—hardly a countercultural type. Alice stayed home to raise her children, and when they reached junior high, she took the first full-time position she'd ever had, at a high-fashion company that made handbags and women's accessories. She adored it. "My job was my identity. That's what made me important, and that's what confirmed my skills." In the ten years she worked for the company, she moved up the ranks, to the position of merchandising director. It was a fast-paced and exciting life. But eventually she found it somewhat disquieting. "I was in the Orient twice a year. I was in Europe

---

TABLE 5.6 Primary Reason for Downshifting Among Voluntary Downshifters

Wanted more time, less stress, and more balance in my life	31%
Wanted to spend more time caring for my children	18
No longer interested in material success	5
Succeeding in today's economy is too difficult	5
Wanted a more meaningful life	15
Wanted a less materialistic lifestyle	3
Other	23

TABLE 5.7 Pre-Downshift Incomes of Voluntary Downshifters

< $10,000	7%
$10,001–25,000	30
$25,001–35,000	18
$35,001–50,000	17
$50,001–75,000	7
$75,001–100,000	6
$100,000+	5
Don't know/refused	11

once a year. I was never not on a plane. And I had children, and I was married, and, I mean, my lifestyle was really pretty strange." She came to realize this strangeness while "walking down a main street in Hong Kong, which is hung with flags and signs and lights all in Chinese. And I felt very much at home. It didn't feel like a strange place. I was halfway around the world. And I didn't miss anything, and I didn't miss anybody."

Everything changed when Alice was laid off, after her company was sold. First she grieved. Then she picked up the pieces and went into job-search mode (counseling, group support, Monday morning meetings dressed for work). She ended up taking a job at a public relations firm, but the price was a $20,000 salary cut, one-third of her former earnings. The PR job didn't work out, but it did teach her about her psychological makeup. When her supervisor let her go, "it was, like, 'Fine, I'm on unemployment, don't bother me for a while. I need to think, about what I want and what I need.'" So she did a little networking, made some contacts, and began freelancing

TABLE 5.8 Post-Downshift Attitudes Among Voluntary Downshifters

I'm happy about the change, and I don't miss the extra income very much.	28%
I'm happy about the change, but I miss the extra income.	35
Losing the income was a real hardship, but I'm still happy about the change.	19
I'm unhappy about the change.	15

TABLE 5.8 Permanent versus Temporary Change among Voluntary Downshifters

Question: *Do you think your lifestyle change will be permanent or just temporary?*

Permanent	55%
Temporary	44

for an advertising company. "Situation assessment kind of writing, which I can do in my sleep. And I was happy as a clam. I could write at midnight, I could write in my jeans. I thought, this is wonderful, this is what I want to do. I want to be left alone." The company liked what she was doing and wanted her on board full-time.

"They had to beg me, because I had cut loose psychologically and emotionally from the working world. I really had." She agreed to work full-time, but only if she could work a four-day week. "I'm not invested, I'm not attached. If they fire me, I will go write. And because I'm not so anxiety-ridden about, am I going to succeed here or not? I think I'm doing good stuff." On the practical side, things have also changed enormously. "My commute is three minutes. I don't travel. Little by little, I've been getting closer to what I want to do. I still haven't figured out how to leave before seven, seven-thirty at night, because yes, I'm certainly cramming five days' work into four days. But padding around in my nightgown on Friday mornings is worth anything." Although Alice was originally downshifted involuntarily, she is among the nearly one-quarter of job losers for whom the experience has been a blessing. She wouldn't even consider going back to the kind of life she had. "I'm not willing to take that pressure anymore—absolutely not willing."

Like most downshifters, Alice has undergone a major change in her relationship to money, time, and work. "Four years ago, if somebody had said to [me], 'What will you do in five years?' that question would have terrified me, because I had no plan, I couldn't see what the future held. And now I do. So the prospect of more time and less money is much more comfortable now for me than it was a couple of years ago." She believes there's an inevitable trade-off between time and money. "That's just it. You know, pick one."

There is no question that Alice Kline has paid a high price for what she has gained. "I've given up money, and I've given up striving to reach top management. I will never be a vice president of a company. I, like, stopped, you know, midclimb. And bailed out."

So how has she been managing, making $20,000 less, putting two children through college? Granted, the Klines are comfortable, and her husband still has his job. But her salary was one-third of the family income. When she lost her first job, her son panicked. Her husband was "hyperventilating, because he didn't really know if we could manage. They couldn't see they wouldn't starve." The family is more relaxed now, but they have had to make significant changes in their spending habits. Alice used to do a lot more impulse buying. "Clothes. Kids. Gadgets, whether it was a VCR or things like that." At the time of our interview, with one child still in college, vacations were limited to nearby Maine. Financially the Klines are doing more thinking about what they spend, more budgeting. "It's like we've let go. We've let go of a lot of things."

Does she feel financially deprived? "In a sense. I can't do things for my kids the way I could without thinking. If somebody wants a piece of stereo equipment, that has to be thought about. It's not like they're never going to get it. There are no extraneous expenses. It's just a much more planned life." Of course, her job-related expenses are lower. As almost all downshifters attest, working costs money, whether it's transportation expenses, child care, takeout food because you're too tired to cook, or a shrink to deal with the pressure.

And for women especially there are always the clothes. Alice's job was in fashion, so her expenditures on clothes were particularly high. "I had to dress. And I had to spend money on clothes because I had to look a certain way." Not that she didn't enjoy buying clothes. "I wasn't in that business by accident. I'm always going to have a funky pair of earrings on. I think it's fun to dress, I love clothes. But I like to do it on my terms, not because of pressure to look a certain way. I have to spend all money on clothes? I don't really want to do that. I'd rather buy something pretty for the house. [Now] the pressure is gone. I don't know when the last time was I bought something." Like many downshifters, Alice is "living off a wardrobe that's fairly deep. But I buy very little for myself. And probably can't afford to buy a lot of stuff for myself."

Learning to live on less is a process. "I think it's like going on a diet. When you're used to spending at a certain level, or you're used to eating at a certain level—which I'm also trying to deal with—I don't know that you can make huge transitions all at once, unless you have to. You kind of do it in stages. So I think that I will keep transitioning to different ways of spending my money or finding certain things that are important. I'm more willing to spend money to entertain people in my home than to put something on my back. So there's changing values within the money."

Alice Kline didn't begin her lifestyle change by questioning her consumer values. "I can't say that I don't think it's fun to do things or that I don't think material things are important. But"—and here I believe Alice describes the quintessential change that most down-shifters go through—"*what I'm willing to do to get there has totally changed.*" The importance of money has fallen relative to "quality of life, what I do for a living, the actual content of what I do, con-nection with friends, connection with other people, connecting up on a personal level even with people that I work with. The quality of my life at work was terrible. It was so tense." Now she is excited about her work, and although she hasn't perfected the routine, "it's coming, little by little."

Alice strongly believes that money is freedom. She found total financial dependence on her husband demeaning and confining. But she has gained other freedoms that she will cling to just as tena-ciously as the financial liberation she gained when she went to work. "I really can say no. I can say, 'I want to do it this way.' I believe that I can structure my life and my work life on my terms. I never believed that." Now she's finding out "how little money can I live on and still have what I define as freedom. It's like finding out how little food can I eat." She laughs.

The Work-and-Spend Cycle in Extremis: Jennifer Lawson

Jennifer Lawson was forty-one when we met and had some months earlier taken a voluntary layoff from a prestigious computer software and consulting firm. She lived with her boyfriend in a condominium in Cambridge. While she was not a typical yuppie—she didn't have a col-lege degree—she was definitely in flight from the excesses of the work-and-spend cycle. She was living on unemployment, doing no extraneous spending, and thrilled to be out of the working world.

Jennifer had grown up in a middle-class family, but as a rebellious teenager, she married a man her parents hated, had a child, and missed out on college. Finding herself a single parent early on, she was forced into low-paid women's factory work in the upstate New York town where she grew up. She fought the company for a higher-paid (male) job driving trucks, but after more than a decade she wanted a change. She moved to the Boston area and serendipitously landed a job at the software firm. She worked there thirteen years, moving up the ranks, despite her lack of a credential, in various technical positions. By the time she left, she was making just over $40,000 a year. She'd come to a dead end in her job, had never really cared about software or computers, and, after so many years, was tired of the weekly grind. Her son was out of college, so she asked for, and was given, the company severance package.

For Jennifer, the upward creep of desire was at the root of her problem. She thinks back to 1980. "At that time, I was thinking that if only I could make $10,000 a year, I'd be fine. And there I was, thirteen years later, making $42,000 a year, and I still wasn't breaking even. I was just about exactly as much in debt as I was when I was making $10,000 a year. It just didn't make any difference. And I'm sure if they had given me a raise to $60,000, I would've managed to spend $65,000. That's just the way I've always been about it. And many people I know are the same way. Once you get to $40,000 a year, then you develop a lifestyle that requires $40,000 a year to support it. And if you keep doing that, then every year when they give you raises you just adjust your spending upward, and it doesn't really help anything."

Like many of the women she knows, Jennifer frequently spent her lunch hour doing recreational shopping. "I'd be in a bad mood, I'd go shopping at lunchtime, I'd try on a dress, I'd say, 'Well, I kind of like it, you know, it's only $89, I'll buy it.' I buy it, I bring it home, and never wear it. I didn't really like it." Or she'd go for one item and return with "seven or eight other things, because I'm easily distracted and I'm not very good at making quick judgments. And so I'd stand there and waffle for a minute, and I'd say, 'Ehh, do we really need another sofa pillow? Oh, all right, I'll take it.' Because it was easier than walking away from it."

If an item cost less than a few hundred dollars, Jennifer would buy it without thinking very long. They'd go to California every year to visit her brother. Eat out. See first-run movies. Like the other dual-earner couples in her building, she and her boyfriend kept the UPS man busy with mail-order shopping. What did she buy? "Small household accessories. There's a company called Horchow that sells gifts and trinkets and objects to put on your bookshelves. Lots of books, lots of records, almost anything you can think of that isn't a major appliance comes mail-order now." My favorite examples were on her terrace. "Even though we don't have a yard, that hasn't kept me from populating the entire porch with expensive gardening accessories. Because I like to garden, so I buy things from Smith and Hawken and Dwight Flower Farms."

Her boyfriend was into consumer electronics. "He loves the Sharper Image catalog and the *Electronics Digest*. He always wants a newer VCR, and we have a laser disc player. It's certainly not necessary. I mean, it's the same kind of machine as a VCR—like, the picture quality is better. And you know, a few people have them. And the discs for them are very expensive, and you can't record your own, but he's a programmer. We have a nice home Macintosh that we mostly just use as a toy. We have a nice printer for it. He likes to mail-order software for it; he's been talking about a new, faster modem to add to it. We don't have a fax machine yet, but he really thinks we need one."

Naturally she was maxed out on her credit cards. "Everyone else I know lives like this too. I mean, I was surrounded by people who do things like using reserve credit to pay their VISA bill at the end of the month, juggling one form of credit, and people kind of laugh about it. Everybody was in way over their heads, and the object of the game was to sort of tread water. Barring disaster, we were all paying.

"So, I felt like I was spending all of my life's energies doing something that I didn't much care about just to get a check every two weeks so that I could go out and buy some more books that I never had the time to read and some more records that I never had the time to listen to. And one of the things that sort of set off alarms was that I realized I had several occasions where I brought home either a new book or a new record and found out that I'd already bought that book or record. Which is really pathetic, you know. I've got stuff stacked up all over the house, and I'm never going to get to read any of them unless I'm in a major car accident."

Quitting her job was a blessing. She was able to calm down and quit smoking. She took up Russian and started to exercise. She no longer collapses into bed Friday evenings, spending the next two days vegging out and spending money. She goes into stores only to buy food. "And it's amazing how painless that has been, because, you see, I'm surrounded by nice objects. I already have a house full of things. I have equipment and supplies for crafts that I was planning to take up years ago and hobbies I was going to try, all carefully mail-ordered and stashed away and never unwrapped. I have hundreds and hundreds of books. I have a television with cable. Unless you insist on seeing something the week that it opens, you can see it on TV a month later anyway. I haven't had any trouble amusing myself at all."

She finds her situation a little scary sometimes, although she realizes that with her boyfriend still earning a good salary she isn't going to be "sleeping on the subway grates." And, she says, their standard of living is still probably better than that of 99½ percent of the population, "so we ought to be able to do fine."

Tales of Workplace Burnout: A Boston Support Group

While Alice and Jennifer are typical of downshifters in many ways, their partners' incomes are sizable enough that their financial adjustments have not been drastic. They live in the same places. Their kids are going to college. Their basics are assured. The four women whose lives I am about to describe were successful professionals whose career changes necessitated major financial retrenchments, for at least some period of time. But each one has found her new life more satisfying, exciting, and fulfilling. These women met through a Boston-area career counselor who ran groups for people interested in changing their work lives. After the six sessions, they continued getting together. I met with them as a group.

Patricia was a divorced mother of two teenagers whose work life was making her "truly miserable." After she left her husband in 1979, she started a career in marketing at one of Boston's largest high-tech companies. Initially she found marketing glamorous and exciting. She wanted "to be where the men are, because that's where the action is and that's where the money is. That was circa 1980. I was relatively successful. I certainly wasn't a superstar, but I did fine." When the company began having problems, so did she. "I had pushed myself beyond my limits. I started to burn out. And [it was] the classic burnout syndrome: forgetting everything and not being able to do the things that you normally could do, being depressed, and all that." She developed a problem with her eye and had to take some time off from work. That's when she realized she wanted to leave.

Instead of quitting the company, she went back, thinking that she could shift into human services. She had decided she wanted a job helping people, having interpreted her eye problem literally. ("I don't like what I see, my eye's bothering me.") But the company was beginning to downsize, and human services was hardly its first priority. She remained in marketing. Work went "from bad to worse. I was in a ridiculous group. They were very much a bunch of young yuppies, very into status and very cutthroat. And I really wasn't interested. I just couldn't get excited about how many computers we . . . well, we never sold computers, but how a product was going to work, or whether we were going to introduce it, or whatever." That's when she went into counseling, thinking that "it would help me do what I wanted to do, because it's really tough to walk away from an income."

Nancy, the registrar at a Boston college, was also stuck in her job. "I had liberal arts degrees and no real direction and sort of fell into that work. And I worked my way up to a certain level where I could really have some impact. It took me until I was forty years old to really deal with the fact that I didn't like my work, and I've spent a long time doing it. I just needed to take a break. I worked all the time."

Her first downshifting move was spontaneous. She quit her job and did some consulting projects for about a year and a half. But she was barely eking out a living, so she went for occupational counseling. "It was like this epiphany, because I realized that I spent my life doing analytical, organizational, rule-bound things. And everything was on the other side. Everything was right brain." She realized that writing had been the one part of her work that she'd always enjoyed. But as the economy turned sour at the beginning of the 1990s, and being "pretty broke" herself, Nancy reluctantly applied for another registrar position. This time, however, the college was far out of town, in a peaceful oceanside area she had been fantasizing about moving to. She took the job without realizing how much she would dislike it.

Ellen was already in therapy when she joined the group. She had been working for fifteen years at a large company that sold building materials. She had stumbled into the job in the late 1970s, on the very day she collected a final unemployment check. But within three years, she was ready to leave. She had been hired for her creative skills but was doing management work. It was a very male company, and she felt like a fish out of water. What kept her there was $40,000 a year and a company car. "I was so afraid of living on the edge again" (as she had when unemployed). It was like being in an "unhappy marriage. [The job] paid the bills." Things clearly weren't working. Sitting in meetings talking about planning for the future, Ellen would get a clutch in her stomach and feel like running away. At about the same time, she went back to school in the evenings, through an independent study program with a new-age feel to it. During one retreat session, she resolved to quit. A few days later, her boss called her in to discuss complaints about her performance. She saw the opportunity she had "visualized" during the retreat, her "golden key." She negotiated a financial settlement and left on the fifteenth anniversary of her hiring.

When Linda came to the group, she was executive director of a nonprofit that focused on neighborhood redevelopment, an organization she'd been working with for about five years. She really believed in what she was doing, but it was consuming her entire life. "[I] had been offered the job before I moved to Boston, so when I moved here, I had known no one. I also lived in the neighborhood where I worked, so it was all-consuming in a lot of different ways." She wanted a life and didn't think it was compatible with that job. So she joined the group and quit her job about a year later.

What ties these stories together? "There was this universal theme among all of us, that, however you put it, we each wanted a life. And the life we wanted was our own. I think we have done that." Patricia believes all four have "walked away from a sure thing, we've all, you know, been willing to take the risk. One of the things that a lot of people don't realize is that you're not going to know, when you jump, what's down there. And I think, for a lot of people, it's just very frightening. You can't go from one sure thing to another sure thing, it just doesn't work out that way. Part of the process is the process."

Job unhappiness was the trigger for each woman. Patricia again: "I think we all got to the point in our jobs where staying with the sure thing was more unbearable than going into the unknown. A lot of people would argue that they can't do it for financial reasons. And I think sometimes it's really the case. But I think a lot of people in our position could say, 'I can't afford to do this.'" But, "we did, and we have, we've all managed." For all four, the group was a crucial part of being able to manage the change. In addition to moral and emotional support, they helped each other with practical advice, such as how to collect unemployment, where to shop to find the best coupon deals, and how to network without spending money.

At the time I met with the group, two of these stories already had happy endings, one looked promising, and the fourth struck me as rather precarious. Patricia quit her job at the high-tech company, but her child support payments also ended, so her income dropped to virtually nothing. Never one to panic, and always resourceful, she took a series of jobs—selling Amway (hated it, could never close a sale), sales clerk at Filene's (hated it as well), outplacement, head hunter (didn't work out), substitute teaching. Eventually she filed a last-minute application for graduate school. When we met, she had recently finished her master's degree in social work, had put together a part-time fellowship and a part-time practice, and was looking for a supplementary part-time job. She had also sold her big house in the suburbs and begun to live out her (although clearly not everybody's) fantasy: she met, fell in love with, and moved in with a shrink in Cambridge. She says that, although her life is still chaotic, she really likes it.

Linda's story also ended happily. After quitting her job, she took a seven-week trip to Asia, where she'd always wanted to go. She came back to the "emotionally draining experience" of unemployment. After turning down some jobs, she decided to set herself up as an independent consultant. She got almost more business than she could handle, was in the process of acquiring some new credentials, and had already matched her previous salary. She also began a serious relationship and was in the process of buying a house, one well within her means. She remains financially quite cautious.

Nancy was also able to find work she loves, but her financial situation was not yet tenable. Her nonfiction writing courses led her to a mentor, some freelance writing, and eventually the editorship of a start-up magazine. Her income was not high enough to cover even her modest expenses, but insurance money from her father's death was tiding her over for the first year. She has come to terms with the fact that she does not own a home, and may never own one. Although her situation is uncertain, she is "trusting that, somehow, it is going to work."

Ellen also went out on her own, but the market for her workshops on creativity and applied imagination is undeveloped. She finds herself volunteering too much of her time and underpricing her services. She worries that she needs more formal credentials. Meanwhile, even though she has become extremely frugal, she can't get her monthly expenses much below $1,200. She had run down her savings and was on the verge of tapping into her retirement accounts. She let her health insurance lapse. She has periodic emotional crises about her situation and gets scared a lot. I felt scared for her too. At the same time, she says she's never felt healthier, or freer. More than the others, she has been grappling with psychological problems that run deeper than the problem of an alienating job. But she feels that her "world is a lot brighter" than it was when she worked fifteen years in a job she hated "in order to feel financially secure. There is some abiding faith that what I'm doing is absolutely right in the larger scheme of things. It's as though I can breathe again—very much so."

How have these women coped with living on less money? Patricia, who is the most financially comfortable of the four, buys fewer clothes and travels less. She paid off her credit cards when she sold the house and now tries to stick to a budget. Though she gave up regular manicures ("that was painful, but I did it"), she still has her hair colored and her skin waxed. Linda cooks more now, something she didn't do when she was working, because she didn't have the time (a common downshifter change). She also buys food in bulk when it's on sale and has made friends with local businesspeople who give her free faxes and other gratis services. She rents out the bottom floor of her two-family house. She brings her lunch to work meetings and is careful not to get parking tickets. Ellen and Nancy are scrutinizing their expenditures much more closely, especially what they spend in restaurants, even on coffee or muffins. Nancy gave up her Boston hairdresser of fifteen years (exceedingly difficult). Ellen meets people over coffee or breakfast rather than lunch.

She is sewing old clothes to make them wearable, having her shoes fixed. And she's buying postcards in hopes of cutting down on long-distance telephone bills. They help each other. When Linda needed a good outfit for a meeting with a CEO, Patricia went with her to Bloomingdale's and negotiated a 15 percent discount. They all spend less on entertainment, use the library more, and pay much more attention to what they buy.

Perhaps more than the others, Nancy now realizes that her previous spending patterns were tied in with her job. "As I worked harder and made more money, I had less to show for that money, because I just spent it, just to kind of keep myself going. I threw money away to compensate for all the emptiness." She also feels that being single is important. "I'm reminded that I'm a woman alone. I think even the notion of time and how I might fill my time would result in buying something. Go out and go to a movie and then maybe go over to the bookstore afterwards, that's what I did with my Saturday afternoon."

Like many downshifters, both she and Ellen are much more appreciative of the small amount of discretionary spending they do. "Everything's juicier for me now." "I'm more discreet now, but I really enjoy it." Nancy again: "It feels different to me because I'm engaged in what I'm doing." Spending less does not feel punitive.

Making It on One Income: Louise and John Mattson

Louise and John Mattson, whom we first met in chapter 4, are what we might call "traditional" downshifters. Louise quit her job working with disabled children just before the birth of their son, and she is planning to stay out of the labor market at least until their second child (on the way at the time of the interview) enters school. John is an engineer at a large company in Seattle. They are in their early thirties, both from middle-class families, both with college educations from the state university. They married young and live near where they grew up, in a middle-class but increasingly trendy neighborhood.

According to Louise, "I've always had in my mind that family is important, and that I would like to stay home with my children, [and that] knowing the people you raise and are married to, that brings a lot of satisfaction in life." She and her husband have no doubts about their decision, but what they anticipated would be "pretty easy" is not. "Not that it's been extremely difficult, but, my gosh, it's really kind of hard to make a one-income family work." John earns in the midforties. They bought a fixer-upper house a few years ago for $140,000 and have put at least another $20,000 into it, plus a tremendous amount of work. They have something under $10,000 in the bank and no consumer debt, and they put away the maximum amount each month into John's 401(k) plan. Louise drives a Ford Taurus wagon, which she considers the minimum she will accept for Adam in terms of safety. John has an "old tin box" for commuting. They watch their money, tracking the big expenditures on a spreadsheet. Louise is always looking for ways to save—reducing the grocery bills, buying children's clothes at garage sales, even doing her own diapers. If they eat out, it's for less than $25. Their only really extravagant expenditure, she feels, was their wedding ($10,000) and honeymoon ($2,500).

I ask them whether they feel concerned about "keeping up with the Joneses," who, in the 1990s, live on two incomes. John answers: "This keeping up with the Joneses has a lot of different angles to it. And one of them I guess I kind of use to make myself feel better is that we're raising Adam in a way that we don't see a lot of other people able to do at this point. And it's really important to us. We look at friends who are making other choices, and it's kind of like, well, we feel like we're doing better at this than you. I don't know, we're into different rewards." Louise concurs that "we do feel, I think, pretty smug" (hardly a word one would associate with two such nice people). "Although it hasn't been ideal the way I'd like it to be in terms of time, because of the remodel, I do feel there's a light at the end of the tunnel. You caught us in the 'we've arrived' mode." She talks about how good it feels not to be dropping Adam off at the baby-sitter's, about wanting to be with him rather than to escape. They relish the fact that he's well behaved and a joy to be around and believe it has to do with the choice they've made. They also note that social comparisons are easier in a neighborhood like theirs, which is homey, not ostentatious.

At the same time, they do feel deprived in some ways; more

would definitely be better. John likes his occasional toys, and he's worried that he may have to give up more of those. This year he was pushing for a computer, partly for Adam, but they bought a new rug instead. John also shares the widespread middle-class fear of falling. "We're both middle-class. But [with] all the different things going on tax-wise, it's just very difficult to stay where we are. There's either a push to go up, by her getting another job, or kind of go down the drain. And we've got friends—I don't want to get into it, but they've been on welfare for five years now. And we live better than them, but we don't live a lot better than them. And they haven't earned a cent for five years." Falling is represented by losing the house, a prospect he concedes is unlikely.

Both Louise and John do have "high expectations of their financial future." But they believe that growth in John's income is not the only source of more leeway. They want to continue to "learn to scale back better on financials and not keep upscaling our home and cars." For now, as they await their second child, they are cautiously optimistic.

Susan Andrews: Struggling on $18,000

Alice Kline and Jennifer Lawson have second incomes to rely on. The members of the support group are motivated by the excitement of the new careers and lives they've been able to construct. John earns a good salary. Susan Andrews's story, still in progress when we met, is more of a cautionary tale—about how difficult it can be to keep up a middle-class existence on a single income in a high-cost city such as Boston.

Susan is a registered nurse, thirty-two, and single. Some years ago, she gave up a job in clinical nursing at Massachusetts General Hospital, Harvard's flagship, where she'd been earning about $45,000 a year. Like many other clinical nurses, she'd burned out working more than fifty hours a week, including nights and holidays, and taking on extra responsibilities. She had lost *balance* in her life, a word that resonates with many downshifters, and one that Susan used repeatedly. Her bottom line is to regain that balance, with a job that provides meaning, challenges her intellectually, and has reasonable hours and stress levels. She has ruled out a return to clinical nursing. "My quote for the last year was, 'They could pay me $100,000, and I wouldn't be here.'"

After leaving MGH, Susan took a job with an insurance company, along with a 15 percent pay cut. When that office closed, she began working on a per diem basis, but she hasn't found much work. The year we met she earned $18,000. "This is not acceptable. I had to question the little lunch maybe once every two weeks, and it's the most inexpensive little turkey sandwich I can get."

The bottom line is that $18,000 can't give her true balance. To find out what annual income would, she asks herself, "What is essential for me? What enhances me?" In the past, the answer has been to travel—"to take your adventure. Europe, $2,000 Caribbean vacations, exploring." As a single woman without much personal life, she found these jaunts essential. Now she can only afford day trips. Even chipping in with friends for a cottage last summer was too stressful—they didn't stay within her limited budget.

Travel aside, the bottom line for Susan is her growing inability to keep up a middle-class lifestyle. Not luxuries, but basics. She comes from an upper-middle-class family. (The neighbors on either side of her parents' suburban home would probably "be considered millionaires.") She is keenly aware of what "society" expects from someone of her level. "I think a lot of the issues that I'm dealing with have to do with what society feels." Discussing the difficulties of keeping up her appearance, she notes that "in this society I find that important, and I struggle with not having the haircut and, you know, needing the contact lenses and not being able to afford the teeth cleaning. My hair's ridiculous now." She is also "embarrassed to be out and about" in "one level" of her wardrobe, describing it as too old and ratty.

She is upset about no longer being able to keep up her customary level of gift giving. "My brother and my sister have had a birthday, and I had a budget of $5–7 for the gift, and that is not acceptable to me. Being a caregiver, I like to give presents. Now I can't go to the card store and buy a $2 card. Christmas has always been a big, big budget thing for me. The people I used to give gifts to I gave cards. The ones I gave cards, they'll get 'Merry Christmas' from me. I feel reduced."

Coming to realize that she may never be a homeowner, Susan is frustrated by "society's" insistence that a person own to be a real part of a community. But in speaking of her relationship to the middle-class society of which she has always been a part, we had entered territory so painful she could no longer speak aloud. "What do you do when your whole peer group and all of society says, 'You're living on $18,000?'" Her voice becomes completely inaudible.

Susan Andrews is living proof of the power of class-based consumption norms. After two years of declining income, she found herself perilously close to the rock bottom of her middle-class world. Her emotional balance, sense of self, and belief in her ability to have a good life were all jeopardized by this experience. The pain, humiliation, and fear silenced her. Her situation became urgent, and despite her deep belief in what she was doing, she felt panic at times. She had reached the limits of her downshift. Meaning, challenge, and reasonable levels of stress were essential in a job. But so too was a salary of at least $30,000 a year.

When $18,000 Feels Luxurious: Jeff Lutz

Susan Andrews saw only one way out of her difficulties. Earn more. Some Americans are pursuing another path. Want less. Live more simply. Slow down and get in touch with nature. A growing "voluntary simplicity" movement is rejecting the standard path of work and spend. This is a committed, self-conscious group of people who believe that spending less does not reduce their quality of life and may even raise it. Their experience is that *less* (spending) is *more* (time, meaning, peace of mind, financial security, ecological responsibility, physical health, friendship, appreciation of what they do spend). Seattle, long a laid-back, nature-oriented city, is home not only to Boeing and Microsoft but also to many of these individuals. I spent nearly a week there in the summer of 1996, meeting people who were living on less than $20,000 a year. Jeff Lutz was one of them.

After graduating from a small college back east, Jeff and his girlfriend Liza moved to Seattle, where they inhabit a nice, spacious old house in a middle-class neighborhood. They share the place with one friend; their rent is $312 per person. Jeff is self-employed as a medical and legal interpreter and is putting a lot of effort into "growing" his business. Nicely dressed and groomed, he doesn't look too different from other twenty-five-year-old graduates of the prep school and college he attended. But he is. Living on about $10,000 a year, he says he has basically everything he wants and will be content to live at this level of material comfort for the rest of his life. Youthful naïveté? Perhaps. But maybe not.

Lutz grew up in Mexico. His mother, a writer and social activist, went to Mexico with her parents, refugees from Franco's civil war. His father was a lawyer from New York. Family role models helped form his commitment to a frugal lifestyle. "My great-grandfather, who escaped czarist jail in Lithuania, lived in Mexico with one lightbulb and a record player. He had three photos behind his bed. One was Tolstoy, and one was Gandhi, and one was Pious XXIII."

As a teenager, Lutz went to a private school in western Massachusetts. There he began to feel like "part of a herd being prodded along to do one thing after the next in semiconscious wakefulness. You go to elementary school, and then you go to junior high, and then you go to high school, and then you go to college in order to get a job, in order to compete with other people in higher salaries, in order to have more stuff. I saw really clearly in high school just where it was leading." At that point, he made up his mind about two things. First, "I needed to find a way to not be in a nine-to-five-until-I-died treadmill. I had a vision of life being much, much more than spending most of my life in a job that was somebody else's agenda." Second, "I wanted to learn how human beings could live more lightly on the earth."

His experiences in Mexico motivated these sentiments. "I spent a week with some Mazotec Indians in the mountains. And some of these kids my age, one of them had a Washington Redskins jersey. I mean, Spanish is their second language; they spoke Mazoteca, and yet they were listening to Michael Jackson and they wanted to buy my sunglasses and they wanted to buy my watch. And they wanted me to bring more sunglasses and watches so that they could resell them to their friends. It was very clear that our culture was sort of surrounding other cultures through the media. I grew up watching *The Love Boat* dubbed in Spanish."

In college, he designed his own major in environmental studies. But unlike many young people who begin their work lives enthusiastically believing they can combine improving the world with making a good salary, Lutz never really considered that path. "The things I was interested in were pretty outside the box." Near the end of his college years, he came across an article by Joe Dominguez, the creator of a nine-step program of "financial independence." Dominguez's program, contained in his best-selling book (with collaborator Vicki Robin) *Your Money or Your Life*, promises freedom from the grind of the working world, not through getting rich but by downsizing desire. Dominguez and Robin believe Americans have been trained to equate more stuff with more happiness. But that is true only up to a point, a point they feel most of us have passed. Doing it their way, you don't need to save a million dollars to retire, but just one, two, or three hundred thousand.

The program involves meticulously tracking all spending. And not just tracking it but scrutinizing it, by comparing the value of whatever you want to buy with the time it takes to earn the money for it. That calculation involves determining your real hourly wage, by taking into account all the hours you work and subtracting all job-related expenses, including the cost of your job wardrobe and takeout food because you're too tired to cook. Equipped with your real wage rate, you can figure out whether a new couch is worth three weeks of work, whether four nights in the Bahamas justify a month of earning, or whether you want to stick with the morning latte (even those half-hours add up). People who follow the program find that when they ask these questions, they spend less. Much less.

Jeff was getting close to financial independence, which entailed earning enough to spend between $800 and $1,200 per month, including health insurance. He says he does not feel materially deprived, and he is careful to point out that voluntary simplicity is not poverty. While he decided against the lattes, he does own a car and a computer, goes out to eat between one and three times a month, rents videos, has friends over for dinner, and buys his clothes both new and used. His furniture is an eclectic mix—nothing fancy, but nothing shabby either. He is convinced that "a higher standard of living will not make me happier. And I'm very clear internally. It's not a belief I picked up from somewhere." It's "something that I've gained an awareness about."

The Voluntary Simplicity Movement

The voluntary simplicity movement is too small to be represented in the downshifter surveys I have conducted. So I cannot estimate its size or demographic composition with any accuracy. Certain demographic features, however, seem salient. Simple-livers tend to be middle-class whites, with at least a college education. They are more likely to be women and are unlikely to have young children living at home. (Although it is possible to live simply with children, financial realities make dramatic downshifts rare.) Simple-livers are more likely to be single, to have grown children, and to be a little bit older.

The circumstances that lead some people to a simple lifestyle do seem similar to those of downshifters. Some simple-livers are reformed shoppers, such as Doris Shepley, whom we met in chapter 3. Oppressed by the prestige house she had bought a few years earlier, she was determined to leave it for some kind of cooperative housing situation, where she would find not only lower monthly expenses but a community of people. Most simple-livers, however, appear to have been prompted to change their lives by their work situation; they opted out of areas such as corporate management, administration, and computers because of stress or a lack of meaning in the job. I found simple-livers in a variety of work situations (working for themselves, out of the labor market during a transitional phase, doing part-time work). Some were already financially independent. A large fraction were involved in some kind of volunteer or service work. The idea of "giving back" after having lived a good material life was a prominent theme.

The movement puts great emphasis on the idea that there is no one way to do this and that each person decides for himself or herself how to spend money. Nevertheless, on such limited budgets individual differentiation is necessarily limited, so common strategies have emerged. Downscaling to smaller houses or apartments and driving used cars are common strategies. In Seattle most take advantage of the many thrift shops and secondhand markets the city offers. (One pregnant woman, facing a tight situation, explained that after some soul-searching she had asked people coming to her baby shower to bring only secondhand gifts. That way their dollars would go further.) Simple-livers commonly talk about what they call "clutter" (an excess of material possessions) and their experiences with divesting. (One couple was progressively selling off their furnishings because they preferred sparse surroundings and moving periodically in order to explore new neighborhoods.) They often socialize with other simple-livers and steer away from restaurants, first-run movies, and expensive entertainment. Having reduced the pressures from the workaday world, simple-livers are able to do much healthier and more time-intensive cooking, so they buy fewer convenience foods. (On the other hand, Cecile Andrews, the doyenne of Seattle's simplicity circles, eats out nearly every evening.) Simple-livers generally take the money-saving habits of downshifters one or more steps further.

While most of the people I interviewed had a strong community orientation, there are aspects of this lifestyle that emphasize separateness, independence, and self-reliance. Couples often keep their finances separately. Simple-livers limit their spending by bartering their services and limiting shared restaurant meals and gifts.

Finally, simple-livers insist that although they might meet the government's criterion, they are not poor. This is true, but for reasons they sometimes do not recognize. Few Americans can thrive on $10,000 a year. Simple-livers can because they are rich in cultural capital (Bourdieu's term) and in human capital (economists' term for education and training). Some started with hefty bank accounts or homes of their own. Because they tend to be at least middle-class and well educated, they are able to manage the world around them. They have social and personal confidence, know how to work the system, and have connections to powerful people and institutions. Unlike the traditional poor, they have *options*—including the option of jumping back into mainstream culture.

Beyond Bourdieu: Can Less Really Be More?

While it's difficult not to be infected by the enthusiasm of this group, their enthusiasm also raises questions. What's different about them that they have been able to buck the national religion? They insist that they're average people, that anyone can do it. Considering that most members of this rapidly expanding movement are relative newcomers, can their lifestyle be successfully maintained over a long period of time? Although most say they don't feel deprived, can this really be true all the time? Doesn't it get tiresome to pinch pennies? Is saving money just another status competition (finding the cheapest car) that is every bit as self-defeating as spending money when people end up spending *less* than they'd like to because of social pressures? And pragmatically, how many Americans with younger children can really save $100,000 or more?

Perhaps the most telling question is the most obvious one. If it's true that less is really more, why isn't everyone trying to live on $15,000 or $10,000 or even $6,000 a year (as some members of this movement do)? Are the rest of us just deluded, slaving away at meaningless jobs, buying a lot of useless junk, as this movement sometimes implies? To use the economists' term, is there really a "free lunch" that most of us can't see? Or does the less-is-more philosophy entail value changes that most Americans have not yet confronted?

To see what those transformations might be, it is helpful to think about the difference between downshifters and simple-livers. Downshifters have experienced a change in which time and quality of life became relatively more important than money. They would prefer more of both, but forced to choose, they make a lifestyle change that increases their time and reduces their earnings. Simple-livers, by contrast, transcend that trade-off. They find a (low) level of sufficiency income, beyond which spending more is no longer positive. Indeed, it may well be negative, because it creates "clutter," stuff that needs taking care of, harms the environment, or alienates them from their peer group. Less is more not only because it allows them freedom, but also because less just becomes more.

Sounds great, but what's the catch? Why couldn't Susan Andrews do it? Susan, like most downshifters, went partway. She barely noticed giving up that part of her spending that went for nightclubs and restaurants. Even giving up the luxury of Caribbean vacations was not a real sacrifice. But beyond a certain point, reduced spending started eating into her basic identity and her ability to maintain her social position. To successfully go beyond the first stage of spending reduction (probably about 20 percent for most people), a more profound values transformation is necessary. Just dropping down doesn't work. To maintain psychological comfort, most of us must transcend the strictures of the current consumption map. We must go "beyond Bourdieu," if you will. The first step is to decouple spending from our sense of personal worth, a connection basic to all hierarchical consumption maps. The second is to find a reference group for whom a low-cost lifestyle is socially acceptable.

In contrast to those of us caught up in the competitive spending process, simple-livers struggle against the dominant cultural assumptions about consumption, continually chipping away at the symbolic meanings of consumer objects. They reject the idea that their worth as a person is determined by the size of their house, or that they are incomplete without good china and a silver service. They symbolically connect their cars with pollution rather than power and sexuality. They no longer feel they have to appear in society in first-run clothes. Rejecting the standard meanings of commodities, they emphasize function over symbolism. How are they able to do this? Granted, it is not easy. The association between consumption and social identity is forged when we are children and exerts a powerful pull on our psyches. Many simple-livers struggle with these issues. As a counterweight, nearly all of them have made a strong moral commitment to what they are doing: they feel that our commercialized culture embodies bad values, they have experienced it as personally dysfunctional, or they are aware of its devastating effects on the environment. "Consumption as usual" comes to feel less and less ethically comfortable. Perhaps most important, they find safety in numbers. In Seattle and the Pacific Northwest, a low-spending, alternative, but decidedly middle-class lifestyle is emerging. The fact that more and more other middle-class people are living this way makes it far easier to deal with the inevitable psychological difficulties of letting go of spending as a way of life.

Of course, for some the inevitable psychological difficulties of reduced consumption are never surmounted. "Simplicity" is involuntarily imposed on millions of Americans. In my survey, 12 percent of the population reported that they had suffered an involuntary income loss in the 1990s. The majority had lost their job and been forced to take a lower-paying position. More than 40 percent had reduced their spending by 50 percent or more. As ethnographic accounts reveal, many of these downward transitions leave permanent scars. For people to whom identity and consumption are deeply fused, losing the symbols of success and personhood is a bitter blow. Marriages founder on such episodes, as divorce lawyers can attest. While husbands and fathers suffer with their reduced manhood, their wives and children may not be able to reconcile to a reduced standard. Sometimes forever.

"Happiness Is Inside": Jonathan Wharton

While simple living has taken off in the Pacific Northwest, simple-living newsletters, study circles, and lifestyles are springing up around the country. Even in a high-cost area such as Boston, I found plenty of people who were transforming their work lives, spending habits, and values. As an industrial designer, Jonathan Wharton was struggling with these issues in both his personal and work life.

A fifty-two-year-old former consultant at Arthur D. Little, Jonathan started his own industrial design consultancy in 1975. It did well, and he lived comfortably in an expensive suburb with his wife and kids. But over time, questions about his work surfaced. "The basic philosophy behind design is that you're developing tools that make a person's life easier to live and more luxurious. [But] it's been my personal experience that that's not necessarily so, that as we acquire these things, they don't necessarily enhance our lives. They become anchors: they don't free us, they hold us down. They require being taken care of. If you buy a boat, you either maintain it yourself, which is okay, or you pay somebody to maintain it, but somewhere along the line the monies necessary to maintain it have to be earned. So I began to look at what is really labor-saving in our society. Do a lot of the time-saving devices that we've developed really save time, or do they just add stress to our lives?"

On an even more basic level, he asks about how products shape our lives. "Do some of the products make the establishment of community difficult, do they separate and isolate people more?" He ruminates about the dishwasher. "Is a dishwasher really necessary for a household of two people?" Now divorced and living with a woman, he recalls the role of the dishwasher in his earlier life. "It was great, but it changed the social interactions of the house. When dishes were done [by hand], there were usually two or three people. When the dishwasher comes into the realm, it's one person who deals with it." And what about the environment? At one time, Jonathan believed that people could learn to appreciate nature through appreciating man-made things. "I wanted to get people to appreciate the aesthetics." Now he worries that the man-made stuff is creating more isolation from nature, and destroying it in the process. He also realizes that there's a strong inertial component to technology. "Over generations, things become part of your expected life—washing machines and dryers, the telephone, electricity. There's a limit to how far people are willing to back up."

Yet he himself has backed up quite a bit, earning only $12,000 the year I interviewed him. There's tremendous ambivalence in his discussion. His income is low because his business is not earning much, but at the same time, he is choosy about what he designs and for whom. The combination of divorce, reduced income, and a personal search for meaning has changed his relationship to products. "I was a thing junkie for a long time, so it's really hard. If there's something that I want, I ask myself what's motivating me, why do I really want this, what am I going to do with it? Just about anything. From a tool to a book to a piece of clothing or a chair, what is the life cycle of this thing going to be for me? How am I going to deal with it? I'm not making a moral judgment, it's the reality of what am I getting by buying this, what am I adding to my life by having it?"

At the same time, he is quite clear that living on less has improved the quality of his life. In the past, he was driven and stressed out. Now he has a sense of personal freedom and possibilities that did not exist before. He is nervous about his financial situation, but "less so" than he's ever been. The change in income has "brought to the foreground for me that happiness is inside, not outside. I really like to live in a nice house, and I really like to have nice things, and I like to stay warm, and I like good food, but those are extras." Even living in a small rented place, driving a 1985 car, no longer patronizing the theater or doing luxury vacations, he believes that he has all those things now. "I have come to believe that you can get those things with less money than you would think if you're willing to work a little bit. The good food if you're willing to put the effort into finding out how to do it rather than always going out to a restaurant. If you want fresh basil in the middle of winter, maybe you have to process it yourself and freeze it." And so on.

Simple living is not mainly about spending less, but about living differently. "If I think, like I did for twenty-five years, that if I keep working at this thing, at this one thing, and keep working at it, then eventually I'll have all these other things, then that's a direction. I'm not sure I believe that anymore. I'm not sure that they can all be purchased. Some of it has to be gotten in another way."

6

Learning Diderot's Lesson:
Stopping the Upward Creep of Desire

INTERNATIONAL
BUY NOTHING DAY

A 24 Hour Moratorium on Consumer Spending

Nov. 28,1997

 Go Ahead–Take the Plunge! Find out what it feels like to go one whole day without shopping. It'll open your eyes to the way we all live.

 Copy this poster, or download posters from www.adbusters.org. Put them up at work, on your fridge, or any-where you like.

 Air the TV uncomercial in your community. Watch quicktime, or real video versions of it at www.adbusters.org

PARTICIPATE BY NOT PARTICIPATING!

In the eighteenth century, the French philosopher Denis Diderot wrote an essay entitled "Regrets on Parting with My Old Dressing Gown." Diderot's regrets were prompted by a gift of a beautiful scarlet dressing gown. Delighted with his new acquisition, Diderot quickly discarded his old gown. But in a short time, his pleasure turned sour as he began to sense that the surroundings within which the gown was worn did not properly reflect the garment's elegance. He grew dissatisfied with his study, with its threadbare tapestry, the desk, his chairs, and even the room's bookshelves. One by one, the familiar but well-worn furnishings of the study were replaced. In the end, Diderot found himself seated uncomfortably in the stylish formality of his new surroundings, regretting the work of this "imperious scarlet robe [that] forced everything else to conform with its own elegant tone."

Today consumer researchers call such striving for conformity the "Diderot effect." And, while Diderot effects can be constraining (some people foresee the problem and refuse the initial upgrading), in a world of growing income the pressures to enter and follow the cycle are overwhelming. The purchase of a new home is the impetus for replacing old furniture; a new jacket makes little sense without the right skirt to match; an upgrade in china can't really be enjoyed without a corresponding upgrade in glassware. This need for unity and conformity in our lifestyle choices is part of what keeps the consumer escalator moving ever upward. And escalator is the operative metaphor: when the acquisition of each item on a wish list adds another item, and more, to our "must-have" list, the pressure to upgrade our stock of stuff is relentlessly unidirectional, always ascending.

To avoid the pitfalls of Diderot, and the new consumerism more generally, requires a new consumer consciousness and behavior. In this chapter, I outline nine principles to help individuals, and the nation, get off the consumer escalator. They are intended as remedies to the problems I have discussed throughout the book: too little saving, a harried lifestyle, a deteriorating environment, the growth of competitive spending, and a lack of consumer control. I anchor my principles in the values of social equity and solidarity, environmental sustainability, financial security, and the need for more family and free time.

Principle 1: Controlling Desire

The first step in avoiding the Diderot effect is to become conscious of the process and the insidious ways it ensnares us. The second step is to rein in desire. Simple livers do it by creating more time and mental space in their lives, by simplifying and concentrating on what really matters to them. Religious leaders, knowing the weakness of the human will in resisting ever-present temptation, advise us to avoid "occasions of sin." Downshifters stay away from malls and upscale shops, knowing that such exposure inevitably creates desire. They stop reading catalogs that come in the mail, chucking them directly into the recycle bin; consciously do less socializing with their shopaholic friends; and learn generally to recognize those first consumption stirrings so as to cut them off before they gain a full head of steam.

Another strategy is to emphasize product durability rather than novelty. If the things you buy last long enough for you to become emotionally attached to them, it will be easier to avoid buying new things. To succeed at this, you need to search for products that will continue to serve you well, both because they will not go out of fashion and because they are physically durable. Are the manufacturers stable, in case repairs are necessary? Is the fabric long-lasting? Will it age well as you age, becoming over time a comfortable and comforting friend, like Diderot's well-worn furnishings? Similarly, it is important to think through the long-term consequences of all significant purchases. If you buy the digital tape deck, will you be led into replacing your tape library with new versions that more fully exploit the capabilities of the new system? If you upgrade the computer, how much of your old software will be usable? If you buy your child a starter set for a Brio train, are you willing to pay for all those expensive add-on pieces? If you start a new sport, ask yourself how much you'll eventually pay out for equipment, lessons, and fees. (And why has it become so imperative to take expensive lessons when picking up a new sport? Maybe a program of relaxation might improve your tennis game more than paying for time with the club pro.) Doing without a contemplated purchase for a certain time may be a good test of whether in fact you need it. Will you really be different from almost everyone else and use that exercise machine for more than the first few months?

Martha Evans, a former accountant, describes her own version of the consumer escalator. "There was a point where I was making a little more money at work, and I was very excited that it was coming. And then it came, and I could hear myself doing this mental tick-tick-tick: I can get this, this, this, and this, this, this. I'm sure it had to do with clothing, with maybe a trip, probably with some household improvements. I really need a kitchen, luxury things that I didn't have." But before too long, Martha learned to control these thoughts. "I would go through a mental exercise where I would say, 'I simply have to stop wanting this, because I know that if I get this, that that's not going to be the end of it.' I could tell where I was getting carried away wanting things, and there was not going to be any end to this wanting."

Principle 2: Creating a New Consumer Symbolism: Making Exclusivity Uncool

Integral to the upward creep is the upscale itself. The new consumerism has taught affluent Americans to covet, and then buy, the Jil Sander suit, the Stickley chair, the SubZero fridge, and the Coach briefcase (with a Montblanc and Filofax to go inside). When they display these products, they project taste, individuality, and exclusivity. But isn't it odd that we must have the things certain others have to establish our credentials as a distinctive person—to avoid being seen as just like everybody else?

Some consumer symbols have become fair game for public scrutiny. Politicians and the media have attacked heroin chic and the anorexic images prevalent in fashion photography. But the symbolism of exclusivity and luxury is still off-limits. No one challenges the *New York Times* for devoting its second page to ads for extraordinarily expensive items affordable to only the top few percent of society. There is as yet no social stigma associated with owning or displaying exclusive products. Indeed, it is rarely even noticed that companies advertise these commodities to a mass consumer audience, large numbers of whom cannot afford them and will go into debt, sacrifice everyday needs, or turn to crime in order to obtain them. When we stop to think about it, what message are we sending here? That being middle-class isn't good enough? That it's okay to wreck your personal or family finances to confirm your social acceptability? That if you are a low-wage earner, you are condemned to a life of inadequacy?

What if public attitudes to status consumption started changing, so that people saw as tacky attempts to buy their way into a personal image of exclusivity? What if a pattern of upscale purchasing became not something to aspire to but something "uncool" in its inegalitarianism? What if wearing the $2,500 Jil Sander suit was no longer looked upon as power dressing but as overkill? What if, when we looked at a pair of Air Jordans, we thought, not of a magnificent basketball player, but of the company's deliberate strategy to hook poor inner-city kids into an expensive fashion cycle? What if more people began thinking like Jennifer Lawson's son, who thinks new clothing is socially ostentatious?

Awareness is the first step in breaking down these associations and immunizing ourselves against symbolic spending triggers. As marketers know full well, these symbols are powerful precisely because they reside partly in the realm of the unconscious. The see-want-borrow-and-buy sequence often does not survive the bright light of day. Denial also helps us live with our ambivalent (sometimes guilty) feelings about consuming exclusively or striving for distinction.

If there's something you really want but don't actually need, there's a good chance that a recurring symbolic fantasy is attached to it. A faster computer? The dream of getting more work done. A remodeled kitchen? The hope of eating proper family dinners. A luxury car? Making VP. Laying bare the fantasy illuminates the often tenuous link between the product and the dream, thereby reducing the power of the object. When identity and consumption are linked, getting too deliberate spoils the symbolism. After doing the cosmetics research, I found myself unable to buy designer-brand cosmetics, not only because I knew I was wasting my money but also because it made me feel foolish.

Not that these symbolic meanings are easy to break down. They are woven deeply into the fabric of our everyday lives. We have profound, if often unrecognized, emotional connections to commodities. On the other hand, Americans will not gain control over their spending habits until they begin to confront that symbolism head on. As the number of prestigious products grows, the financial pressures on people increase. Less and less of what we have remains mere background—things valued for their function, for what having them to use adds to our daily lives, rather than for what they convey about us as quality human beings. The classic pantheon of house, car, and wardrobe has been joined by all manner of new status symbols: stoves come in restaurant quality to signal the requisite level of commitment to good cooking (for the really upscale, there's the $10,000+ Aga, the model favored by the queen of England); wooden swing sets become an aesthetic (class) item that status-conscious association trustees are ready to go to court over; water (once a free, abundantly available noncommodity) has become classed into brand names, with a select few becoming status symbols; and a recent ad suggests that if no one has mentioned the distinctiveness of your garage door lately, it's time to have it redone. It is only by becoming aware of the thousand and one little ways that consumption is connected to distinction and status that we can begin to break down those barriers and consume in less socially exclusive (and expensive) ways.

Principle 3: Controlling Ourselves: Voluntary Restraints on Competitive Consumption

Imagine the following. A community group in your town organizes parents to sign a pledge agreeing to spend no more than $50 on athletic shoes for their children. The staff at your child's day-care center requests a $75 limit on spending for birthday parties. The local school board rallies community support behind a switch to school uniforms. The PTA gets 80 percent of parents to agree to limit their children's television watching to no more than one hour per day.

Do you wish someone in your community or at your children's school would take the lead in these or similar efforts? I think millions of American parents do. Television, shoes, clothes, birthday parties, athletic uniforms—these are areas where many parents feel pressured into allowing their children to consume at a level beyond what they think is best, want to spend, or can comfortably afford. In contrast to the fashionable ideology that a "free market" is the best response to society's needs because it allows the freest expression of the public will, in these examples the self-control of a group of people leads to a better outcome for everyone. Voluntary restrictions on individual liberty can make sense. Giving up your right to spend $100 on athletic shoes *may* make you—and your child—better off.

The foregoing examples are the obvious, and easy, ones, in part because they involve adult spending on children. But if the argument of this book is correct—that America suffers from too much competitive consumption—there should be plenty of other areas where collective restrictions would work.

What about adults spending on themselves? Situations in which people spend together come readily to mind. Everyone agrees that it's reasonable to put limits on the office Christmas gift exchange. Why not do the same for holiday spending within families? While some families already explicitly set limits, many do not but would appreciate the chance to reduce the value of both what they spend and receive. Voluntary agreements to limit the amounts spent almost certainly make people better off on other occasions as well: weddings, birthdays, baby showers. So too with various types of clubs. How many book club members would prefer to put new hardbacks off-limits and confine their choices to paperbacks? Isn't it better when a wine-tasting group operates with spending guidelines?

Other areas of social spending are also ripe for collective restraints. Do you have a group of friends with whom you regularly get together? What about keeping expenditures for an evening below a certain level? Try second- rather than first-run movies, or patronizing only restaurants where the entrées are below a certain price. Sometimes these customs evolve naturally, particularly when only a few people are involved and they know each other's financial situations. But at other times, restraint fails and spending can gradually escalate. It can be embarrassing to raise the issue; we fear we may be signaling that we are petty, cheap, or in an inferior economic position. If it were customary to be explicit about spending limits, the pressure on the individual would be lifted. Frugality could become a socially acceptable consideration.

The most difficult type of situation arises when private spending supports a previously developed social need for the product. I would prefer not to get a cell phone, an answering machine, or a home-based fax. But as these products become universal, I can be seen as refusing to contribute my share to the new scheme of things if I resist adding them to my own stock of stuff.

I believe there are now many middle-class Americans who would welcome a deceleration or even a decline in the consumption standards of their reference groups. They don't want to give up their friends. They don't want to risk being seen as not "one of us." But they would like more financial leeway. Would you prefer that your associates not replace their cars too frequently? Or that your friends not remodel their kitchens, so you don't become ashamed of your own? Would you like to travel in circles in which it is normal not to have a house with a downstairs bathroom for guests? Do you wish that your neighbors dressed their children in hand-me-downs or with patches on the knees of their jeans? Do you wish you didn't feel like your child needs the latest computer software at home?

In these kinds of examples—cell phones, clothing standards, kitchen remodeling—explicit collective agreements are less workable. But more subtle shifts in the culture of consumption can achieve similar results. Steering the dinner party conversation around to these questions might get your friends thinking. Devoting your annual Christmas letter to issues of "stabilizing" consumption might start a conversation among your correspondents. Organizing a clothing swap among your friends is a perfect opportunity for an initial discussion about spending on clothes. Getting the PTA to organize forums about lifestyles and values allows the community to work through the issues together.

In the past, collective limitations on spending were much more powerful. In traditional societies, various spending taboos and invocations of the "evil eye" restrained competitive consumption. In Europe and North America, dress, housing, and other types of consumption have been restricted. And throughout history, religious ideology has served as an additional brake: nearly all the world's religions have stressed the sacredness of simplicity and moderation. Coveting our neighbor's belongings was so important a no-no that it qualified as one of the Ten Commandments; when in the movie *Wall Street* the antagonist announces that "greed is good," he is talking about one of the seven deadly sins. But by the early twentieth century, these restraints had been largely lifted. The notion of sufficiency, which long had regulated consumption, was discarded in the face of the promise of mass prosperity. Spending, even spending to excess, was extolled as good for the ego, if not for the soul. Consumerism became the new, therapeutic belief system. Religious, folk, and legal impediments to consumption declined markedly. Most insidious of all, aggressive spending was made patriotic. It spread the wealth, we were told, creating jobs for the unemployed as well as profits for American industry. The movies contributed to the shift in values. An inclination to spend too much was cast as an attractive trait. If it was a fault, it was the fault of an open, honest, generous person; frugality was portrayed as the proclivity of a small, pinched personality. The result, at the century's end, is that almost half the population of the world's richest country say that they have just enough income to get by.

The hallmark of the kinds of controls I have been talking about is that they are mainly voluntary. If people don't welcome them, they won't work. They also need to be instituted collectively. While individuals *can* buck the system, few of us are so inclined. Because consuming is a social act, so too is consuming differently. This is one lesson we can learn from the Pacific Northwest, where simple living is going mainstream. Feeling like a part of a trend is a lot more comfortable than being an oddball. The social support possible in places like Seattle makes a world of difference. While the Northwest may have a culture and history more conducive to downshifting than, say, the culture of New York City, the initiatives I am suggesting are possible anywhere. Within the space of a few short years, millions of Americans joined a movement to turn off their televisions for a week in April. Pledging to limit purchases of athletic shoes, or Christmas gift giving, or birthday party competitions is equally possible.

Principle 4: Learning to Share: Both a Borrower and a Lender Be

The latest trend in lawn mowers is big and expensive—the riding mower. Here the dynamics are pretty clear. You saw your neighbor roll out his last summer. He first got the idea from his cousin, who was crowing about it. Of course, you really *need* the riding mower. You wouldn't have bought it otherwise, right? The question is, do you really need it twenty-four hours a day, seven days a week? Or could you be satisfied just having it when you want to mow?

Instead of joining the stampede for expensive riding mowers, what if you and a dozen of the families on the street got together and bought a couple of mowers for everyone's use? Call it a product "library." Set up on the model of the public library, it gives people the functional benefits of products without having to purchase them privately. How about a toy exchange? Your children could get the variety in toys they need, and you wouldn't have to be continually buying new ones. Or an athletic equipment library: you could try out cross-country skiing for a season *before* investing in your own skis. Lending libraries make sense for products that are not in use all the time (mowers, snow blowers, boats, athletic equipment) and for relatively inexpensive products that may be of limited usefulness to the individual but do not wear out quickly (books, toys, videos, CDs, clothes). The specifics of the library would vary with the product. With expensive items like mowers, a common fund would purchase the products. Members of the program would be responsible for keeping the mower in good shape and returning it on time (or be fined). Reservations could be required for popular times. Mowers could be kept in private garages, to make access easy. For smaller products, like toys, donations may be sufficient to get the program going.

Why not just rely on rentals or secondhand shops for these products? For some products, rental and secondhand markets do work. But for others, a lending library approach is better. Because people pay into the common fund and are part owners, they take better care of the products. This is especially important for expensive equipment, such as mowers, snow blowers, boats, and some athletic equipment. Plus, there's the added savings of forgoing the rental chain's profit. For inexpensive products such as toys or CDs, an exchange (housed for convenience at the local library, the town hall, or another public building) allows frequent trading, avoids the cumbersome steps of selling and buying, and allows you to use popular items again and again.

The fact that such initiatives have been very limited suggests they need a jump-start. Public libraries, which have already branched out into videos and CDs, might begin by extending the repertoire of products they provide. Local governments could provide technical assistance for neighborhood groups to get going. In low-income communities, government monies could justifiably be used for the initial purchase of some products.

Would lending libraries for products other than books actually work? They would naturally be susceptible to the tensions that can come with cooperative efforts, such as squabbling and freeloading. Moreover, Americans tend to be highly possessive, preferring to own above all else. But the success of libraries suggests that this mentality does not extend to all commodities and that cooperative efforts can succeed. Lending libraries would help people save money, use fewer environmental resources, and free up closet and garage space. They may also increase neighborliness—sharing a mower with your neighbors is likely to lead to other kinds of social interaction. They're at least worth a try.

Principle 5: Deconstruct the Commercial System: Becoming an Educated Consumer

The next time you watch TV, try an experiment. Instead of zapping the commercials, or watching them mindlessly, try to deconstruct them. Watch the Jeep drive out to the edge of the Grand Canyon. What do you see? A chance to get closer to nature? Freedom and individuality? Or a gas-guzzling commodity that fills the air with smog, helps turn wilderness into cement, and is a leading cause of accidental death? As the Swoosh swooshes by, consider whether Nike really stands for women's power, independence, and hipness, as it wants us to believe. Or is the $2 million a day it spends promoting women in sports a sham in light of the $1.60 a day it gives its female Vietnamese workers? As you look closely at the ad, ask yourself whether you really want to join a fashion trend that hooks lower-income youth into products that their parents cannot possibly afford. Or would you rather join an international community of people who are urging us to "Just Do It"—"it" being a boycott of Nike? When De Beers's diamond ads come on, with the beautiful musical backdrop of violins, think hard about what the imperative of a "carat or more" ("so rare it will be worn by fewer than 1 percent of women") really means. If you, along with the rest of the 99 percent, haven't yet received one from your spouse, are you really unloved? And if you do wear that dazzling rock, how is it making your friends feel?

Once you've learned to "read" a commercial, to anesthetize yourself to its subtle messages, move on to other aspects of the commercial system. Investigate the commodities that you buy and use. Learn what they didn't teach you in school. And figure out what you *did* learn.

Even in the days before schools became adjunct marketing arms of corporations (with Channel One and force-feeding of commercials, educational materials produced by corporations, and school buses covered with ads), students were absorbing an apparently upscale consumer attitude. Indeed, one of the ironic results of our educational system is that the people with the highest degrees are the most susceptible to paying extra for designer names, status, and prestige. As chapter 4 detailed, they shop more, are more influenced by their reference groups, and feel more pressure to keep up. Perhaps that's because school has taught us more about how to want things than about how to choose wisely. But what if that started to change? What if we became interested in new kinds of consumer education, learning about a product's "total package" and not just the price and the fancy features? To become good consumers, we need to know more about how products are produced and what tax the manufacturing process levies on the planet, as well as about the health, safety, and environmental impacts of a product and its true long-term costs. We need to get beyond the seductive but superficial appearance of the commodities on the airwaves and the shelves.

Americans love the Gap. We load up on Gap jeans, pocket-Ts, and accessories and aspire to the Gap look. In many circles, BabyGap gets as many oohs and aahs at a shower as frilly embroidered dresses did in an earlier era. Even that bastion of conservative dress, the New York Stock Exchange, donned khakis for its first-ever casual Friday. How many of us stop to consider, before buying these fashionable products, where and how they are made? We prefer not to think about the fact that they are produced by women (and even children) slaving away for nearly nothing in sweatshops where unions are often outlawed and workplace control is Draconian. The Nike employees who make the products we just "have to have" cannot even properly feed themselves, much less buy the shoes they produce. The globalization of the world economy has produced, in industry after industry, a proliferation of low-wage sweatshops, far out of view of the final consumer. Clothes, shoes, toys, knickknacks, furniture—you name it, sweatshops are fueling our consumer boom. These issues have attracted some public attention, and some companies are making efforts to police conditions in the sweatshops with which they contract. They are more interested in PR, however, than lasting change. The companies' rationalization that, no matter how low the wages the workers are better off than they would be having no job at all, is just not the point. What the employees need, and deserve, is a job *and* a paycheck that supports them. Companies and consumers alike need to wean themselves off low wages and cheap production costs.

The ways in which consumption degrades the environment is another area we need to educate ourselves about. Americans know very little about the ecological impacts of their lifestyles beyond the obvious (cars are bad, recycling is good, excessive packaging is bad). We are oblivious to some of our most damaging consumer habits: air conditioning, jet travel, meat, household toxins, and the sheer volume of resources consumed each day (120 pounds). We are unaware that even seemingly innocuous products like coffee (new growing methods are reducing species diversity) and hamburgers (cattle grazing is causing desertification, and pesticides for corn feed are damaging human reproductive systems) have significant impacts. A necessary first step toward becoming an educated consumer is to learn about the impact your consumption has on the environment. Only then can you make responsible and informed choices.

To become educated, you cannot rely solely on the information that manufacturers provide. As I am writing this, a jury has found Dow Corning guilty of withholding information about the adverse health effects of breast implants. The tobacco and asbestos companies have done the same thing. In other industries (chemical, pharmaceutical, bioengineering, agribusiness, furniture and automobiles, to name only a few), health and safety studies are sometimes faulty, incomplete, or nonexistent. With the exception of a few federally mandated measures (gas mileage, energy use information on appliances), environmental impacts are rarely revealed to the consumer. Companies do not want to uncover or publicize negative information about the products they sell.

How can consumers get the facts without time-consuming searches through literature that is often too technical for the layperson? Historically, consumers have become informed by creating consumer organizations and movements. By banding together and putting public pressure on manufacturers and retailers, consumer organizations help protect people from dangerous products, unscrupulous selling practices, and insufficient information. But the few familiar examples (Ralph Nader's fight for auto safety in the 1960s, Consumers Union's *Consumer Reports*) point up how rare independent consumer organizations are today. Most of the product information we have is sponsored indirectly by the manufacturers, through magazines that review products (autos, computers, home furnishings, fashion) but are supported by industry ad revenues.

Americans also need to learn how *not* to spend—how to budget, plan their finances, be patient, and save. Most American households don't have a family budget, and those who do tend not to follow them. The saving ethic has become so alien that many of us think of it in terms only of paying less than full price—as "getting a good deal." Financial management is neglected by the U.S. education system. My Dutch students were shocked to find that their American counterparts are not taught in school how to save. While we've got the energy for a raging controversy about sex education, we have paid almost no attention to the ignorance of our youth when it comes to practicing "safe spending." All schools should offer a basic course in money and spending. In addition to straightforward material such as the economics of compound interest and how to evaluate the long-term consequences of different savings patterns, young people also need to be taught about basic monthly expenses, how to make and stick to a budget, how to calculate what it takes to rent an apartment, and the true costs of owning a car. They need to learn long-term planning, how to prepare for education expenses, homeownership, and the costs of raising children. They need to be exposed to basic facts about the finances of retirement, life insurance, and disability.

We must also teach our kids to be savvy consumers, forewarning them especially about the risks of credit cards. They must know that when they buy on credit, they may end up paying two, three, or four times the sticker price. They need to be able to figure out, *in the store*, how much more. Other important lessons include learning to arm themselves against the temptations of easy money, delaying gratification, and—because young people have been shown to be particularly vulnerable to the pitches of ad men—deconstructing the powerful symbolism that the commercial culture throws at them every day.

For the generations of adults who missed this course, remedial education is in order. Many of us, and especially women, entered adulthood knowing little or nothing about the value of money or how to manage it. We failed to realize that our understanding about how and when to use money can make or break our lives. We need to become conscious of the financial costs of the work-and-spend lifestyle: job-related expenses, beyond the obvious costs of child care and transportation; of the ways in which time and money substitute for each other; and of how stress and exhaustion almost inevitably lead to spending pressures.

Principle 6: Avoid "Retail Therapy": Spending Is Addictive

Millions of Americans use consuming as a way to fight the blues, to savor a happy moment, to reward themselves, to enhance self-esteem, or to escape from boredom. Indeed, consumerism is so pervasive that "retail therapy" is a response to just about *any* mood state or psychological problem. But it carries considerable risk. As with consumption of drugs, alcohol, and food, millions of Americans are experiencing spending control problems. Some have developed a psychological disorder called "compulsive buying tendency." While reports of oniomania, or buying mania, can be found in psychiatric texts in the early part of the century, experts believe its prevalence has increased markedly in recent years, although no hard numbers exist.

Conforming to the stereotype, the paradigmatic case of compulsive buying tendency is a thirty-six-year-old educated woman whose problem developed in her late teens. (Not a likely reader of this book, by the way, because books are at the bottom of the acquisition chain, and even if she bought it, she probably wouldn't read it: it's the act of acquiring that matters.) Compulsives prefer clothes, and after clothes, shoes, jewelry, and makeup—classic appearance- or identity-related items. By the time the typical sufferer comes in for help, she is using half her household income to pay the bills and a variety of severe personal problems have surfaced.

No one knows exactly how many Americans suffer from compulsive buying tendency. Ronald Faber of the University of Minnesota classified between 1.8 percent and 6 percent of his sample (or up to fifteen million) as suffering or at serious risk. Using the same test on a group of mostly college students in Arizona, Allison Magee estimated 15–16 percent. (We know the tendency is greater among youth.) On the other hand, clinically defined compulsives may not be fundamentally different from "normal" consumers. They're just the extreme cases. Millions of ordinary people also exhibit high "generalized urges to buy." Indeed, an innocuous form of compulsive buying appears to afflict one-quarter of us. This should probably come as no surprise in a country where 41 percent of the population age 22–61 (and nearly half of all young adults) say that "shopping makes me feel good."

The downshifter Patty Fuller fit the innocuous buyer profile. Because her buying was well within the limits of her substantial income, she never faced financial difficulties. "I used to go mall shopping," she says. "My husband called it 'medicinal spending.' It used to take up a lot of my time. Everybody knew I was a shopaholic. It was the joke, when Patty comes to visit, you take her shopping. I loved it. It was my hobby." Like the clinical cases, Patty could lose interest in what she bought. Sometimes she'd buy clothes she never wore. "Or I'd wear them once. I gave a lot of stuff away to friends, just take it, take it. And I'd buy gifts for relatives and friends." Eventually the combination of overwork and shopping led her to a radical change of lifestyle. "I don't go into malls anymore." And she doesn't give Christmas gifts. "Because it just doesn't feel right anymore. When you sit down and think about the meaning of life, it's just not mainstream America, it's not what we purport in this country."

How to avoid even the appearance of a problem? First, analyze your personal habits. People who score high on the compulsive spending scale also score high on the see-want-borrow-and-buy sequence. They are more oriented to fantasy and daydreaming. They are more materialist. And they tend to believe that consuming is a mark of social status. Figure out what kind of consumer you are. Second, avoid excessive exposure to tempting situations. New York, the nation's fashion capital, is known as a breeding ground for compulsive buyers. (Of course, with the country turning into one enormous shopping arcade, open twenty-four hours a day, avoidance is getting harder.) Finally, avoid impulse buying. It's a common habit, and not just for potato chips and Twinkies. Try locking up the plastic for six months and use only cash so that the costs of purchases will seem real. Don't use cards over the phone or on the Internet; send a check instead. If you desperately want something, force yourself to sleep on it for a night, or, if it's a major item, a week. Buy only from lists thoughtfully constructed before going to stores. Make yourself wait for things so that you appreciate them. Participate in Buy Nothing Day, the annual day-after-Thanksgiving ritual of zero shopping that is fast becoming an international movement. Take the money you would have spent and put it in the bank. Or better yet, commit yourself to an automatic withdrawal savings plan—the method that, for most people, is the only way to ensure that saving actually happens. Then make sure your best friend has done the same.

Of course, the vast majority of us are not in danger of becoming compulsive consumers with a stash of cubic zirconia necklaces in the basement. (Television shopping is a magnet for problem overconsumers.) Nor are we likely to receive, as Patty Fuller did, a cautionary newspaper clipping from her mother-in-law with the headline "Woman Loses Husband While Shopping in the Mall." But we can all learn from the experiences of compulsive buyers. Spending can be addictive. It can absorb your consciousness, become a substitute for other activities, and start to take over your life.

Principle 7: Decommercialize the Rituals

Even for the most determined among us, holidays and life rituals represent a formidable challenge to frugality. In an era when bar and bat mitzvahs cost as much as weddings, and weddings require practically a trust fund to manage, control can seem out of reach. Even families who want something simple and shun ostentation find themselves almost inexplicably shelling out thousands, or tens of thousands. There's a built-in upward creep to the process that catering managers put to work for themselves.

Large numbers of Americans express support for downscaling and decommercializing our ritual celebrations. A recent poll conducted by the Center for a New American Dream found that 39 percent of Americans would "welcome lower holiday spending and less emphasis on gift giving a lot." But many find it hard to do on an individual basis. When John and Louise Mattson tried to limit their family's Christmas giving, John's stressed-out sister resisted, despite the fact that the overtime she worked to buy her gifts was making her sick. Arguments ensued, and in the end John and Louise dropped the idea and went along, against their better judgment.

Like many, the Mattsons feel that Christmas has become unacceptably commercialized, an orgy of shopping and spending. Even Halloween, once a simple holiday, now gobbles up $2.5 billion in soft drink, candy, costume, decoration, and beer spending. Many Americans yearn for holidays that feel authentic and true to earlier, noncommercial traditions. But what they, and many Americans, don't realize is the extent to which many of our most cherished holiday traditions have been commercialized for quite some time. And therein lies much of the difficulty of creating another way. Rudolph the Red-Nosed Reindeer was invented by an ad man for Montgomery Ward. Even Thanksgiving, arguably our most authentic holiday, was moved a week earlier by Franklin Roosevelt in 1939 at the urging of a department store owner hoping to lengthen the shopping season.

The first step in downsizing a holiday is to recognize the ways in which commercial interests have shaped our rituals and habits. Once you realize that large inventories of toys for children are a recent phenomenon, or that our ancestors didn't wrap gifts, it's easier to do things differently. Diamond engagement rings are not a time-honored tradition but a product of recent vintage, brought to us by—who else—the diamond manufacturer. So too the knowledge that bridal registries were not the usual practice of the turn-of-the-century rich; they're also relatively new. Bride magazines, wedding consultants, wear-it-once dresses—new, new, new. When you know how weddings used to be celebrated, it's easier to close *Bride* magazine and be satisfied with an inexpensive affair. Learning the histories of holidays and then sharing the information with friends and family may help to take away some of the imperative of costly "traditions." Various simple-living groups and manuals suggest alternative, noncommercial ways to celebrate the holidays. They propose spending limits on gifts, limiting the number of gifts, spending time together as an alternative to gifts, making rather than buying tree ornaments, and giving gifts of time and labor. Reorienting celebrations around home-prepared food rather than store-bought commodities is one way to get back to authentic holiday experiences, because food and drink have been at the center of most historical traditions. Such a shift is likely to bring more creative satisfaction, less stress on the pocketbook, and more social togetherness. (Thanksgiving has always been my favorite holiday—just food and family.) But, of course, such a change takes more time. To figure that one out, read on.

Principle 8: Making Time: Is Work-and-Spend Working?

As most people who have thought seriously about how to reduce their spending know, spending less requires time. It requires not only shopping more carefully or doing research, but acknowledging that the cheaper way to do something is usually more time-consuming. What's true in cooking (preparing dried beans, baking homemade bread, making a cake from scratch) is also true in general: cheaper transport is usually slower, making a Halloween costume takes more time, and ordering by mail (to avoid shopping) incurs shipping costs. While there are certainly exceptions, the principle is that you pay for convenience. People who work in stressful, time-consuming jobs know the drill well. It's hard to reduce spending because they need to "buy" time—by getting others to do their housework, gardening, food preparation, chauffeuring, even shopping. And then they need to earn the paycheck to pay for all those services.

For some of us, spending less requires breaking out of this harried, convenience-oriented lifestyle. It requires taking control of our lives on a daily basis, so that shifting to a more time-intensive but cheaper (and incidentally, more ecologically sound) lifestyle is possible. Of course, that is not easy to do. Most jobs do not offer "downward flexibility" in hours, allowing the employee to work a little less, with a little loss in pay. Many, particularly the better-remunerated ones, are all-or-nothing propositions. At Telecom, 85 percent of all respondents said that reducing hours in their job would be either impossible or fairly difficult.

However, it can be done. Millions of downshifters are finding ways. If you find yourself working long hours but spending everything you make, if you are stressed out and not even enjoying the consumer goodies you do have, then the work-and-spend cycle is not working for you. Start thinking seriously about a change that may entail earning less but will give you back control of your time and your life.

Principle 9: The Need for a Coordinated Intervention

A central argument of this book has been that competitive consumption creates a "prisoner's dilemma"—both prisoners would be better off if neither one talked, but only the one who talks first gets a good deal from the prosecutor. The well-being of everyone could be improved if there were a way to harmonize individual behavior and minimize the competitive incentives. If the Joneses could be induced not to upgrade their car or house or whatever, then the Smiths wouldn't have to either, and both would be happier. But central to the prisoner's dilemma is the inability of the two prisoners to bring about the best outcome because they are not allowed to confer and devise a common position. One way to make that happen is with a central coordinating entity—like the government.

The traditional route has been taxation. Consider the sport utility vehicle. As it has become the latest status symbol, individuals feel pressure to acquire one. While some people truly benefit from owning such a vehicle, others who never go camping or hunting or embark on off-road journeys end up on the bandwagon because that's what the with-it people are now buying. And it's not all image. Who wants to be in the car-sized Corolla that a Land Cruiser just plowed into? Who wants to be the only parent in the class who can't accommodate the kids after the soccer game? For an individual, it's sometimes hard to escape the logic. But for the public, the trend is a definite negative.

If large vehicles were taxed more heavily than lighter, energy-efficient cars (instead of the other way around), the competitive spiral leading to the acquisition of more and more Land Cruisers, Explorers, and Suburbans might slow down. If individuals were forced to be accountable for the effect of their vehicles on others' safety, they might be less likely to choose the five-thousand-pound gorilla. The roads would be safer, the environment cleaner, and many families' bank accounts larger.

Lest luxury taxes sound intrusive, unfair, or even un-American, remember that we already do a tremendous amount of "social engineering" through subsidizing and taxing specific commodities, including items designated as luxuries. In my state, a piece of clothing that costs above $175 incurs sales tax, but less expensive items do not. There is also an extensive network of subsidies for tobacco and sugar farmers, energy conservation, military production, homeownership, child care, charitable giving, and the like. Consider also that higher taxes on some items could be counterbalanced by lower levies on others. If you bought the small, energy-efficient car, the sales tax could be waived altogether. When insurance companies raised the liability insurance rates for owners of sport utility vehicles, they implied that the rates on cars that do not do so much damage in collisions would be lowered.

The principle would be that the high-end, status versions of certain commodities would pay a high tax, the midrange models would pay midrange taxes, and low-end versions would be exempt. Property taxes could also be progressively structured, so that if you opt for a living room, family room, library, and glassed-in porch to go with the seven bedrooms and bathrooms in your new dream house, you'll face a higher tax rate than a family whose house is of median square footage.

Consumption taxes are a start. But mitigating the factors that give rise to competitive spending in the first place is also important. That starts with reversing thirty years of growing inequality in the distribution of income and wealth. It's not surprising that the upper-middle class has become "the one to watch" (as NBC touts about itself): its members receive almost half of the nation's annual income and use it to create a compelling consumer lifestyle. What if tax and other government policies improved the distribution of income so that wealth and income were more fairly shared? The gap between aspirations and incomes would narrow, and people might choose to work less, borrow less, and slow down their daily lives. (Government policies can also affect these choices.) They'd also have to worry less about protecting their possessions, since fewer individuals would steal the things the culture tells them they must have to be whole. Competitive spending pressures would ease—a rarely recognized side benefit of a more equal distribution of income.

A final area is advertising. Ad expenditures have skyrocketed in recent years and now stand at more than $2,000 per family. These expenditures are fully subsidized by taxpayers: advertising costs are deductible from corporate profits. If this write-off were revoked, it's likely there would be fewer ads, which nearly everyone but Madison Avenue probably agrees would be a good thing. (Sixty-five percent of the public already agree with such an idea, and 80 percent believe that prime-time advertising should be limited.) It's time to get this giveaway on the congressional docket.

Filling the Void

The message children used to get from their bedtime stories was that money doesn't buy happiness. Though the new governess for our children, Miss Television, has a more modern message, an accumulating body of economic literature supports the old notion. Being poor, or devoid of possessions, does greatly impair one's well-being, but *beyond a certain point*, having more stuff doesn't seem to help. A fivefold increase in Japan's average income made its citizens no better off in terms of happiness. The postwar threefold increase in American incomes had the same result. On average, we're long past the point where additional income, or consumption, yields much psychic benefit. In large part, it is this evidence that makes me feel comfortable advocating the changes I do. Our history shows that the extra spending won't be missed.

On the other hand, a serious turning away from consumerism, as an ideology and a way of life, raises a whole set of issues that scholarly research has not really addressed. While it may be true that reorienting our emotional lives away from the symbolism of products would be liberating (I for one would welcome less pressure about the fabric I choose for my couch, or whether I'm keeping up technologically), such a shift would probably leave a void. James Twitchell overstates the case when he asserts that "getting and spending is what gives our lives order and meaning." But he does have a point. If we aren't flipping through catalogs or daydreaming about the perfect living room, what will we be doing?

The cynical answer is: watching television. Perhaps. But then again, television yields relatively low satisfaction and is often used by adults as a way to unwind after a stressful and exhausting day at work. It is often background, or company, a sort of white noise and light show. (Even now, 39 percent of the population say they watch too much TV.) If we had more time off from working and could plan more satisfying recreation, we might well spend less time in front of the tube. The experiences of downshifters suggest there are plenty of satisfying ways to fill the void. They have the time to do the things the rest of us keep putting off, such as gardening, cooking, quilting, writing books, mountain biking, opening bed and breakfasts, socializing, playing music, joining book clubs, exercising, learning a language, taking care of their children, and spending lots of time volunteering. Yes, yes, I know what you're thinking. Some of these activities, like gardening, can be terribly expensive. But remember, you don't need to be fully outfitted by Smith and Hawken, and maybe you could even get a garden tool library started. There really are cheap ways to do most things. Besides, with all the money you're saving, you can afford to splurge on something you really love.

Another option is civic reengagement. Many of the people I interviewed have connected up with others who are also trying to live differently. There is now an expanding movement for new, less consumerist lifestyles, fueled by organizations such as the Center for a New American Dream, the New Road Map Foundation, the Northwest Earth Institute, the Cultural Environment Movement, the Center for the Study of Commercialism, Unplug, TV Turn-Off Week, and the Media Foundation (see the resources listing at the end of the book). These groups are addressing the environmental, cultural, and social effects of the old American dream and trying to devise a new one. They organize discussion groups, public forums, newsletters, and community events. They are eager for new recruits.

I remain optimistic that we *can* fill the void. It can hardly be possible that the dumbing-down of America has proceeded so far that it's either consumerism or nothing. We remain a creative, resourceful, and caring nation. There's still time left to find our way out of the mall.

EPILOGUE: WILL CONSUMING LESS WRECK THE ECONOMY?

Everyone knows that spending equals jobs. What will happen when people hold on to their cars longer, opt for the $35 athletic shoes, and start eating food they cooked themselves, at home? Given that consumer spending is the main force behind economic growth, won't this "new consumer" wreak havoc on the economy?

There's little question that if a large number of Americans suddenly cut up their credit cards, the economy would go into recession. A large and unexpected decline in consumer spending would send sales, and employment, down. But that apocalyptic scenario is unrealistic. If Americans begin to consume differently, they will do so gradually. Actually, they already are. Among the fifth of the population that downshifted in the first half of the 1990s, 30 percent cut their spending by one-quarter, and 30 percent by one-half or more. Meanwhile, the economy is roaring along.

To figure out the impact of new consumer patterns, we need to start with some reasonable assumptions about how behavior, and spending, will change. Will consumption fall absolutely? Will it stabilize? Or will it just grow more slowly than it has? What will happen to hours of work and the supply of labor? How much capital investment is business making? Once we settle on the basic assumptions, we also need to consider economists' legendary differences of opinion. We must realize

there are no simple answers to this question. The bottom line, however, is that retaining a healthy economy is possible if consumer spending slows considerably or even drops in real terms. To see why, let's
consider the key economic variables at stake: savings and consumption, growth and productivity, and hours and employment.

The jobs question is probably the simplest. At any point in time,
employment (and conversely, unemployment) depends on three factors: the level of production, the number of people who want jobs,
and the number of hours they work. If consumer spending slows,
production will go down. But employment can be maintained if
fewer people want jobs or hours of work fall.

There are good reasons to believe that a gradual reduction in consumer spending will not cause much unemployment. The most
important one is that the trend toward buying less is likely to be
associated with a trend toward working less. That's because downshifting is primarily driven by the desire for more free time. The
most plausible scenario for the emergence of a less consumerist culture is the growing popularity of downshifting. With such impetus,
the transition could be accomplished without a rise in unemployment. Fewer people would want jobs, and the hours worked *per* job
could fall. The other reason to be sanguine about the employment
situation is that the U.S. economy has become reasonably good at
creating jobs. (It has been much less good at creating jobs that pay
decent wages and benefits and offer a long-term future. Doing that
requires changes I have not touched on here.)

What if people don't downshift but do decide to spend less? What
impact will a sudden attack of frugality have on the economy? The
conventional wisdom is that this is a good thing. Most economists
and many others believe the country hasn't been saving *enough*.
Some worry that consumer credit has reached unhealthy levels and
that a credit collapse is all too likely. There is concern that households have developed an unsustainable gotta-have-it-now attitude to
buying, as well as ongoing concern that the nation borrows too much
from abroad and is underinvesting in the future. Within this camp,
the neoclassical approach worries less about employment, believing
that if the labor market is flexible, there will always be enough work
for people.

Of course, not everyone thinks this way. Keynesian-oriented

economists warn that too much saving does terrible damage. When consumers don't spend enough, businesses stop investing because demand for their products has fallen. This in turn leads to recession and unemployment.

I have always believed there is great merit in the Keynesian view. Businesses *do* respond to market conditions, and a downturn in demand often leads companies to lay off workers and postpone capital improvements. Unemployment can be a persistent problem. But here again, timing is everything. If the shift to saving is gradual, companies can develop new customers. With the globalization of the economy, such market diversification is more feasible. Downturns in demand can also lead to consolidations and efficiency gains, especially in industries where production capacity is already too high. Finally, while the economy's rate of growth may be lower under this scenario, unemployment does not have to rise. If companies respond to reduced demand by cutting hours of work, they can cut their production without reducing personnel. Since the mid-1990s, Volkswagen has been doing this, shifting to a popular four-day schedule and avoiding layoffs.

Now we come to the long-run questions of growth and productivity. It is relatively uncontroversial that in an economy in which people work less and consume less, the rate of economic growth will also be lower. We can already see this in those Western European countries with large numbers of "postmaterialists," people who are not terribly concerned with making money, getting ahead, or consuming a lot. Places like the Netherlands and Denmark, which are high on the postmaterialism index, have had relatively lower growth rates. Is this cause for concern? On the one hand, the answer is no. In these countries, the slow growth rate merely means that people are not so intent on making a high income or consuming a lot. As long as unemployment does not become a problem, slow (or no) growth is a perfectly acceptable reflection of people's choices and priorities. They prefer more time off from work. Or more environmental protection. They opt for more financial security. There is no economic commandment that says we must maximize the growth rate.

On the other hand, there is a price to be paid. If the economy grows slowly, productivity also grows slowly. For reasons economists don't fully understand, labor productivity is highly correlated with economic growth. So when the economy roars along, it tends to become more efficient. Labor productivity matters both in itself (as the factor determining how much worktime is necessary to produce any given quantity of products) and because it is the major determinant of competitiveness. If productivity growth is reduced, a country's competitive position tends to worsen. And in an increasingly globalized world, that matters more. In my mind, this would be the most significant effect of a shift to less consumerism.

But significant does not mean insurmountable. On the one hand, if any country can afford to take risks, it's the United States. Its competitive position has soared in the 1990s, with American companies beating out the competition around the world. Second, there *are* ways to compensate for the productivity improvements that would be lost through slower growth. If average hours of work fall, the rate of hourly productivity typically rises, as people tend to work harder or more efficiently within a shorter space of time. (When you take Friday afternoon off, don't you make it up somewhere in the week?) It is also possible to be more proactive with respect to productivity, as many other countries are. The Netherlands, despite its high number of postmaterialists and relatively slow growth, has extremely high labor productivity. It also has a government that invests heavily in education, research, and development. The United States could do this too.

Finally, we need to reexamine the structure of international competition itself. The relentlessly increasing competitiveness of the world economy in recent years is not an inevitable effect of technology, as many would have it, but has in large part been caused by the deliberate actions of companies and governments—American corporations and the U.S. government, more specifically. U.S. companies have been remaking foreign consumer markets in their own, hypercompetitive image. And the U.S. government has largely rewritten the global rules of the game. If keeping up now seems to take an exhausting, indeed overwhelming amount of effort, we have mostly ourselves to blame.

But we can also do something about it. Throughout Europe, people are wondering whether the globalization of consumer markets isn't proceeding too rapidly, with too little thought. They are worried that they will not be able to maintain their quality of life in a world where making as much money as possible has become the reigning religion. And they are trying to find another way, a model of a decently functioning economy coexisting with a decent cultural and daily life experience. Isn't it time Americans started asking some of these same questions?

Abel, Andrew B. 1990. "Asset Prices Under Habit Formation and Catching up with the Joneses." *American Economic Review* 80 (2): 43–47.

Ackerman, Frank, Neva R. Goodwin, and David Kiron. 1997. *The Consumer Society*. Washington, D.C.: Island Press.

ACORN (A Classification Of Residential Neighborhoods). 1994. *User's Guide*. Arlington, Va.: CACI Marketing Systems.

Advisory Commission to Study the Consumer Price Index (1996). *Toward a More Accurate Measure of the Cost of Living*. Washington, D.C. Senate Finance Committee.

Allen, Douglas E., and Paul F. Anderson. 1994. "Consumption and Social Stratification: Bourdieu's *Distinction*." In Chris T. Allen and Deborah Roedder-John, eds., *Advances in Consumer Research* (21:70–74). Provo, Utah: Association for Consumer Research.

Allen, Margaret. 1981. *Selling Dreams: Inside the Beauty Business*. New York: Simon and Schuster.

Alessie, Rob, and Arie Kapteyn. 1991. "Habit Formation, Interdependent Preferences, and Demographic Effects in the Almost Ideal Demand System." *Economic Journal* 101 (May): 404–19.

Allison, Ralph I., and Kenneth P. Uhl. 1964. "Influence of Beer Brand Identification on Taste Perception." *Journal of Marketing Research* 1 (August): 36–39.

Andrews, Cecile. 1997. *The Circle of Simplicity: Return to the Good Life*. New York: HarperCollins.

Appadurai, Arjun. 1986. *The Social Life of Things: Commodities in Cultural Perspective*. New York: Cambridge University Press.

Attanasio, Orazio, and Steven J. Davis. 1994. "Relative Wage Movements and the Distribution of Consumption." NBER Working Paper 4771. Cambridge, Mass.: National Bureau of Economic Research.

Ausubel, Lawrence M. 1991. "The Failure of Competition in the Credit Card Market." *American Economic Review* 81 (March): 50–81.

———. 1995. "The Credit Card Market, Revisited." Unpublished paper, University of Maryland (July).

Averett, Susan, and Sanders Korenman. 1993. "The Economic Reality of *The Beauty Myth.*" NBER Working Paper 4521. Cambridge, Mass.: National Bureau of Economic Research.

Baker, Dean. 1996. "Getting Prices Right: A Methodologically Consistent Consumer Price Index, 1953–1994." EPI Technical Paper. Washington, D.C.: Economic Policy Institute (12 April).

Basmann, Robert L., David J. Molina, and Daniel J. Slottje. 1988. "A Note on Measuring Veblen's Theory of Conspicuous Consumption." *Review of Economics and Statistics* 70 (August 1998): 531–35.

Baudrillard, Jean. 1988. *Selected Writings.* Stanford, Calif.: Stanford University Press.

Baugh, Dawna F., and Leslie L. Davis. 1989. "The Effect of Store Image on Consumers' Perceptions of Designer and Private Label Clothing." *Clothing and Textiles Research Journal* 7(3): 15–21.

Bearden, William O., and Michael J. Etzel. 1982. "Reference Group Influence and Product and Brand Purchase Decisions." *Journal of Consumer Research* 9 (September 1982): 183–94.

Bearden, William O., Richard G. Netemeyer, and Jesse E. Teel. 1989. "Measurement of Consumer Susceptibility to Interpersonal Influence." *Journal of Consumer Research* 15 (March 1989): 473–81.

Behling, Dorothy U., and Jennette Wilch. 1988. "Perceptions of Branded Clothing by Male Consumers." *Clothing and Textiles Research Journal* 6(2): 43–47.

Belk, Russell W. 1978. "Assessing the Effects of Visible Consumption on Impression Formation." In H. Keith Hunt, ed., *Advances in Consumer Research* (5:39–47). Ann Arbor, Mich.: Association for Consumer Research.

———. 1980. "Effects of Consistency of Visible Consumption Patterns on Impression Formation." In Jerry Olson, ed., *Advances in Consumer Research* (7:365–71). Ann Arbor, Mich.: Association for Consumer Research.

———. 1981. "Determinants of Consumption Cue Utilization in Impression Formation: An Association Derivation and Experimental Verification." In Kent B. Monroe, ed., *Advances in Consumer Research* (8:170–75). Ann Arbor, Mich.: Association for Consumer Research.

———. 1985a. "Third World Consumer Culture." In Erdoğan Kumcu and A. Fuat Firat, eds., *Marketing and Development: Toward Broader Dimensions* (103–27). Greenwich, Conn.: JAI Press.

———. 1985b. "Materialism: Trait Aspects of Living in the Material World." *Journal of Consumer Research* 12 (December): 265–80.

————. 1986. "Yuppies as Arbiters of the Emerging Consumption Style." In Richard J. Lutz, ed., *Advances in Consumer Research* (13:514–19). Provo, Utah: Association for Consumer Research.

————. 1988. "Possessions and the Extended Self." *Journal of Consumer Research* 15 (September): 139–68.

————. 1990. "Halloween: An Evolving American Consumption Ritual." In Gerald Gorn, Marvin Goldberg, and Richard Pollay, eds., *Advances in Consumer Research* (17: 508–17). Provo, Utah: Association for Consumer Research.

————. 1995. *Collecting in a Consumer Society*. London: Routledge.

Belk, Russell W., Kenneth D. Bahn, and Robert N. Mayer. 1982. "Developmental Recognition of Consumption Symbolism." *Journal of Consumer Research* 9 (June): 4–17.

Belk, Russell W., Robert Mayer, and Kenneth Bahn. 1982. "The Eye of the Beholder: Individual Differences in Perceptions of Consumption Symbolism." In Andrew Mitchell, ed., *Advances in Consumer Research* (9:523–30). Ann Arbor, Mich.: Association for Consumer Research.

Belk, Russell, Robert Mayer, and Amy Driscoll. 1984. "Children's Recognition of Consumption Symbolism in Children's Products." *Journal of Consumer Research* 10 (March): 386–97.

Berhau, Pat. Forthcoming. "The Other Side of Class Stratification: Social Class and the Experiences of Consumers." Ph.D. dissertation, Temple University.

Bickman, Leonard. 1971. "The Effect of Social Status on the Honesty of Others." *Journal of Social Psychology* 85 (October): 87–92.

Birdwell, Al E. 1968. "A Study of the Influence of Image Congruence on Consumer Choice." *Journal of Business* 41 (January): 76–88.

Bishop, Doyle W., and Marasu Ikeda. 1970. "Status and Role Factors in the Leisure Behavior of Different Occupations." *Sociology and Social Research* 54 (January): 190–208.

Blanchard, Elisa A. 1994. "Beyond Consumer Culture: A Study of Revaluation and Voluntary Action." Thesis, Tufts University (November).

Blix, Jacqueline, and David Heitmiller. 1997. *Getting a Life: Real Lives Transformed by Your Money or Your Life*. New York: Viking Penguin.

Blumberg, Paul. 1974. "The Decline and Fall of the Status Symbol: Some Thoughts on Status in a Post-Industrial Society." *Social Problems* 21 (April): 490–98.

Bolonik, Kera, and Jennifer Griffin. 1997. *Frugal Indulgents: How to Cultivate Decadence When Your Age and Salary Are Under 30*. New York: Henry Holt.

Boorstin, Daniel. 1968. *The Consuming Public*. New York: H. W. Wilson.

Bosman, Ciska M., Gerard A. Pfann, Jeff E. Biddle, and Daniel S. Hammermesh. 1997. "Business Success and Businesses' Beauty Capital." NBER Working Paper 6083. Cambridge, Mass.: National Bureau of Economic Research.

Boston Globe. 1997. "Inside the Self-storage Boom: The Stuff America's Made Of." *Boston Globe*, 23 November, A25.

Bourdieu, Pierre. 1984. *Distinction: A Social Critique of the Judgement of Taste*. Cambridge, Mass.: Harvard University Press.

Bradley, Sam. 1995. "Prospecting for the Fortune of Youth." *Brandweek*, 13 February.

———. 1996. "Hallmark Enters $20B Pet Category." *Brandweek*, 1 January.

Bradsher, Keith. 1997. "A Deadly Highway Mismatch Ignored." *New York Times*, 24 September, A1.

Bragg, Rich. 1996a. "In the Family the Good Life Lost." *New York Times*, 5 March, A1.

———. 1996b. "More Than Money, They Miss the Pride a Good Job Brought." *New York Times*, 5 March, A17.

Braun, Ottmar L., and Robert A. Wicklund. 1989. "Psychological Antecedents of Conspicuous Consumption." *Journal of Economic Psychology* 10: 161–87.

Brewer, John, and Roy Porter, eds. 1993. *Consumption and the World of Goods*. London: Routledge.

Brown, Clair. 1994. *The Standard of Living*. Cambridge, Mass.: Blackwell.

Bryce, Robert. 1995. "Here's a Course in Personal Finance 101, the Hard Way." *New York Times*, 30 April, 11.

Burke, Peter. 1993. "*Res et Verba*: Conspicuous Consumption in the Early Modern World." In John Brewer and Roy Porter, eds., *Consumption and the World of Goods* (148–61). London: Routledge.

Calder, Bobby J., and Robert E. Burnkrant. 1977. "Interpersonal Influence on Consumer Behavior: An Attribution Theory Approach." *Journal of Consumer Research* 4 (June): 29–38.

Calmes, Jackie. 1996. "Good News for Clinton: Voters Feel Better Off." *Wall Street Journal*, 20 September, R2.

Campbell, Colin. 1987. *The Romantic Ethic and the Spirit of Modern Consumerism*. Oxford: Blackwell.

———. 1996. "The Meaning of Objects and the Meaning of Actions: A Critical Note on the Sociology of Consumption and Theories of Clothing." *Journal of Material Culture* 1(1): 93–105.

Campbell, John Y., and John H. Cochrane. 1995. "By Force of Habit: A Consumption-Based Explanation of Aggregate Stock Market Behavior." NBER Working Paper 4995. Cambridge, Mass.: National Bureau of Economic Research.

Canner, Glenn B., Arthur B. Kennickell, and Charles A. Luckett. 1995. "Household Sector Borrowing and the Burden of Debt." *Federal Reserve Bulletin* (April): 323–38.

Caughey, John L. 1984. *Imagining Social Worlds: A Cultural Approach*. Lincoln: University of Nebraska Press.

Center for a New American Dream. 1997. "Holiday Spending Poll." Takoma Park, Md.: Center for a New American Dream (October).

Central Statistical Office. 1995. *National Accounts*. New Delhi: Government of India Printing Office.

Chao, Angela, and Juliet B. Schor. 1998. "Empirical Tests of Status Consumption: Evidence from Women's Cosmetics." *Journal of Economic Psychology* 19(1): 1–30.

Chapin, F. Stuart. 1928. "A Quantitative Scale for Rating the Home and Social Environment of Middle-class Families in an Urban Community: A First Approximation to the Measurement of Socioeconomic Status." *Journal of Educational Psychology* 19(2): 99–111.

———. 1935. "A Measurement of Social Status." Chapter 19 in *Contemporary American Institutions: A Sociological Analysis* (373–97). New York: Harper and Brothers.

Cherulnik, Paul D., and John K. Bayless. 1986. "Person Perception in Environmental Context: The Influence of Residential Settings on Impressions of Their Occupants." *Journal of Social Psychology* 126(5): 667–73.

Childers, Terry L., and Akshay R. Rao. 1992. "The Influence of Familial and Peer-Based Reference Groups on Consumer Decisions." *Journal of Consumer Research* 19 (September): 198–211.

Christenson, Gary, et al. 1994. "Compulsive Buying: Descriptive Characteristics and Psychiatric Comorbidity." *Journal of Clinical Psychiatry* 55 (January): 5–11.

Clark, Andrew E., and Andrew J. Oswald. 1994. "Unhappiness and Unemployment." *Economic Journal* 104 (May): 648–59.

Cobb, Clifford, Ted Halstead, and Jonathan Rowe. 1995. *The Genuine Progress Indicator: Summary of Data and Methodology.* San Francisco: Redefining Progress.

Cocanougher, A. Benton, and Grady D. Bruce. 1971. "Socially Distant Reference Groups and Consumer Aspirations." *Journal of Marketing Research* 8 (August): 379–81.

Coleman, Richard P. 1982. "The Continuing Significance of Social Class to Marketing." *Journal of Consumer Research* 10 (December): 265–80.

Congleton, Roger. 1989. "Efficient Status Seeking: Externalities, and the Evolution of Status Games." *Journal of Economic Behavior and Organization* 11: 175–90.

Consumer Reports. 1988 (February), 1989 (June), 1991 (February).

Council of Economic Advisers. 1995, 1996, 1997. *Economic Report of the President.* Washington, D.C.: U.S. Government Printing Office.

Cox, Dena, Anthony D. Cox, and George P. Moschis. 1990. "When Consumer Behavior Goes Bad: An Investigation of Adolescent Shoplifting." *Journal of Consumer Research* 17 (September): 149–59.

Craik, Jennifer. 1994. *The Face of Fashion: Cultural Studies in Fashion.* London: Routledge.

Crispell, Diane. "We Don't Need Much to Have It All." *Wall Street Journal,* October 21, B1.

Cross, Gary. 1993. *Time and Money: The Making of Consumer Culture.* New York: Routledge.

———. 1997. *Kids' Stuff: Toys and the Changing World of American Childhood*. Cambridge, Mass.: Harvard University Press.

Cutler, David M., and Lawrence F. Katz. 1992. "Rising Inequality: Changes in the Distribution of Income and Consumption in the 1980s." NBER Working Paper 3964. Cambridge, Mass.: National Bureau of Economic Research.

Danziger, Sheldon, and Peter Gottschalk. 1993. *Uneven Tides: Rising Inequality in America*. New York: Russell Sage.

d'Astous, Alain. 1990. "An Inquiry into the Compulsive Side of 'Normal' Consumers." *Journal of Consumer Policy* 13: 15–31.

Davis, Fred. 1992. *Fashion, Culture, and Identity*. Chicago: University of Chicago Press.

Davis, James A. 1956, "Status Symbols and the Measurement of Status Perception." *Sociometry* 19(3): 154–65.

Deaton, Angus. 1992. *Understanding Consumption*. Oxford: Clarendon Press.

de Certeau, Michel. 1984. *The Practice of Everyday Life*. Berkeley: University of California Press.

Dholakia, Ruby Roy, and Sidney J. Levy. 1987. "Effect of Economic Experiences on Consumer Dreams, Goals, and Behavior in the United States." *Journal of Economic Psychology* 8: 429–44.

Diderot, Denis. 1964. "Regrets on Parting with My Old Dressing Gown." In Jacques Barzun and Ralph H. Bowen, trans., *Rameau's Nephew and Other Works by Denis Diderot* (309–17). New York: Bobbs-Merrill.

Diener, Ed, Ed Sandvik, Larry Seidlitz, and Marissa Diener. 1993. "The Relationship Between Income and Subjective Well-being: Relative or Absolute?" *Social Indicators Research* 28: 195–223.

DiMaggio, Paul, and Michael Useem. 1978. "Social Class and Arts Consumption: The Origins and Consequences of Class Differences in Exposure to the Arts in America." *Theory and Society* 5: 141–161.

Dittmar, Helga. 1992. *The Social Psychology of Material Possessions*. New York: St. Martin's.

———. 1994a. "Material Possessions as Stereotypes: Material Images of Different Socioeconomic Groups." *Journal of Economic Psychology* 15: 561–85.

———. 1994b. "To Have Is to Be: Materialism and Person Perception in Working-class and Middle-class British Adolescents." *Journal of Economic Psychology* 15: 233–51.

Dolich, Ira J. 1969. "Congruence Relationships Between Self-images and Product Brands." *Journal of Marketing Research*, 6 (February): 80–84.

Dominguez, Joe, and Vicki Robin. 1992. *Your Money or Your Life*. New York: Penguin.

Doob, Anthony N., and Alan E. Gross. 1968. "Status of Frustrator as an Inhibitor of Horn-Honking Responses." *Journal of Social Psychology* 76: 213–18.

Douglas, Mary, and Baron Isherwood. 1996. *The World of Goods: Towards an Anthropology of Consumption*. London: Routledge.

Douty, Helen I. 1963. "Influence of Clothing on Perceptions of Persons." *Journal of Home Economics* 55 (March): 197–202.

Driscoll, Amy M., Robert N. Mayer, Russell W. Belk. 1985. "The Young Child's Recognition of Consumption Symbols and Their Social Implications." *Child Study Journal* 15(2): 117–30.

Duesenberry, James S. 1949. *Income, Saving, and the Theory of Consumer Behavior.* Cambridge, Mass.: Harvard University Press.

Durning, Alan Thein. 1991. "Asking How Much Is Enough." In Lester R. Brown et al., *State of the World 1991* (153–69). New York: Norton.

———. 1992. *How Much Is Enough? The Consumer Society and the Future of the Earth.* Washington, D.C.: Worldwatch Institute.

Easterlin, Richard A. 1973. "Does Money Buy Happiness?" *Public Interest* 30 (Winter): 3–10.

———. 1995. "Will Raising the Incomes of All Increase the Happiness of All?" *Journal of Economic Behavior and Organization* 27: 35–47.

Easterlin, Richard A., and Eileen M. Crimmins. 1991. "Changes in the Values of American Youth." *Public Opinion Quarterly* 55: 499–533.

Ehrenreich, Barbara. 1990. *Fear of Falling: The Inner Life of the Middle Class.* New York: HarperCollins.

"The 18-Minute Mile." 1997. *TV-Free American* 3(2): 2.

Elgin, Duane. 1993. *Voluntary Simplicity: Toward a Way of Life That Is Outwardly Simple, Inwardly Rich.* New York: Morrow.

Englis, Basil G., and Michael R. Solomon. 1995. "To Be and Not to Be: Lifestyle Imagery, Reference Groups, and *The Clustering of America*," *Journal of Advertising* 24 (Spring): 13–28.

Ewen, Stuart. 1988. *All Consuming Images: The Politics of Style in Contemporary Culture.* New York: Basic.

Ewen, Stuart, and Elizabeth Ewen. 1992. *Channels of Desire: Mass Images and the Shaping of American Consciousness.* Minneapolis: University of Minnesota Press.

Faber, Ronald J. 1992. "Money Changes Everything: Compulsive Buying from a Biopsychosocial Perspective." *American Behavioral Scientist* 35 (July): 809–19.

Faber, Ronald J., Gary A. Christenson, Martina De Zwaan, and James Mitchell. 1995. "Two Forms of Compulsive Consumption: Comorbidity of Compulsive Buying and Binge Eating." *Journal of Consumer Research* 22 (December): 296–304.

Faber, Ronald J., and Thomas C. O'Guinn. 1992. "A Clinical Screener for Compulsive Buying." *Journal of Consumer Research* 19 (December): 459–69.

Faber, Ronald J., Thomas C. O'Guinn, and Raymond Krych. 1987. "Compulsive Consumption." In Melanie Wallendorf and Paul Anderson, eds., *Advances in Consumer Research* (14:132–35). Provo, Utah: Association for Consumer Research.

Farkas, Steve, and Jean Johnson. 1997. *Miles to Go: A Status Report on Americans' Plans for Retirement.* New York: Public Agenda Foundation.

Featherstone, Michael. 1991. *Consumer Culture and Postmodernism.* London: Sage.

Feinberg, Richard A. 1986. "Credit Cards as Spending Facilitating Stimuli: A Conditioning Interpretation." *Journal of Consumer Research* 13 (December): 348–56.

Felson, Marcus. 1976. "The Differentiation of Material Life Styles: 1925 to 1966." *Social Indicators Research* 3: 397–421.

———. 1978. "Invidious Distinctions Among Cars, Clothes, and Suburbs." *Public Opinion Quarterly* 42 (Spring): 49–58.

Festinger, Leon. 1954. "A Theory of Social Comparison Processes." *Human Relations* 7(2): 117–40.

Financial Markets Center. 1997. *FOMC Alert.* Philomont, Va.: Financial Markets Center (18 August).

Fine, Ben, and Ellen Leopold. 1990. "Consumerism and the Industrial Revolution." *Social History* 15(20): 151–79.

———. 1994. *The World of Consumption.* London: Routledge.

Firat, A. Fuat, and Alladi Venkatesh. 1995. "Liberatory Postmodernism and the Reenchantment of Consumption." *Journal of Consumer Research* 22 (December): 239–67.

Fish, Stanley. 1994. "The Unbearable Ugliness of Volvos." In *There's No Such Thing as Free Speech . . . and It's a Good Thing Too* (273–79). New York: Oxford University Press.

Fitzgerald, Kathryn A. 1995. "Experiential Aspects of Elementary School Choice for Upper-middle-class Urban Americans: How Tough Choices Can Lead down the Path to 'Power Kindergarten.'" In Frank R. Kardes and Mita Sujan, eds., *Advances in Consumer Research* (22:633–39). Provo, Utah: Association for Consumer Research.

Fournier, Susan. 1996. "The Consumer and the Brand: An Understanding Within the Framework of Personal Relationships." Working Paper 97–024. Boston: Harvard Business School (September).

Fournier, Susan, and Michael Guiry. 1991. "A Look into the World of Consumption Dreams, Fantasies, and Aspirations." Research report, University of Florida (December).

———. 1993. "An Emerald Green Jaguar, a House on Nantucket, and an African Safari: Wish Lists and Consumption Dreams in Materialist Society." In Leigh McAlister and Michael L. Rothschild, eds. *Advances in Consumer Research* (20: 352–58) Provo, Utah: Association for Consumr Research.

Fox, Richard Wrightman and T.J. Jackson Lears, eds. 1983. *The Culture of Consumption.* New York: Pantheon.

Frank, Robert H. 1985a. *Choosing the Right Pond: Human Behavior and the Quest for Status.* New York: Oxford University Press.

———. 1985b. "The Demand for Unobservable and Other Nonpositional Goods." *American Economic Review* 75(1): 101–16.

Frank, Robert, and Philip J. Cook. 1995. *The Winner-Take-All Society.* New York: Free Press.

Freund, Thatcher. 1993. *Objects of Desire: The Lives of Antiques and Those Who Pursue Them.* New York: Pantheon.

Gabriel, Yiannis, and Tim Lang. 1995. *The Unmanageable Consumer: Contemporary Consumption and Its Fragmentations.* London: Sage.

Galbraith, John Kenneth. 1984. *The Affluent Society.* Boston: Houghton Mifflin.

Galí, Jordí. 1994. "Keeping up with the Joneses: Consumption Externalities, Portfolio Choice, and Asset Prices." *Journal of Money, Credit, and Banking* 26(1): 1–8.

Gelsi, Steve. 1995. "Sneaking into Third." *Brandweek,* 4 December, 24–25.

Givhan, Robin D. 1995. "Birth of a Salesman: How Tommy Hilfiger Got Everyone from Snoop to Springsteen to Buy His Clothes." *Washington Post,* 24 November, D1.

Gladwell, Malcolm. 1997. "The Coolhunt." *New Yorker,* 17 March, 78–88.

Goethals, G. R. 1986. "Social Comparison Theory: Psychology from the Lost and Found." *Personality and Social Psychology Bulletin* 12: 261–78.

Goffman, Erving. 1951. "Symbols of Class Status." *British Journal of Sociology* 2 (December): 294–304.

———. 1959. *The Presentation of Self in Everyday Life.* Garden City, N.Y.: Anchor.

Goldberg, Carey. 1995. "The Shopping Addicts: When the Urge to Spend Overtakes the Rational Processes of Mind and Budget." *New York Times,* 8 October, 1.

Gonzalez, David. 1990. "Teenagers Play the Odds in a Violent World." *New York Times,* 19 December, 1.

Gordon, David M. 1996. *Fat and Mean: The Corporate Squeeze of Working Americans and the Myth of Managerial "Downsizing."* New York: Free Press.

Gordon, Robert J. 1990. *The Measurement of Durable Goods Prices.* Chicago: University of Chicago Press.

———. 1995. "The American Real Wage Since 1963: Is It Unchanged or Has It More Than Doubled?" Unpublished paper, Northwestern University.

Gould, Stephen J., and Benny Barak. 1988. "Public Self-consciousness and Consumption Behavior." *Journal of Social Psychology* 128(3): 393–400.

Graham, Ellen. 1996. "What Money Just Can't Buy," *Wall Street Journal,* 20 September, R4.

Greenhouse, Steven. 1997. "Nike Supports Women in Its Ads but Not Its Factories, Groups Say." *New York Times,* 26 October, A30.

Greve, Karen. 1995. "The Impact of Parental Working Hours on Discretionary Expenditures on Children in Upper Income Families." Undergraduate honors thesis, Harvard University.

Grossman, Gene M., and Carl Shapiro. 1988. "Foreign Counterfeiting of Status Goods." *Quarterly Journal of Economics* 103(1): 79–100.

Grubb, Edward L. 1965. "Consumer Perception of 'Self-concept' and Its Relation to Brand Choice of Selected Product Types." In P. D. Bennett, ed., *Marketing and Economic Development* (419–24). Chicago: American Marketing Association.

Grubb, Edward L,. and Harrison L. Grathwohl. 1967. "Consumer Self-concept, Symbolism, and Market Behavior: A Theoretical Approach." *Journal of Marketing* 31 (October): 22–27.

Halle, David. 1993. *Inside Culture: Art and Class in the American Home.* Chicago: University of Chicago Press.

Hamlin, Suzanne. 1996. "Behind Americans' Love of Bottled Water." *New York Times*, 11 December, Style sect., 10.

Harris, Hamil R. 1996. "Council Seeks to Rid Streets of Bad Goods." *Washington Post*, 25 July, J1.

Hennigan, Karen M., et al. 1982. "Impact of the Introduction of Television on Crime in the United States: Empirical Findings and Theoretical Implications." *Journal of Personality and Social Psychology* 42 (March): 461–77.

Herbert, Bob. 1997. "Making Billions on the Backs of Hungry Women." *International Herald Tribune*, 1 April, 9.

Hewitt, Paul S. 1989. "Something's Gone Terribly Wrong with Being 'Rich.'" *Los Angeles Herald Tribune*, 7 January.

Higgins, E. Tory. 1987. "Self-discrepancy: A Theory Relating Self and Affect." *Psychological Review* 94(3): 319–40.

Hilts, Philip J. 1984. "Six-and-a-Half-Year Boycott of Nestle Is Ended as Firm Adopts Baby-Formula Code." *Washington Post*, 27 January, A1.

Hirsch, Fred. 1976. *Social Limits to Growth.* Cambridge, Mass.: Harvard University Press.

Hirschman, Elizabeth C. 1985. "Primitive Aspects of Consumption in Modern American Society." *Journal of Consumer Research* 12 (September): 142–54.

———. 1992. "The Consciousness of Addiction: Toward a General Theory of Compulsive Consumption." *Journal of Consumer Research* 19 (September): 155–79.

Hirschmann, Albert O. 1982. *Shifting Involvements: Private Interests and Public Action.* Princeton, N.J.: Princeton University Press.

Hochschild, Arlie Russell. 1997. *The Time Bind: When Work Becomes Home and Home Becomes Work.* San Francisco: Henry Holt.

Holman, Rebecca H. 1980. "Clothing as Communication: An Empirical Investigation." In Jerry C. Olson, ed., *Advances in Consumer Research* (7:372–77). Ann Arbor, Mich.: Association for Consumer Research.

———. 1981. "Product Use as Communication: A Fresh Appraisal of a Venerable Topic." In B. M. Enis and K. J. Roering, eds., *Review of Marketing* (106–19). Chicago: American Marketing Association.

Holt, Douglas B. 1997a. "Poststructuralist Lifestyles Analysis: Conceptualizing the Social Patterning of Consumption in Postmodernity." *Journal of Consumer Research* 23 (March): 326–50.

———. 1997b. "Distinction in America? Recovering Bourdieu's Theory of Taste from Its Critics." *Poetics* 25 (November): 93–120.

———. 1998. "Does Social Class Structure Contemporary American Consumption?" *Journal of Consumer Research* 25 (June).

Hyman, Herbert H. 1942. "The Psychology of Status." *Archives of Psychology* 269: 94–102.

Inglehart, Ronald. 1977. *The Silent Revolution*. Princeton, N.J.: Princeton University Press.

———. 1990. *Culture Shift*. Princeton, N.J.: Princeton University Press.

Ireland, Norman. 1994. "On Limiting the Market for Status Signals." *Journal of Public Economics* 53(1): 91–110.

Jacobson, Michael F., and Laurie Ann Mazur. 1995. *Marketing Madness: A Survival Guide for a Consumer Society*. Boulder, Colo.: Westview.

Jager, Michael. 1986. "Class Definitions and the Esthetics of Gentrification: Victoriana in Melbourne." In Neil Smith and Peter Williams, eds., *Gentrification of the City* (78–91). London: Unwin Hyman.

James, Jeffrey. 1987. "Positional Goods, Conspicuous Consumption, and the International Demonstration Effect Reconsidered." *World Development* 15(4): 449–62.

———. 1993. *Consumption and Development*. London: Macmillan.

Johnson, Gail. 1997. "Is Nike Losing Its Swoosh?" *Adbusters: Journal of the Mental Environment* (Autumn): 57.

Jordan, Miriam. 1996. "In Rural India, Video Vans Sell Toothpaste and Shampoo." *Wall Street Journal*, 10 January, B1.

Kacen, Jacqueline J. 1997. "Retail Therapy: Consumers' Shopping Cures for Negative Moods." Unpublished paper, University of Michigan-Dearborn.

Kapteyn, Arie, and F. G. van Herwaarden. 1980. "Interdependent Welfare Functions and Optimal Income Distribution." *Journal of Public Economics* 14: 375–97.

Kapteyn, Arie, and Tom Wansbeek. 1982. "Empirical Evidence on Preference Formation." *Journal of Economic Psychology* 2: 137–54.

Kasser, Tim, and Richard M. Ryan. 1993. "A Dark Side of the American Dream: Correlates of Financial Success as a Central Life Aspiration." *Journal of Personality and Social Psychology* 65(2): 410–22.

Kelly, Robert F. 1987. "Museums as Status Symbols II: Attaining a State of Having Been." In Russell Belk, ed., *Advances in Non-Profit Marketing* (2:1–38). Greenwich, Conn.: JAI Press.

Kennickell, Arthur B., Martha Starr-McCluer, and Annika E. Sundèn. 1997. "Family Finances in the U.S.: Recent Evidence from the Survey of Consumer Finances." *Federal Reserve Bulletin* 80 (January): 1–24.

Khermouch, Gerry. 1996. "Water Cooler: Naya Aim: Be Like Nike." *Brandweek*, 20 May.

Kleine, Susan Schultz, Robert E. Kleine III, and Chris T. Allen. 1995. "How Is a Possession 'Me' or 'Not Me'? Characterizing Types and an Antecedent of Material Possession Attachment." *Journal of Consumer Research* 22 (December): 327–43.

Kleine, Robert E., III, Susan Schultz Kleine, and Jerome B. Kernan. 1993. "Mundane Consumption and the Self: A Social-Identity Perspective." *Journal of Consumer Psychology* 2(3): 209–35.

Kline, Stephen. 1993. *Out of the Garden: Toys and Children's Culture in the Age of TV Marketing.* New York: Verso.

Knight, Deborah. 1997. "Make Way for Mansions." *Boston Sunday Globe Magazine,* 19 October.

Kosicki, George. 1987. "A Test of the Relative Income Hypothesis." *Southern Economic Journal* 54: 422–33.

Kroeger, Broeke. 1987. "Feeling Poor on $600,000 a Year." *New York Times,* 26 April.

Krugman, Paul. 1994. *Peddling Prosperity: Economic Sense and Nonsense in the Age of Diminished Expectations.* New York: Norton.

———. 1996. "The CPI and the Rat Race." *Slate,* 21 December, 24–25.

LaBarbera, Priscilla A. 1988. "The Nouveaux Riches: Conspicuous Consumption and the Issue of Self-fulfillment." In Jagdish N. Sheth, *Research in Consumer Behavior* (3:179–210). Greenwich, Conn.: JAI Press.

Lamont, Michèle, and Annette Lareau. 1988. "Cultural Capital: Allusions, Gaps, and Glissandos in Recent Theoretical Developments." *Sociological Theory* 6(2): 153–68.

Lamont, Michèle, and Marcel Fournier, eds. 1992. *Cultivating Differences: Symbolic Boundaries and the Making of Inequality.* Chicago: University of Chicago Press.

Lamont, Michèle, et al. 1996. "Cultural and Moral Boundaries in the United States: Structural Position, Geographic Location, and Lifestyle Explanations." *Poetics* 24: 31–56.

Landon, E. Laird, Jr. 1974. "Self-concept, Ideal Self-concept, and Consumer Purchase Intentions." *Journal of Consumer Research* 1 (September): 44–49.

Lane, Robert. 1991. *The Market Experience.* Cambridge: Cambridge University Press.

———. 1994. "The Road Not Taken: Friendship, Consumerism, and Happiness." *Critical Review* 8(4): 521–54.

Larson, Erik. 1992. *The Naked Consumer: How Our Private Lives Become Public Commodities.* San Francisco: Henry Holt.

Laumann, Edward O., and James S. House. 1970. "Living Room Styles and Social Attributes: The Patterning of Material Artifacts in a Modern Urban Community." *Sociology and Social Research* 54 (April): 321–42.

Leach, William. 1993. *Land of Desire: Merchants, Power, and the Rise of a New American Culture.* New York: Pantheon.

Lears, T. J. Jackson. 1983. "From Salvation to Realization: Advertising and the Therapeutic Roots of the Consumer Culture." In Richard Wightman Fox and T. J. Jackson Lears, eds., *The Culture of Consumption* (1–38). New York: Pantheon.

———. 1984. *No Place of Grace: Anti-modernism and the Transformation of American Culture.* New York: Pantheon.

———. 1994. *Fables of Abundance.* New York: Basic.

Lebergott, Stanley. 1993. *Pursuing Happiness: American Consumers in the Twentieth Century.* Princeton, N.J.: Princeton University Press.

Lee, Martyn J. 1993. *Consumer Culture Reborn: The Cultural Politics of Consumption.* London: Routledge.

Leete, Laura, and Schor, Juliet B. 1994. "Assessing the Time-Squeeze Hypothesis: Hours Worked in the United States, 1969–1989." *Industrial Relations* 33(January): 24–43.

Leibenstein, Harvey. 1950. "Bandwagon, Snob, and Veblen Effects in the Theory of Consumers' Demand." *Quarterly Journal of Economics* 64 (May): 183–207.

Leiss, William. 1976. *The Limits to Satisfaction.* Toronto: University of Toronto Press.

Leiss, William, Stephen Kline, and Sut Jhally. 1990. *Social Communication in Advertising: Persons, Products, and Images of Well-being.* New York: Routledge.

Levering, Frank, and Wanda Urbanska. 1992. *Simple Living: One Couple's Search for a Better Life.* New York: Viking.

Levy, Frank. 1995. "Incomes and Income Inequality." In Thomas Reynolds Farley, ed., *State of the Union: America in the 1990s,* vol. 1, *Economic Trends* (1–57). New York: Russell Sage.

———. 1996. "Where Did All the Money Go? A Layman's Guide to Recent Trends in U.S. Living Standards." Working Paper 96–008. Cambridge, Mass.: Massachusetts Institution of Technology, Industrial Performance Center.

Levy, Sidney J. 1959. "Symbols for Sale." *Harvard Business Review* (July-August): 117–24.

Lieberson, Stanley. 1992. "Einstein, Renoir, and Greeley: Some Thoughts About Evidence in Sociology." *American Sociological Review* 57 (February): 1–15.

Lipovetsky, Gilles. 1994. *The Empire of Fashion: Dressing Modern Democracy.* Princeton, N.J.: Princeton University Press.

Luhrs, Janet. 1997. *The Simple Living Guide.* New York: Broadway Books.

Lurie, Alison. 1992. *The Language of Clothes.* London: Bloomsbury.

Lury, Celia. 1996. *Consumer Culture.* New Brunswick, N.J.: Rutgers University Press.

MacCannell, Dean. 1989. *The Tourist: A New Theory of the Leisure Class.* New York: Schocken.

Macklin, M. Carole. 1996. "Preschoolers' Learning of Brand Names from Visual Cues." *Journal of Consumer Research* 23 (December): 251–61.

Madrick, Jeff. 1997. "The Cost of Living: A New Myth." *New York Review of Books*, 6 March, 18–24.

Magee, Allison. 1994. "Compulsive Buying Tendency as a Predictor of Attitudes and Perceptions." *Association for Consumer Research* 21: 590–94.

Malhotra, Naresh K. 1988. "Self-concept and Product Choice: An Integrated Perspective." *Journal of Economic Psychology* 9: 1–28.

Marchand, Roland. 1985. *Advertising the American Dream: Making Way for Modernity 1920–1940*. Berkeley: University of California Press.

Mason, Roger. 1981. *Conspicuous Consumption: A Study of Exceptional Consumer Behavior*. New York: St. Martin's.

McAdams, Richard H. 1992. "Relative Preferences." *Yale Law Journal*: 1–104.

McAllister, Matthew P. 1996. *The Commercialization of American Culture: New Advertising, Control, and Democracy*. Thousand Oaks, Calif.: Sage.

McCracken, Grant. 1990. *Culture and Consumption: New Approaches to the Symbolic Character of Consumer Goods and Activities*. Bloomington: Indiana University Press.

McGrath, Mary Ann, Basil G. Englis, and Michael R. Solomon. 1997. "Beautiful Houses, Beautiful People: Social Categorization and Styles of Interior Decor." Paper presented at the annual meeting of the Association for Consumer Research, Denver (October).

McKeage, Kim K. R., Marsha L. Richins, and Kathleen Debevec. 1993. "Self-Gifts and the Manifestation of Material Values." In Leigh McAlister and Michael L. Rothschild, eds., *Advances in Consumer Research* (20:359–63). Provo, Utah: Association for Consumer Research.

McKendrick, Neil, John Brewer, and J. H. Plumb. 1982. *The Birth of Consumer Society: The Commercialization of Eighteenth-Century England*. London: Europa.

McKenna, Elizabeth Perle. 1997. *When Work Doesn't Work Anymore: Women, Work, and Identity*. New York: Delacorte.

McKenzie, Evan. 1994. *Privatopia: Homeowner Associations and the Rise of Residential Private Government*. New Haven, Conn.: Yale University Press.

McKnight, Gerald. 1989. *The Skin Game: The International Beauty Business Brutally Exposed*. London: Sedgwick & Jackson.

Mediamark Research Inc. 1989–91. *Mediamark Survey: Adult Personal Care Annual Report*. New York: Mediamark Research Inc.

Mick, David Glen, and Michelle DeMoss. 1990a. "To Me from Me: A Descriptive Phenomenology of Self-Gifts." In Marvin E. Goldberg, Gerald Gorn, and Richard W. Pollay, eds., *Advances in Consumer Research* (17:677–82). Provo, Utah: Association for Consumer Research.

———. 1990b. "Self-Gifts: Phenomenological Insights from Four Contexts." *Journal of Consumer Research* 19(3): 322–32.

Mick, David Glen, and Susan Fournier. 1996. "Garden of Paradise or Paradox? Copying with Technological Consumer Products in Everyday Life." Unpublished paper, Harvard University (August).

Miller, Daniel. 1987. *Material Culture and Mass Consumption.* Oxford: Basil Blackwell.

——. 1992. "'The Young and the Restless' in Trinidad: A Case of the Local and the Global in Mass Consumption." In Roger Silverstone and Eric Hirsch, eds., *Consuming Technologies: Media and Information in Domestic Spaces* (163–82). London: Routledge.

——, ed. 1993. *Unwrapping Christmas.* Oxford: Oxford University Press.

——, ed. 1995. *Acknowledging Consumption: A Review of New Studies.* London: Routledge.

Miringoff, Mark. 1997. *1997 Index of Social Health: Monitoring the Social Well-being of the Nation.* Tarrytown, N.Y.: Fordham Institute for Innovation in Social Policy.

Mishel, Larry, Jared Bernstein, and John Schmitt. 1996. *The State of Working America 1996–1997.* Washington, D.C.: Economic Policy Institute.

Mitchell, Arnold. 1978. *Consumer Values: A Typology.* Menlo Park, Calif.: SRI International.

Mommaas, Hans. 1990. "Leisure Culture and Lifestyle: Veblen, Weber, and Simmel Revisited." Unpublished paper, Tilburg University.

Morin, Richard, and John M. Berry. 1996. "As for the Economy, Public Sees Thorns." *International Herald Tribune,* 14 October, 1.

Mort, F. 1988. "Boys Own? Masculinity, Style, and Popular Culture." In Rowena Chapman and Jonathan Rutherford, eds., *Male Order: Unwrapping Masculinity* (193–225). London: Lawrence and Wishart.

Moschis, George P. 1976. "Social Comparison and Informal Group Influence." *Journal of Marketing Research* 13 (August): 237–44.

Mukerji, Chandra. 1983. *From Graven Images: Patterns of Modern Materialism.* New York: Columbia University Press.

Munson, J. Michael, and W. Austin Spivey. 1981. "Product and Brand User Stereotypes Among Social Classes." In Kent B. Monroe, ed., *Advances in Consumer Research* (8:696–701). Provo, Utah: Association for Consumer Research.

Natarajan, Rajan, and Brent C. Goff. 1991. "Compulsive Buying: Towards a Reconceptualization." In F. W. Rudmin, ed., *To Have Possessions: A Handbook on Ownership and Property,* special issue of *Journal of Social Behavior and Personality* 6(6): 307–28.

——. 1992. "Manifestations of Compulsiveness in the Consumer-Marketplace Domain." *Psychology and Marketing* 9 (January): 31–44.

National Accounts Data. 1997. GDP news release (26 November).

Neumark, David, and Andrew Postlewaite. 1995. "Relative Income Concerns and the Rise in Married Women's Employment." NBER Working Paper 5044. Cambridge, Mass.: National Bureau of Economic Research.

Newman, Katherine S. 1989. *Falling from Grace: The Experience of Downward Mobility in the American Middle Class*. New York: Vintage.

Nightingale, Carl Husemoller. 1993. *On the Edge: A History of Poor Black Children and Their American Dreams*. New York: Basic.

O'Guinn, Thomas C., and Ronald J. Faber. 1989. "Compulsive Buying: A Phenomenological Exploration." *Journal of Consumer Research* 16 (September): 147–57.

O'Guinn, Thomas C., Ronald J. Faber, Nadine J. J. Curias, and Kay Schmitt. 1989. "The Cultivation of Consumer Norms." In Gerald Gorn and Richard W. Pollay, eds., *Advances in Consumer Research* (16:779–85). Provo, Utah: Association for Consumer Research.

O'Guinn, Thomas C., and L. J. Shrum. 1997. "The Role of Television in the Construction of Consumer Reality." *Journal of Consumer Research* 23 (March): 278–94.

Ohmann, Richard. 1996. *Selling Culture: Magazines, Markets, and Class at the Turn of the Century*. London: Verso.

Olson, James M., and J. Douglas Hazlewood. 1986. "Relative Deprivation and Social Comparison: An Integrative Perspective." In James M. Olson, C. P. Herman, and M. P. Zanna, eds., *Relative Deprivation and Social Comparison: The Ontario Symposium* (4:1–15). Hillsdale, N.J.: Lawrence Erlbaum.

Otnes, Cele, and Tina M. Lowrey. 1993. "'Till Debt Do Us Part: The Selection and Meaning of Artifacts in the American Wedding." In Leigh McAlister and Michael L. Rothschild, eds., *Advances in Consumer Research* (20:325–29). Provo, Utah: Association for Consumer Research.

Packard, Vance. 1959. *The Status Seekers*. New York: McKay.

Park, C. Whan, and V. Parker Lessing. 1977. "Students and Housewives: Differences in Susceptibility to Reference Group Influences." *Journal of Consumer Research* 4 (September): 102–10.

Pearlstein, Stephen. 1996. "For Richer, for Poorer: An Election-Year Primer." *Washington Post*, 5 May, H1.

Peterson, Richard A., and Roger M. Kern. 1996. "Changing Highbrow Taste: From Snob to Omnivore." *American Sociological Review* 61 (October): 900–907.

Peterson, Richard A., and Albert Simkus. 1992. "How Musical Tastes Mark Occupational Status Groups." In Michèle Lamont and Marcel Fournier, eds., *Cultivating Differences: Symbolic Boundaries and the Making of Inequality* (152–86). Chicago: University of Chicago Press.

Pollak, Robert A. 1976. "Interdependent Preferences." *American Economic Review* 66 (June): 309–20.

Pollan, Michael. 1997. "Confidence Builder." *House and Garden* (September): 128–32.

Porter, James N., Jr. 1967. "Consumption Patterns of Professors and Businessmen: A Pilot Study of Conspicuous Consumption." *Sociological Inquiry* 37 (Spring): 255–65.

Potter, David Morris. 1954. *People of Plenty: Economic Abundance and the American Character.* Chicago: University of Chicago Press.

Rademaekers, William. 1996. "Going Gaga over the Aga." *Time*, 23 December, 40–42.

Rahn, Wendy, and John Transue. 1997. "The Decline of Social Trust Among American Youth: The American Economy, Value Change, and Social Capital." Unpublished paper, University of Minnesota (21 May).

Ramirez, Maria Fiorini. 1997. "Americans at Debt's Door." *New York Times*, 14 October, A35.

Rauscher, Michael. 1992. "Keeping up with the Joneses: Chaotic patterns in a status game." *Economics Letters* 40: 287–90.

———. 1993. "Demand for Social Status and the Dynamics of Consumer Behavior." *Journal of Socioeconomics* 22(2): 105–13.

Ray, Paul H. 1997. "The Emerging Culture." *American Demographics* (February): 29–34.

Reinhold, Robert. 1981. "Furor over Baby Formulas—Where, When, and How." *Washington Post*, 24 May, 9.

Richins, Marsha L. 1991. "Social Comparison and Idealized Images of Advertising." *Journal of Consumer Research* 18 (June): 71–83.

———. 1994. "Special Possessions and the Expression of Material Values." *Journal of Consumer Research* 20 (December): 522–33.

———. 1995. "Social Comparison, Advertising, and Consumer Discontent." *American Behavioral Scientist* 38(3): 593–607.

Rimer, Sara. 1996. "In the Community, Fraying Bonds." *New York Times*, 6 March, A1.

Roberts, Scott D. 1991. "Consumer Responses to Involuntary Job Loss." In Rebecca H. Holman and Michael R. Solomon, eds., *Advances in Consumer Research* (18:40–42). Provo, Utah: Association for Consumer Research.

Robinson, John P. 1989. "When the Going Gets Tough." *American Demographics* (February): 50.

———. 1990. "I Love My TV." *American Demographics* (September): 24–27.

Robinson, John P., and Geoff Godbey. 1997. *Time for Life.* State College: Pennsylvania State University Press.

Rook, Dennis W. 1987. "The Buying Impulse." *Journal of Consumer Research* 14 (September): 189–99.

Roper Survey Organization. 1993. "How We Classify Ourselves." *American Enterprise* (May-June): 87.

Rosencranz, Mary Lou. 1962. "Clothing Symbolism." *Journal of Home Economics* 54 (January): 18–22.

Rosenfeld, Lawrence B., and Timothy G. Plax. 1977. "Clothing as Communication." *Journal of Communication* 27(2): 24–31.

Ryan, John C., and Alan Thein Durning. 1997. *Stuff: The Secret Lives of Everyday Things.* Report 4. Seattle: Northwest Environment Watch.

Sachs, Jeffrey, and Wing Thye Woo. 1996. "China's Transition Experience, Reexamined." *Transition* 7(3). Washington, D.C.: World Bank.

Sahlins, Marshall. 1976. *Culture and Practical Reason.* Chicago: University of Chicago Press.

Saltzman, Amy. 1991. *Downshifting: Reinventing Success on a Slower Track.* New York: HarperCollins.

Samuelson, Robert. 1995. *The Good Life and Its Discontents: The American Dream in the Age of Entitlement 1945–1995.* New York: Times Books.

Schaninger, Charles. 1982. "Social Class Versus Income Revisited: An Empirical Investigation." *Journal of Marketing Research* 18 (May): 192–208.

Scherhorn, Gerhard. 1990. "The Addictive Trait in Buying Behavior." *Journal of Consumer Policy* 13: 33–51.

Schmidt, Leigh Eric. 1995. *Consumer Rites: The Buying and Selling of American Holidays.* Princeton, N.J.: Princeton University Press.

Schor, Juliet B. 1992. *The Overworked American: The Unexpected Decline of Leisure.* New York: Basic.

———. 1995. "Can the North Stop Consumption Growth?: Escaping the Cycle of Work and Spend." In V. Bhaskar and Andrew Glyn, eds., *The North, the South, and the Environment* (68–84). London: Earthscan.

———. 1997a. "Do Americans Keep up with the Joneses?: The Impact of Consumption Aspirations on Savings Behavior." Unpublished paper, Tilburg University (May).

———. 1997b. "New Analytic Bases for an Economic Critique of Consumer Society." In David Crocker and Toby Linden, eds., *The Ethics of Consumption: The Good Life, Justice, and Global Stewardship* (131–38). Lanham, Md.: Rowman and Littlefield.

———. 1997c. *Beyond an Economy of Work and Spend.* Tilburg, Netherlands: Tilburg University Press.

———. 1998. "New Strategies for Everyday Life: The Impact of Globalization on Time and Consumption." *Time and Society* 7(1): 119–27.

Schouten, John W. 1991. "Selves in Transition: Symbolic Consumption in Personal Rites of Passage and Identity Reconstruction." *Journal of Consumer Research* 17 (March): 412–23.

Schouten, John W., and James H. McAlexander. 1995. "Subcultures of Consumption: An Ethnography of the New Bikers." *Journal of Consumer Research* 22 (June): 43–61.

Schudson, Michael. 1984. *Advertising, the Uneasy Persuasion: Its Dubious Impact on American Society.* New York: Basic.

———. 1991. "Delectable Materialism: Were the Critics of Consumer Culture Wrong All Along?" *American Prospect* (Spring): 26–35.

Scitovsky, Tibor. 1976. *The Joyless Economy.* New York: Oxford University Press.

Segal, Jerome M. 1995. "Money and Our Economic Life." *Tikkun* 10(6): 59–62.

———. 1996. "The Politics of Simplicity." *Tikkun* 11(4): 20–25.

Seiter, Ellen. 1993. *Sold Separately: Children and Parents in Consumer Culture*. New Brunswick, N.J.: Rutgers University Press.

Semon, Thomas T. 1979. "On Felson's 'Invidious Distinctions.'" *Public Opinion Quarterly* 43: 119–20.

Sen, Amartya. 1983. "Poor, Relatively Speaking." *Oxford Economic Papers* 35 (March): 153–69.

———. 1987. *The Standard of Living*. Cambridge: Cambridge University Press.

Shammas, Carole. 1990. *The Pre-Industrial Consumer in England and America*. Oxford: Clarendon Press.

Shapiro, Matthew D., and David W. Wilcox. 1996. "Mismeasurement in the Consumer Price Index: An Evaluation." NBER Working Paper 5590. Cambridge, Mass.: National Bureau of Economic Research.

Shavitt, Sharon, Pamela M. Lowrey, and James E. Haefner. 1997. "Public Attitudes Toward Advertising: More Favorable Than You Might Think." Unpublished paper, University of Illinois at Urbana-Champaign.

Sherry, John F., ed. 1995. *Contemporary Marketing and Consumer Behavior*. Thousand Oaks, Calif.: Sage.

Sherry, John F., Jr., Mary Ann McGrath, and Sidney J. Levy. 1995. "Monadic Giving: Anatomy of Gifts Given to the Self." In John F. Sherry, Jr., ed., *Contemporary Marketing and Consumer Behavior* (399–432). Thousand Oaks, Calif.: Sage.

Shi, David. 1985. *The Simple Life: Plain Living and High Thinking in American Culture*. New York: Oxford University Press.

Shrum, L. J., Thomas C. O'Guinn, Richard J. Semenik, and Ronald J. Faber. 1991. "Processes and Effects in the Construction of Normative Consumer Beliefs: The Role of Television." In Rebecca H. Holman and Michael R. Solomon, eds., *Advances in Consumer Research* (18:755–63). Provo, Utah: Association for Consumer Research.

Siebert, Charles. 1996. "The Cuts That Go Deeper." *New York Times Magazine*, 7 July, 20–25.

Simmel, George. 1957. "Fashion." *American Journal of Sociology* 62(6): 541–58.

Singletary, Michelle, and Albert B. Crenshaw. 1996. "Plastic Credit: Opium of the People." *International Herald Tribune*, 25 November, 11.

Slater, Don. 1997. *Consumer Culture and Modernity*. Cambridge: Polity Press.

Smith, Adam. 1976. *The Wealth of Nations,* ed. Campbell and Skinner (869–71). Oxford: Oxford University Press.

Solomon, Michael R. 1983. "The Role of Products as Social Stimuli: A Symbolic Interactionism Perspective." *Journal of Consumer Research* 10 (December): 319–29.

———., ed. 1985. *The Psychology of Fashion*. Lexington, Mass.: Lexington Books.

———. 1988. "Counselors of Taste." *Psychology Today* (January): 51–53.

Solomon, Michael R., and Bruce Buchanan. 1991. "A Role-Theoretic Approach to Product Symbolism: Mapping a Consumption Constellation." *Journal of Business Research* 22: 95–109.

Solowij, Anna-Marie. 1996. "Would You Pay £330 for a Pot of Face Cream?" *Guardian*, 11 December.

Sommers, Montrose S. 1964. "Product Symbolism and the Perception of Social Strata." In Stephen A. Greyser, ed., *Toward Scientific Marketing* (200–216). Chicago: American Marketing Association.

Sommers, Montrose S., and Grady D. Bruce. 1968. "Blacks, Whites, and Products: Relative Deprivation and Reference Group Behavior." *Social Science Quarterly* 49 (December): 631–42.

Spence, A. Michael. 1974. *Market Signalling: Informational Transfer in Hiring and Related Screening Processes*. Cambridge, Mass.: Harvard University Press.

Stanley, Thomas J., and William D. Danko. 1996. *The Millionaire Next Door: The Surprising Secrets of America's Wealthy*. Marietta, Ga.: Longstreet Press.

Steinhauer, Jennifer. 1997. "Halloween Buying: How Sweet It Is." *New York Times*, 2 November, sect. 4, p. 2.

Stipp, David. 1996. "Farewell, My Logo." *Fortune*, 27 May, 128.

St. James, Elaine. 1994. *Simplify Your Life: 100 Ways to Slow Down and Enjoy the Things That Really Matter*. New York: Hyperion.

Strasser, Susan. 1989. *Satisfaction Guaranteed: The Making of the American Mass Market*. New York: Pantheon.

Tedlow, Richard S. 1990. *New and Improved: The Story of Mass Marketing in America*. New York: Basic.

Tefertiller, Tracy. 1994. "Children of Abundance: Exploring the Consumption Patterns of Teenage Girls." Undergraduate honors thesis, Harvard University.

Thompson, Craig J., and Diana L. Haytko. 1997. "Speaking of Fashion: Consumers' Uses of Fashion Discourses and the Appropriation of Countervailing Cultural Meanings." *Journal of Consumer Research* 24 (June): 15–42.

Thompson, Craig J., Howard R. Pollio, and William B. Locander. 1994. "The Spoken and the Unspoken: A Hermeneutic Approach to Understanding the Culture Viewpoints That Underlie Consumers' Expressed Meanings." *Journal of Consumer Research* 21 (December): 432–52.

Tomes, Nigel. 1986. "Income Distribution, Happiness, and Satisfaction: A Direct Test of the Interdependent Preferences Model." *Journal of Economic Psychology* 7: 425–46.

Toobin, Jeffrey. 1996. *The Run of His Life: The People Versus O. J. Simpson*. New York: Random House.

Turow, Joseph. 1997. *Breaking up America: Advertisers and the New Media World*. Chicago: University of Chicago Press.

Twitchell, James B. 1996. *ADCULTusa: The Triumph of Advertising in American Culture*. New York: Columbia University Press.

Uchitelle, Louis, and N. R. Kleinfield. 1996. "On the Battlefields of Business, Millions of Casualties." *New York Times*, 3 March, A1.

Underwood, Elaine. 1994. "Luxury's Tide Turns." *Brandweek*, 7 March, 18–22.

———. 1995. "Sweatsuit." *Brandweek*, 20 February, 24–28.

———. 1996a. "Low-key Luxury." *Brandweek*, 1 July, 23–28.

———. 1996b. "Tommy Hilfiger on Brand Hilfiger." *Brandweek*, 5 February, 23–27.

U.S. Department of Commerce. 1996. *Statistical Abstract of the United States*. Washington, D.C.: U.S. Government Printing Office.

Valence, Gilles, Alain d'Astous, and Louis Fortier. 1988. "Compulsive Buying: Concept and Measurement." *Journal of Consumer Policy* 11: 419–33.

van Biema, David. 1996. "They Didn't Pay Retail." *Time*, 23 December, 43.

Veblen, Thorstein. 1967. *The Theory of the Leisure Class*. New York: Penguin.

Veenhoven, Ruut. 1991. "Is Happiness Relative?" *Social Indicators Research* 24: 1–24.

Vincent, J. M. 1934. "Sumptuary Legislation." *Encyclopedia of the Social Sciences* 14: 464–66.

Wachtel, Paul. 1989. *The Poverty of Affluence: A Psychological Portrait of the American Way of Life*. Philadelphia: New Society Publishers.

Wachtel, Paul L., and Sidney J. Blatt. 1990. "Perceptions of Economic Needs and of Anticipated Future Income." *Journal of Economic Psychology* 11: 403–15.

Waldfogel, Joel. 1993. "The Deadweight Loss of Christmas." *American Economic Review* 83(5): 1328–36.

Warner, W. Lloyd, Marchia Meeker, and Kenneth Ells. 1960. *Social Class in America: The Evaluation of Status*. New York: Harper & Row.

Weinberg, Daniel H. 1996. "A Brief Look at Postwar U.S. Income Inequality." *Current Population Reports* P60–191 (June).

Weiss, Michael J. 1988. *The Clustering of America*. New York: Harper & Row.

———. 1994. *Latitudes and Attitudes: An Atlas of American Tastes, Trends, Politics, and Passions*. Boston: Little, Brown.

Wheeler, Ladd, and Kunitate Miyake. 1992. "Social Comparison in Everyday Life." *Journal of Personality and Social Psychology* 62(5): 760–73.

Wicklund, Robert A., and Peter M. Gollwitzer. 1982. *Symbolic Self-Completion*. Hillsdale, N.J.: Lawrence Erlbaum.

Wilk, Richard R. 1996. "A Critique of Desire: Distaste and Dislike in Consumer Behavior." Unpublished paper, Indiana University.

Wise, Gordon L. 1974. "Differential Pricing and Treatment of New Car Salesmen: The Effect of the Prospect's Race, Sex, and Dress." *Journal of Business* 47: 218–30.

Wittmayer, Cecelia, Steve Schulz, and Roert Mittelstædt. 1994. "A Cross-cultural Look at the 'Supposed to Have It' Phenomenon: The Existence of a Standard Package Based on Occupation." In Chris T. Allen and Deborah Roedder-John, eds., *Advances in Consumer Research* (21:427–35). Provo, Utah: Association for Consumer Research.

Wolf, Naomi. 1991. *The Beauty Myth: How Images of Beauty Are Used Against Women.* New York: Doubleday.

Wolff, Edward N. 1994. "Trends in Household Wealth in the United States, 1962–1983 and 1983–1989." *Review of Income and Wealth* Series 40(2): 143–74.

———. 1995. *Top Heavy: A Study of the Increasing Inequality of Wealth in America.* New York: Twentieth Century Fund.

———. "Recent Trends in the Size Distribution of Household Wealth." Unpublished mimeo, New York University.

Wuthnow, Robert. 1996. *Poor Richard's Principle: Recovering the American Dream Through the Moral Dimension of Work, Business, and Money.* Princeton, N.J.: Princeton University Press.

Appendix A. Cosmetics Research

For more details on the results discussed in chapter 3, see Chao and Schor (1998). Here I provide a condensed description of that research. Brand-buying data are from Mediamark Research Inc. (1989–91). Price and quality data are from *Consumer Reports* (1988, 1989, 1991). We matched the two data sources by product and year. Where the two data sets did not match exactly, we averaged the prices of the various lines to arrive at an average brand price. *Consumer Reports* ranked thirty-nine lipsticks, thirty-four mascaras, thirty-one eye shadows, and thirty-six facial cleansers. Matching these against the Mediamark data, we were left with twenty-two lipsticks, sixteen mascaras, eighteen eye shadows, and five facial cleansers. We distinguish between "products" (particular types of cosmetics), "brands" (the name or marketer of the product), and "lines" (specific varieties of product *within* a brand).

VISIBILITY RANKINGS

Our a priori view was that lipsticks would have the highest level of visibility, because women take lipsticks out in public, and that facial cleansers, ordinarily left at home, would have the lowest level.

Eye shadows and mascaras are in an intermediate category. Our a priori ranking was confirmed in an informal survey of twenty female students at Harvard University. Lipstick was ranked most visible by all twenty respondents; facial cleansers were ranked least visible by eighteen of twenty. Mascara was ranked second, and eye shadow third.

QUALITY RANKINGS

Consumer Reports publishes the results of product quality tests, using testers who were not given the identity of the brands. The method of evaluation varied by product. For lipsticks and eye shadows, professional makeup artists evaluated the products. For mascaras, twenty-two women who ordinarily wear mascara used and evaluated the products. For facial cleansers, ninety women were recruited to use the products over a ten-week period. Laboratory tests were also conducted on mascaras. In all cases, testers were asked to rank the products on a variety of dimensions. The results of these rankings are presented in figure 3.1. All lipstick brands are ranked equally. *Consumer Reports* also conducted a one-on-one test between Flame Glow (a low-end brand with little name recognition) and Chanel (perhaps the most prestigious of major brands), using the brand containers but switching half the lipsticks inside. About as many women preferred Flame Glow as preferred Chanel. In the eye shadow tests, identical quality rankings also emerged for all brands. With mascaras, a .424 correlation between price and quality was found; for facial cleansers, the correlation was .408.

PATTERNS OF BRAND BUYING

To assess differences in patterns of brand buying, we used the Mediamark survey. For lipsticks, the data are from 1989 and cover 12,573 respondents. For mascaras and lipsticks, the data were gleaned in 1990 from 12,724 respondents. And for facial cleansers, there were 12,146 respondents in 1991. The published data are available only in cross-tabulated format. Thus, for each brand, we know the percentage of women (among the 12,000+) who bought that brand. For each of the demographic or socioeconomic categories, we have the fraction of women in that group who bought each brand.

Figure 3.2 shows the brand-buying patterns for the four products among the entire sample of women. We used two statistical measures to determine the existence of status consumption. First, we tested whether the percentage of women buying expensive brands (defined as the top three brands) increases with the visibility of the product. The percentage of women buying the top three brands of facial cleansers, eye shadows, mascaras, and lipsticks was 10.88 percent, 13.19 percent, 16.19 percent, and 17.94 percent, respectively. The chi-square statistic indicates significant differences by product visibility in the percentage of women buying the top three brands, with a p-value less than .0005. Second, we tested whether women within each income level bought more of the most expensive brands (defined as the top fifth of a product's brands, ranked by price). Again, the chi-square statistic is highly significant, with a p-value of less than .0005. Within each income level, the fraction of women buying an expensive visible product is significantly greater than the fraction of those buying the less visible product.

Ordinary least squares regressions for each of the four products (not shown here) also support the above conclusions. See Chao and Schor (1998) for a presentation and discussion of those estimates, as well as results that show the propensity to engage in status purchasing by income, education, race, and location. There we find that educational level is positively correlated to the propensity to engage in status consumption.

Appendix B. The Telecom Survey

The survey described in chapter 4 took place between November 1994 and May 1995 at a telecommunications company with more than eighty thousand employees located in the southeastern United States. The survey, entitled "Time, Money, and Values Questionnaire," was carried out with the cooperation of the management, which allowed employees to fill it out during worktime. (The estimated time for completing the survey was forty-five minutes.) The survey was distributed through the company mail room and returned by post to Boston University. Strict guarantees of confidentiality were given to respondents, who were also informed that the company would not be receiving any of the data. After a pilot test at a New England company, surveys were distributed in two units of Telecom. The first wave, in November 1994, went to four hundred employees in a five-thousand-person unit. The second wave, which went to sixteen hundred employees in May 1995, was selected from an employee pool of eighty thousand (the company's main unit). It was distributed to equal numbers of men and women, and the sample procedure replicated the occupational distribution of the U.S. workforce at the 1-digit level. There were 834 usable surveys returned, for a response rate of 42 percent. The sample overrepresents women (57.3 percent) as compared to the U.S. population on account of the high fraction of women in the first wave.

The savings variable was generated from a series of questions about anticipated borrowing and saving behavior in the survey year. (A second savings measure was also solicited, but it appeared to

---

APPENDIX TABLE B.1 Descriptive Statistics—Telecom Survey

Sex	
Male	42.7%
Female	57.3%
Median age	40
Mean education	some college
Mean years with company	16–20
Marital status	70.5% married
Place of dwelling	
suburb	66%
city	15%
Mean hours of television/week	11.5
Median household income	$60,000–75,000
Home ownership rate	87%
Race	
White	77%
African American	17%

have been subject to significantly more measurement error and was therefore not used.) Anticipated annual saving is the sum of additions to nonretirement savings plus additions to retirement savings minus reductions in existing savings accounts plus reductions in existing debt minus additions to debt. This measure excludes all changes in the value of mortgage debt. (Because of an oversight, the survey did not ask about withdrawals from personal retirement accounts (IRAs, 401[k]s, and so on. However, borrowings against these accounts were included.) Respondents who did not believe

---

APPENDIX TABLE B.2 Frequency Distributions for Selected Questions—Telecom Survey

---

How does your financial status compare to that of most of the members of the reference group you chose?

Much worse	1.1%
Worse	13.8
Same	57.4
Better	23.3
Much better	1.9
NA	2.5

In the past two years, to what extent have you personally felt pressure to "keep up with the Joneses"?

(1) None	62.0%
(2)	28.0
(3)	8.8
(4) A great deal	1.2

Annual savings

Dissaving or 0	7.9%
$0–2,500	11.4
$2,501–5,000	12.3
$5,001–10,000	20.6
$10,001–25,000	34.2
$25,000+	13.6

they had the requisite detailed knowledge about their household's financial situation were permitted to omit this section of the questionnaire; sixty-three respondents did so. Anticipated levels of saving may not have been accurate for the second wave because it was conducted so early in the year (May), as compared to November for the first wave. As a check, all equations were estimated for the first and second waves separately. We did not find appreciable differences in results between the two waves.

Copies of the questionnaire are available from the author. A scholarly paper containing the savings functions (Schor 1997a) is also available.

APPENDIX TABLE B.3 Variable Definitions

Dependent variable is annual household saving: Q119 + Q124 − Q123 − (Q120 * Q121) + Q122

Q119: "How much money do you estimate your household will add to savings this year, excluding official IRS-defined retirement accounts such as IRAs, 401(k)s, etc?" Answer categories are 1 = $0; 2 = $1–500; 3 = $501–1,000; 4 = $1,001–2,000; 5 = $2,002–5,000; 6 = $5,001–7,500; 7 = $7,501–10,000; 8 = $10,001–25,000; 9 = $25,001–50,000, 10 = $50,001 or above (coded as dollar value midpoints).

Q124: "With the exclusion of mortgage debt, how much money will your household be paying off this year?" Answer categories/coding as in Q119.

Q123: "With the exclusion of mortgage debt, how much money will your household be adding to debt this year?" Answer categories/coding as in Q119.

Q120: "If you answered 'zero' to Q119, will your household be spending any of the savings that you had before [year of survey]?" 1 = yes; 0 = no.

Q121: "If yes, to Q120, how much?" Answer categories 1= $1–1,000; 2 = $1,001–3,500; 3 = $3,501–5,000; 4 = $5,001–10,000; 5 = $10,001–$20,000; 6 = $20,001 or above (coded as midpoints of ranges).

Q122: "How much money do you estimate your household will add to official IRS-defined retirement accounts this year?" Answer categories as in Q119.

Annual household income (Q111): Coded as 1–10 where 1 = less than $20,000; 2 = $20,001–30,000; 3 = $30,001–45,000; 4 = $45,001–60,000; 5 = $60,001–75,000; 6 = $75,001–90,000; 7 = $90,001–110,000; 8 = $110,001–150,000; 9 = $150,001–250,000; 10 = $250,001 or above.

Household net worth: total financial assets minus liabilities, in dollars.

Number of dependents: total number of children and relatives who are financially dependent on respondent.

Sex (Q212): 1 = male; 2 = female

Race/ethnic background (Q213): 0 = African, African American, Hispanic, Native American, Mixed race, or Other; 1 = Caucasian; 2 = Asian or Asian-American.

Age (Q214): 1 = less than 20; 2 = 21–30; 3 = 31–40; 4 = 41–50; 5 = 51–60; 6 = more than 60.

Occupation (Q220): 1 =production/manufacturing; 2 = clerical office worker; 3 = professional; 4 = technical; 5 = service worker; 6 = sales; 7 = manager; 8 = other.

Educational level (Q217): 1 = some high school; 2 = high school diploma; 3 = some college; 4 = four-year college degree; 5 = postgraduate degree; 6 = other.

Satisfaction with Income (Q161): "On the whole, how satisfied are you with your income?" 1 = very dissatisfied; 2 = somewhat dissatisfied; 3 = somewhat satisfied; 4 = very satisfied.

Financial status compared to reference group (Q105): "How does your financial status compare to most of the members of the reference group you chose above?" 1 = much worse; 2 = worse; 0 = same; 4 = better; 5 = much better.

Television watching (Q26): hours spent per week watching television.

Permanent household income: Author's calculation of lifetime expected income. See Appendix to Schor (1997a) for detailed calculations.

Felt Pressure to Keep Up (Q174): "In the past two years, to what extent have you personally felt to 'keep up with the Joneses'?" Answers 1–4 labeled as "none" to "a great deal." Low-pressure sample are respondents answering 1 and 2; high-pressures are 3 and 4.

APPENDIX TABLE B.4 Multiple Regression Analysis of Saving Among Telecom Employees

Independent Variable[a]	Coefficient	(White's t-statistics)[b]
Constant term	$19,995.00	(1.31)
Household income	.112	(4.46)
Permanent household income	.025	(0.50)
Household net worth	.016	(0.85)
Sex	-3,763.00	(-1.72)
Age	-9,916.00	(-1.49)
Age-squared	1,140.00	(1.21)
Race	-204.00	(-0.12)
Occupation	-174.00	(-0.41)
Educational level	-1,448.00	(-1.06)
Number of dependents	-1,232.00	(-3.35)
Satisfaction with income	629.00	(0.82)
Hours per week watching TV	-208.00	(-2.87)
Financial status compared to reference group	2,953.00	(3.83)

[a] Dependent Variable is annual household saving.

[b] T-Statistics are White's t's, because equation shows presence of heteroskedasticity. White statistic = 247

APPENDIX TABLE B.5 Multiple Regression Analysis of Saving Among "Low-Pressure" Telecom employees

INDEPENDENT VARIABLE[a]	COEFFICIENT	(WHITE'S T-STATISTICS)[b]
Constant term	$25,094.00	(1.56)
Household income	.106	(4.25)
Permanent household income	.037	(0.71)
Household net worth	.013	(0.63)
Sex	-4,513.00	(-1.94)
Age	-12,168.00	(-1.66)
Age-squared	1,465.00	(1.43)
Race	-589.00	(-0.33)
Occupation	-200.00	(-0.44)
Educational level	-1,595.00	(-1.14)
Number of dependents	-1,326.00	(-3.45)
Satisfaction with income	523.00	(0.62)
Hours per week watching TV	-225.00	(-2.90)
Financial status compared to reference group	2,938.00	(3.69)

[a] Dependent variable is annual household saving.

[b] T-statistics are White's t's, because equation shows presence of heteroskedasticity. White statistic = 232. Sample is too small for heteroskedasticity correction for high-pressure group.

Appendix C. The Downshifter Survey

The downshifter survey discussed in chapter 5 was conducted by EDK Associates, Inc., of New York. The results are based on eight hundred telephone interviews with adults nationwide. All interviews were conducted 15–17 November 1996. For a sample of this size, we can say with 95 percent certainty that the error due to sampling could be plus or minus 3.5 percentage points.

A number of the basic questions from the November 1996 survey were included in the Merck Family Fund survey in February 1995. At that time, the voluntary downshifter question yielded a positive response rate of 28 percent, rather than the 19 percent rate found in November 1996. The difference may be partly due to the different survey dates. (The question is retrospective and covers the "last five years.") It is also possible that the Merck poll was subject to a higher response rate bias because downshifters may be more likely to be found at home during the evening. To minimize this bias, a large fraction of the interviews in the 1996 poll were done on Sunday evening, when it was hypothesized that downshifters and non-downshifters would be most equally likely to be home.

THE INTERVIEWS AND THE WRITTEN QUESTIONNAIRE

During the summer and fall of 1994 and the summer of 1996, I conducted twenty-seven interviews with individuals who had undergone downshifts, both voluntary and involuntary. All interviews (with the exception of one phone interview) were taped, and those I have discussed in the book were subsequently transcribed. With the exception of one group interview and two couples, all interviews took place with one individual and me. They lasted from one to two hours. (The group interview was two to three hours.) These were unstructured interviews, with only a few common questions. For the most part, I asked the interviewees to tell me their life stories as they related to issues of work and consumption.

I found interviewees in a nonrandom fashion. For that reason, the resulting sample of interviewees is not likely to be statistically representative of the population of downshifters. In comparison to results from the quantitative survey, the interview sample is more female, far less likely to be married, higher-earning, more educated, and geographically unrepresentative. (It includes only individuals from the Seattle and Boston areas.) Furthermore, the interview sample also includes individuals who began their downshift with an involuntary event (typically a layoff).

In the Boston area, I attended a workshop at a local unemployment office entitled "How to Live Well on Practically Nothing," described my research project, and asked people who would be willing to be interviewed to sign a sheet. From that list, I interviewed all individuals (eleven) whom we could contact and who had undergone some sort of downshift. One interviewee subsequently invited me to her "support group," where I held a group interview with four women. I interviewed one additional downshifter (Jennifer Lawson), who approached me at one of my public lectures. These interviews took place in 1994.

In the Seattle area, I contacted the New Road Map Foundation, which provided me with a list of individuals from its mailing list. I contacted a number of them and interviewed them in their homes or in a few cases in cafés. I was also given one name by Janet Luhrs, the editor of the *Simple Living* newsletter. In addition, I did one phone interview and one in-person interview with individuals who responded to a notice about my research that I placed in the New Road Map Foundation newsletter. I also attended and taped a voluntary simplicity circle attended by approximately fifteen people. This research was done in 1996.

In response to the notice I placed in the New Road Map Foundation newsletter, I received approximately twenty-five replies. All of these individuals subsequently filled out a written questionnaire and responded to a request for their personal stories.

Individuals differed in whether they wished to remain anonymous. However, I have used pseudonyms in all cases. All interviewees were informed about the nature of the research and were aware that their stories might be contained in this book.

Appendix D. The Merck Family Fund Poll and Focus Groups

The Merck Family Fund commissioned a poll and focus groups in early 1995. The poll and focus groups were conducted by the Harwood Group, a survey research firm. The survey was conducted in February 1995 and involved a random telephone sample of eight hundred households. I was involved in the formulation of a number of the survey questions. The focus groups were held in January 1995 in Dallas; Los Angeles; Frederick, Maryland; and Indianapolis. Basic results, cross-tabulations, and the data from the survey as well as the focus group transcripts were made available to me. Some of the calculations reported in the text are my own.

Center for a New American Dream
6930 Carroll Avenue
Suite 900
Takoma Park, MD 20912
301-891-3683 (tel)
newdream@newdream.org

The Media Foundation
1243 W. 7th Avenue
Vancouver, BC V6H 1B7
Canada
604-736-9401 (tel)
604-737-6021 (fax)
www.adbusters.org
editor@adbusters.org
tvturnoff@org
buynothingday@org

New Road Map Foundation
PO Box 15981
Seattle, WA 98115
206-527-5114 (tel)
206-526-0437 (fax)
newroadmap@igc.apc.org

Northwest Earth Institute
921 SW Morrison, Suite 532
Portland, OR 97205
503-227-2807
info@nwei.org

Center for the Study of Commercialism
1875 Connecticut Avenue, NW, Suite 300
Washington, DC 20009
202-332-9110 (tel; press option 6)
202-265-4954 (fax)
studycommerc@igc.org

Center for Media and Values
1962 S. Shenandoah Street
Los Angeles, CA 90034
213-202-1936

Co-op America
1612 K Street
Washington, DC 20006
202-872-5307 (tel)
202-331-8166 (fax)
www.coopamerica.org

TV-Free America
1322 18th Street, NW
Washington, DC 20036
202-887-0436
tvfa@essential.org
http://www.essential.org/orgs/tvfa

Unplug
360 Grand Avenue, Box 385
Oakland, Ca 94610
510-268-1100
peacenet.unplug@igc.org

Center for New Work
Ann Arbor, MI
734-998-0111 (tel.)
newwork@cyberspace.org

Chapter One: Introduction

3 On *The Millionaire Next Door:* see Stanley and Danko (1996).

5 On the *faux* life: see Bolonik and Griffin (1997).

5 On the targeting of upscale items: see Turow (1997).

5 These and other figures on subjective income adequacy are from the Merck Family Fund poll, February 1995 (see appendix D for details). Of course, the relation between yearly income and its adequacy is complex. In addition to social factors, adequacy also depends on family size, housing costs, the presence of children, and whether that year's income is typical.

6 On middle-class dissatisfaction: data are from my Telecom survey. Only 19.5 percent of respondents with annual incomes exceeding $75,000 reported being "very satisfied" with their incomes, and 29 percent of them reported being either very dissatisfied or dissatisfied. In the $60,000–75,000 category, the fraction of dissatisfied (including very dissatisfied) respondents was 24 percent. In the $45,000–60,000 category, 52 percent felt dissatisfied.

6 On wish lists: see the discussion of Fournier and Guiry's (1991, 1993) work in chapter 4.

6 On savings rates: see U.S. Department of Commerce (1996), table 1336 (p. 837), for comparable wealthy countries. The U.S. rate in 1995 was 4.5 percent, while it was 14.3 percent in France, 12.3 percent in Germany, 13.1 percent in Italy, 10.1 percent in the United Kingdom, 13.4 percent in Japan, 7.3 percent in Canada, and 11.3 percent in the Netherlands (in 1994). For poorer countries' savings rates, see for example on China, Sacks and Woo (1996). On Indian thriftiness, see

Jordan (1996), and for savings data, see Central Statistical Office (1995).

7 "creditable day-laborer would be ashamed": Smith (1976, ch. 5, bk. 2, p. 869). Smith defines necessaries as "that which the rules of decency have rendered necessary to the lowest rank of people" (p. 871). I am indebted to Amartya Sen for this reference. Marx, Mill, Pigou, and Keynes made similar observations. See McAdams (1992).

8 On the Italian nobles' palaces: see Burke (1993, p. 155).

8 On "ancestor portraits": see Packard (1959, pp. 66–68).

8 On Duesenberry: see his 1949 book *Income, Saving, and the Theory of Consumer Behavior*.

8 On the 1950s: see also classic consumer critiques of this period, such as John Kenneth Galbraith's *The Affluent Society* (1984), David Potter's *People of Plenty*, and Vance Packard's *The Status Seekers* (1959). In 1976 Fred Hirsch returned to Duesenberry's theme of relative position, arguing that people were increasingly desiring goods that were inherently in short supply (like oceanfront property or front-row seats), thereby leading to *Social Limits to Growth*. Ten years later, Robert Frank's *Choosing the Right Pond* (1985a) analyzed the consequences of this orientation, showing that it had led us to too much private consumption and not enough public spending on goods—such as environmental protection, occupational safety, and savings—that do not carry status. See also Scitovsky (1976) and Hirschmann (1982). See Schudson (1991) for an interesting discussion of critiques of consumerism.

9 On Galbraith, Hirsch, et al.: see Galbraith (1984), Hirsch (1976), Scitovsky (1976), Easterlin (1973, 1995), Sen (1983, 1987), Brown (1994), and Frank (1985a, 1985b). See chapter 2 for citations from the economics literature, which, however, are not numerous. Although Veblen had an enormous impact on views of consumption, empirical studies of status consumption are rather rare within economics. In view of the extraordinary number of empirical studies of consumption in the postwar era, the discipline's failure to pursue the social and competitive dimensions is striking. Economists devoted enormous attention to studying the timing of consumption over the life cycle and attempting to disprove the idea that the rich and the poor save different fractions of their incomes. But the fact that one person's spending might influence another person's (that is, the interdependence of preferences), while taken as obviously true by many outside the field, has been virtually ignored by economists of consumer behavior. For a survey of economic research on consumption, see Deaton (1992).

9 For white-collar employees: I use the word *most* because in many blue- and pink-collar jobs workplace contacts still tend to be mainly with those who share a common economic status.

9 On the winner-take-all society: see Frank and Cook (1995).

10 On clustering: see Weiss (1988, 1994).

11 On "middle Americans," "twenty-somethings," and so on: these cluster names are from the ACORN (1994) consumer classification system, a residential neighborhood classification system. Beginning with "radical feminists," the group names are fictitious.

11 The rise in middle-class consumption: it is important to note that not all Americans have been consuming more. A worsening income distribution has left a significant fraction worse off in absolute terms, although experts disagree about how large that fraction is. For one of the few studies to look at how the distribution of consumption, rather than income, has changed, see Cutler and Katz (1992), who find that the consumption of the bottom 20 percent declined absolutely as well as relatively. For similar results, by educational category, see Attanasio and Davis (1994). On aggregate trends in consumption, see Levy (1996). See notes to p. 12 for references on the debate about real incomes and possible bias in the consumer price index.

11 On the expanding American dream: all data are from U.S. Department of Commerce (1996). On travel, see table 423 (p. 264), and table 428 (p. 265); see also table 424 (p. 265), which shows a large divergence in travel behavior for households above and below $40,000; on recreation spending, see table 401 (p. 252).

12 On the rise in spending: the 30 percent figure is per capita personal consumption expenditures in 1992 dollars and comes from *Economic Report of the President* (1996, table B–27, p. 311; author's calculations). The 70 percent figure uses estimates of the possible bias in the consumer price index, which may be described as "consensus" among those who believe the CPI is overstated (taken from Shapiro and Wilcox 1996). However, the possible bias in the CPI is a contentious issue. On CPI overstatement, see Gordon (1990, 1995) and Shapiro and Wilcox (1996). For the case against overstatement, see Baker (1996). The "consensus" estimate is contained in the report of the Advisory Commission to Study the Index, known as the "Boskin" commission (1996). However, for a critique of the Boskin Commission and its conclusions, see Madrick (1997). I believe there are good reasons to think that the CPI has overstated inflation for at least some significant portions of the population, in particular for better-off consumers. Differential rates of price inflation by income group is an underexamined dimension of this debate. Finally, it is worth noting that consumption has grown more than income. (The respective rates are 23.7 percent and 29.8 percent [author's calculations from above data].)

12 For a review of the literature on income stagnation: see Frank Levy (1996). On consumers' anxiety and economic pessimism, see David Gordon (1996). For alternative perspectives, see Samuelson (1995), which bears some similarity to my own, and Segal (1995), who argues

that the income needed to maintain a constant quality of life has risen. For a journalistic synthesis of some of these issues, see Pearlstein (1996). On pessimism, see also the *New York Times* series "The Downsizing of America," commencing with Uchitelle and Kleinfield (1996).

12 On the rise in income to the top 1 percent: see Mishel, Bernstein, and Schmitt (1996, table 1.10, p. 59). The exact figures are $279,122 and $523,499. On the changing distribution, see also Levy (1995), Krugman (1994), Danziger and Gottschalk (1993), and Weinberg (1996).

12 On the rise in wealth of the top 1 percent: see Wolff (1995, pp. 10–11). The share of the top 1 percent in terms of net worth rose from 34 percent to 39 percent, and in terms of financial wealth from 43 percent to 48 percent between 1983 and 1989 (see also Wolff 1994 and 1997 for the most recent data).

12 On "feeling poor" articles: see Kroeger (1987) and Hewitt (1989). For an excellent account of this period, focusing on the professional-managerial class, see Ehrenreich (1990). See also Belk (1986) and LaBarbera (1988).

12 On the top 20 percent of households and what they earn: see Mishel, Bernstein, and Schmitt (1996, table 1.7, p. 53). In 1994 the upper limit of the fourth quintile was $71,982. Thus, the top 20 percent begins at $72,000. The midpoint is found by interpolating from table 1.9 (p. 58). The average income of the top 5 percent of families is $253,670. For the top 1 percent, only the 1989 figure is given, which is $523,449, so that it is not possible to calculate mean incomes in the 95–99 percent range from this table.

13 On gazing at the top of the pyramid: see Fournier and Guiry (1991, pp. 16–17) for all figures. Asked to estimate the fraction of U.S. households in the "really made it" group and the "doing very well" group, respondents answered 6 percent and 12 percent, respectively. Like most samples in the consumer research field, this one was not randomly generated and was more heavily female than the overall population (62 percent). For sample characteristics, see Fournier and Guiry (1991, p. 7).

14 On the growing incomes of the top 20 percent: see Mishel, Bernstein, and Schmitt (1996), table 1.6, p. 51. Households between the eightieth and ninety-fifth percentile went from 25.9 percent to 27.1 percent (or 26.8 percent, depending on how the top code is calculated). See the text for explanation.

14 On falling behind: see Mishel, Bernstein, and Schmitt (1996) and Gordon (1996).

14 On one in four believing the standard of living would rise: see Morin and Berry (1996, p. 1).

14 On half believing their children's living standard will be lower: see Calmes (1996, R2). The exact figure is 47 percent.

14 On income necessary to fulfill dreams: data from files of Roper Center, University of Connecticut. Figure from 1994 from Crispell (1994).

15 On "the good life": data from files of Roper Center, University of Connecticut. Data for earlier years are also available in Roper (1993).

15 Changing definitions of necessities: data from files of Roper Center, University of Connecticut.

16 On McMansions and the rise in square footage in Wellesley: see Knight (1997). See also Pollan (1997).

17 On income needed to reach satisfaction: data are from my Telecom survey. Among those making $30,000 a year or less, 81 percent said they'd need less than 20 percent more income to be satisfied, while only 40 percent of those in the $75,000+ category would be satisfied with a 20 percent increase. By contrast, in the $30,000 group, only 18 percent felt they would need 50 to 100 percent more, while 63 percent in the $75,000+ category believed they needed that much. For a study showing that perception of economic needs exceeds anticipated incomes among students, see Wachtel and Blatt (1990).

18 For the anthropological literature on the impact of *Dallas* in developing countries: see the citations, as well as a discussion of other soap operas, in Miller (1992).

18 On pundits missing this dynamic: for a notable exception from a prominent economist, see Krugman (1996), who emphasizes the positional character of consumer desire.

19 On being "ruined in school": see Belk, Mayer, and Driscoll (1984). Belk reports similar complaints from children about unfashionable jeans labels. On preschoolers and brand names, see Macklin (1996).

19 On the growth in consumer credit: see Council of Economic Advisers (1997) or Singletary and Crenshaw (1996).

19 On the rise in consumer debt among households earning $50,000–100,000: see Council of Economic Advisers (1997, ch. 2). On the fraction of $50,000–100,000 households in credit card debt, see Kennickell, Starr-McCluer, and Sundén (1997, table 11, p. 19).

19 On debt service as a percentage of disposable income: see Financial Markets Center (1997, p. 9) and Ramirez (1997).

19 On the rise in working hours: see Schor (1992), Leete and Schor (1994), and, for an update to 1994, Mishel, Bernstein, and Schmitt (1996, table 3.1, p. 132). The 10 percent figure is from author's calculations.

20 On living paycheck to paycheck: the exact number of paycheck-to-paycheck households is not well established. This figure is from a 1996 poll by Peter Hart and Robert Teeter, reported in Graham (1996), with the category defined as those whose earnings provide "just enough to pay bills, with nothing to spare." Another 8 percent report that their incomes are "not enough to pay bills."

20 On personal bankruptcies: which reached their highest quarterly level ever in 1996, see Council of Economic Advisers (1997, ch. 2).

20 On household savings rate: see the "preliminary" estimates for third

quarter 1997 in National Accounts Data (1997). For earlier years, see Council of Economic Advisers (1996). The causes of the decline in savings are not well understood by economists.

20 On 55 percent of households not saving in 1995: see Kennickell, Starr-McCluer, and Sundén (1997, table 1, p. 3).

20 On foreign savings rates: see U.S. Department of Commerce (1996, table 1336, p. 837).

20 On Chinese savings rates: see Sachs and Woo (1996).

20 On $9,950 as median value of household financial assets: see Wolff (1997, table 1, p. 27).

20 On baby boomers' retirement savings: see Farkas and Johnson (1997, p. 10). Baby boomers are defined as individuals aged 33–50 in 1997.

20 On families' reserves lasting only 1–3 months: see Wolff (1997, table 9, p. 35).

20 On college-educated heads and savings: see Kennickell, Starr-McCluer and Sundén (1997, table 1, p. 3).

20 On the vast majority who could save more: see Farkas and Johnson (1997). They report that 68 percent of Americans aged 22–61 said they could save more if they made the effort. But relatively few indicated that they would. The study concludes: "Most people say they could save more but they are reluctant to do so if it means cutting back on the new 'essentials' of middle-class life." Those new essentials? "Eating out, extras for the children, vacations, movies and entertainment, clothing extras, and less than careful grocery shopping." The respective percentages of those who say (1) they can cut back on these items and (2) they are very likely to cut back on these items: restaurant meals, 60/16 percent; doing more careful grocery shopping, 49/17 percent; extras for the kids, 53/10 percent; clothing, 36/18 percent; vacation or travel, 32/22 percent; movies, 28/20 percent; beauty care products and services, 25/22 percent (p. 17). The fractions of those who can and will cut back were all significantly lower in 1997 than in 1994. In 1995 the Merck Family Fund poll found even more people saying they could cut back—72 percent agreed that, "if I wanted to, I could choose to buy and consume less than I do."

20 On the vast majority who say they should be saving more: see Farkas and Johnson (1997, p. 31), who find that just over three-quarters (76 percent) of Americans think they should be saving more for retirement than they actually are. Among households making between $25,000 and $35,000, 59 percent reported that they had saved less than $10,000 for their retirement. Among those in the $35,000–50,000 bracket, the fraction is 41 percent. And even among those making between $50,000 and $75,000, just over one-fifth have put aside less than $10,000. (These figures may actually be much higher because a large fraction of the respondents either didn't know what they had

saved or refused to answer the question.) Graham (1996) also reports on a *Wall Street Journal* poll that found that 58 percent of the population is "very or somewhat" dissatisfied with the amounts they are saving. At Telecom, 80 percent reported that their household saves "too little" compared to what they would like to save.

20 On overspending: I intend this term to apply to those with reasonable amounts of discretionary income, not people with low incomes who cannot afford even a decent standard of living.

21 On the genuine progress indicator: see Cobb, Halstead, and Rowe (1995).

21 On the index of social health: see Miringoff (1997).

22 On downshifting: see chapter 5, where I document these claims and provide results of my survey and interviews (including the finding that downshifters are not more likely to be women).

23 On previous "downshifter" movements: see Shi (1985).

24 On Americans' growing uneasiness with consumerism: see first note of chapter 5.

24 On attitudes toward materialism and its perceived effects on families: see Wuthnow (1996, p. 246).

24 On the history of consumer culture: see the work of, among many others, Lears (1984, 1994), Shammas (1990), Leach (1993), Ohmann (1996), Mukerji (1983), Brewer and Porter (1993), Boorstin (1968), McKendrick, Brewer, and Plumb (1982), Cross (1993), Fox and Lears (1983).

24 On experiencing consumer society as something natural: it will perhaps be useful to define "consumption," "consumer society," and "consumer culture," as there are wide differences in how these terms are used in the literature. I define consumption as economists do, to mean all monetary expenditure. I define consumer society as a society in which discretionary consumption has become a mass phenomenon, not just the province of the rich or even the middle classes. Thus, while consumerism as a way of life and an ideology began very early in some places (the Dutch golden age, late Ming China, Georgian England), consumerism as a mass phenomenon started in the United States in the 1920s. By my definition, a *society* only becomes consumerist when consumerism is a mass phenomenon. So I believe we can only speak of "consumer society" in the twentieth century. In the United States, the 1920s is the crucial turning point when changes in production made middle-class lifestyles possible for nearly everyone. Second, consumer society is based on continuous growth in consumption expenditures, and such growth is central to the economic functioning of the system. Furthermore, culture, ideology, and morality develop along with this economic arrangement. Nonsatiation becomes the general norm. Social and political stability thus come to be dependent on the delivery of consumer goods.

24 On students and commercials: see Twitchell (1996, pp. 6–7).

Chapter Two: Communicating with Commodities

27 On lack of desire: see Wilk (1996), which is a good counterweight to the literature's focus on desire. See also Englis and Solomon (1995), who look at the reference group their subjects are most concerned with *not* being like.

27 On what compels us to consume: I should forewarn the reader that my account is necessarily limited. I do not address a range of motives that a growing interpretive consumer literature has highlighted. The purpose of this chapter is to present a view of consuming that centers on the idea that what we consume has social meaning; that the spending habits of others affect our consumer desires; that novel and more expensive products are more highly valued by most people; and that lifestyles distinguish social groups along a prestige hierarchy. Most consumption, I would argue, conforms to this general characterization. I take this approach not because I believe in a mono-causal theory of consumption, but because I take social and comparative aspects to be very important in explaining motives for a wide range of products and a large fraction of expenditure, and for their role in the escalation of consumption norms. I should also note that I do not say much about the supply side of the picture (marketers, advertisers, salespeople, taste-makers), not because I do not believe it is important, but because others have focused on it. However, I believe that most of these accounts have not adequately explained why consumers go along with these marketing efforts. For accounts that focus mainly on the supply side, see, among others, Ewen (1988) and Ewen and Ewen (1992), and some analyses of advertising, such as that of Leiss, Kline, and Jhally (1990). For historical accounts of marketing, see Strasser (1989) and Tedlow (1990) and, for advertising, Marchand (1985) and Lears (1994). For recent surveys and general accounts of consumerism and consumer culture, see Miller (1995), Gabriel and Lang (1995), Slater (1997), Lee (1993), Sherry (1995), Lury (1996), Ackerman, Goodwin, and Kiron (1997) and Brewer and Porter (1993). The literature on consumption is now vast. Among those important accounts I have not cited elsewhere are Douglas and Isherwood (1996), Campbell (1987), James (1993), Fine and Leopold (1994), Featherstone (1991), Leiss (1976), Appadurai (1986), and Miller (1987). This list is by no means exhaustive. See the works just cited for bibliographic completeness.

27 "situations where others are close": Festinger (1954, p. 123). The reference-group literature within psychology is very large; for a bibliography, see Olson and Hazlewood (1986). A recent contribution is Wheeler and Miyake (1992). Most of the studies refer to subjects other than consumption comparisons. For the original use of the "reference group" term, see Hyman (1942). See also Goethals (1986). Within the consumer field, see

Moschis (1976), Bearden and Etzel (1982), Bearden, Netemeyer, and Teel (1989), Park and Lessing (1977), Childers and Rao (1992), Cocanougher and Bruce (1971), Sommers and Bruce (1968), Calder and Burnkrant (1977), Porter (1967), and Braun and Wicklund (1989). See also Richins (1991, 1995). The economic literature on relative, or positional, consumption is relatively limited. In addition to the classic works cited in chapter 1, I refer the reader to Frank (1985b), Mason (1981), Congleton (1989), Rauscher (1992, 1993), Pollak (1976), James (1987), Ireland (1994), Campbell and Cochrane (1995), Galí (1994), Abel (1990), and Sen (1983, 1987). Empirical studies include Easterlin (1973, 1995), Brown (1994), Alessie and Kapteyn (1991), Tomes (1986), Kapteyn and van Herwaarden (1980), Kapteyn and Wansbeek (1982), Kosicki (1987), Basmann, Molina, and Slottje (1988), Neumark and Postelwaite (1995), and Clark and Oswald (1994).

27 On reference groups: see also Cocanougher and Bruce (1971), who found that male students aspire to the stereotyped consumer products possessed by a business executive, concluding that for young people at least reference groups can be socially distant, based on aspirations rather than current status.

28 For a critique of Bourdieu's results on painter preferences: see Lieberson (1992). These are among Bourdieu's weakest correlations. See Bourdieu's appendix table 2 (1984, p. 527). Class differences stand out more strongly in aesthetic judgments of photographic subjects (table A.2, p. 526).

28 On antiques: see Freund (1993).

29 On disdain for upper-class tastes among those of lower cultural capital: see Holt (1998).

29 On the role of cultural capital in reproducing class inequalities: I am putting forward the weak version of this argument. For discussions of Bourdieu on consumption, see, among others, Holt (1997b), Allen and Anderson (1994), Lamont and Fournier (1992), and Lamont and Lareau (1988). See the next few notes, especially "on Bourdieu and social differentiation," for further discussion.

30 On research into some areas of American consumption: the area that has been studied is art and culture. See, for example, the collection by Lamont and Fournier (1992), DiMaggio and Useem (1978), Halle (1993), Lamont et al. (1996). Some of these writers interpret their evidence as not supportive of Bourdieu. However, Holt argues for alternative interpretations. My reading suggests that this literature provides a mixed case with respect to class patterning in the arts. Perhaps the most difficult case for Bourdieu is Halle's study of fine art. While he finds evidence of common tastes across class (for instance, everyone likes landscapes), he does find strong differentiation in the case of abstract art (a key category for Bourdieu). However, while Halle claims that his data show less class variation

than Bourdieu's theory predicts, he never specifies how much variation is enough but assumes the standard is self-evident (it is not). Furthermore, Halle's discussion downplays class differences in tastes in favor of similarities. In the absence of objective criteria, the discussion has a certain "is the glass half empty or half full?" character.

Notably, all these studies cover only art and culture. This is not surprising, since Bourdieu devoted much attention to art and culture; however, as Holt (1997b) argues, this may not be the most relevant area for the United States, which has traditionally had a less important art and cultural field than France. Holt argues—correctly, I believe—that a proper test of Bourdieu would encompass a broader consumption field that includes travel, reading, clothing, dining, interior decoration, and so on. Such research, of course, would be far more ambitious than any that has yet been undertaken, with the exception of Holt's own qualitative research (see Holt 1997a, 1997b, 1998).

30 On PBS and art museums: see Lamont et al. (1996), who use 1993 data.

30 On a prestige index of musical taste: see Peterson and Simkus (1992), whose data are from 1982; see tables 2 and 3 on preferences (pp. 157–58), and table 4 on attendance (p. 162). They find that higher-status occupational groups have more varied tastes than lower-status groups, prompting the idea of high-status "omnivores" and lower-status "univores" (a pyramidal structure of taste). On status attendance, see Peterson and Simkus (1992, appendix A, pp. 170–71). See also Peterson and Kern (1996) and DiMaggio and Useem (1978), who find that social class is correlated with more elite forms of cultural consumption, such as art museums, theater, classical music, and science museums. By contrast, certain activities, such as movies and musicals, are "popular" across social classes. See also Coleman (1982) and Schaninger (1982).

30 On "doing" a museum: see Kelly (1987). Studies of leisure activities generally have showed variation by class, although they are now dated. See Bishop and Ikeda (1970), who found that 28 percent of the variance in activities is accounted for by a prestige measure.

30 On Bourdieu and social differentiation: before I present evidence for the claim that consumption is both a source and an indicator of social differentiation, it may be helpful to spell out some of the theoretical issues in the debate. Holt (1997b, 1988) has argued that, in contrast to earlier writers such as Veblen and Warner, Bourdieu is not arguing that consumption *objects* are socially patterned by a process of overt status display and hierarchical emulation, but that Bourdieu emphasizes taste rather than possession—*how* things are consumed, and the socialization processes by which taste comes to be experienced as a natural category rather than a conscious instrument of class domination. While I agree that these issues are important in Bourdieu, I think Holt has drawn the lines too sharply. I read Bourdieu more as a reformulation

and updating of the perspectives of Veblen, Warner, and others—all of whom, after all, wrote decades earlier. So, while Bourdieu often discusses style and taste, this should not be seen as an alternative to class patterning of *objects*. Rather, both *practices* and *objects* structure the consumption field. Bourdieu may put less emphasis on visible status goods not because he dismisses them but rather because their role had long been acknowledged. (On the importance of objects, see the evidence discussed later in this chapter, including the work of Belk, McCracken, and others.) I also do not believe that the evidence supports the common claim that a hierarchical process of emulation and acquisition no longer occurs. Analysis of the product ownership data over time provides evidence against that view.

Perhaps the most obvious difference between Bourdieu and Veblen has to do with the psychological aspects of class distancing. Veblenian status-seekers are far more conscious of what they are about, whereas Bourdieu shows how taste has become naturalized and individuals are not as conscious of the class implications of their choices. (Although it is important to avoid caricaturing Veblen. His view was more sophisticated than is sometimes recognized.) Again, this is a reasonable updating, based on the rise of democratic and populist ideologies. Here I agree with Holt's claim that class differences have "gone underground." However, it is important not to go too far in this argument: to say that there is no consciousness of class distancing in contemporary America is too strong a claim. (See chapter 4 for a discussion of the psychology of competitive consumption.)

On the question of the extent to which the social patterning of the consumption field reproduces social inequality, I subscribe to a weak version of the hypothesis. It is now easier for individuals to use consumption to transcend a lower-class background, and there is more tolerance in the consumption field than in the past. On the other hand, I believe that the extreme alternative, that there is no role for consumption in social reproduction, is exaggerated. Thus, I would claim that both objects and practices display a hierarchical socioeconomic patterning. This patterning is both reflective of class and has a weak effect in reproducing it. This patterning is furthermore reproduced dynamically as standards of living rise. (See chapter 4 on the dynamic aspects.)

31 On Warner's classic ethnography: see Warner, Meeker, and Eells (1960, p. 23).

31 To raise sales, write the ad in French: see Packard (1959, p. 62).

31 "buy a pair of ancestor portraits": ibid., p. 67.

31 On the mania for Victoriana among the new middle classes: see Jager (1986). Superfluity and nonfunctionality have historically been important in establishing high-class credentials.

31 For the studies I refer to: see Felson (1976, 1978). In the former, Felson

used a telephone survey to elicit prestige rankings of automobile models, department stores, and Chicago suburbs. While he did find some degree of common ranking, the large number of "don't know" answers led him to conclude that consumption patterns no longer reflected social strata. This conclusion was premature. First, Felson made the mistake of assuming that everyone in the status hierarchy was familiar with all the items in it. But on the basis of what we know about reference groups, we would expect people to be familiar with products "in the neighborhood" of their standard of living, not with those far away from it. Furthermore, there is evidence that high-status people are better predictors of low-status consumer patterns than the reverse (see Sommers 1964). Second, the reliance on telephone, rather than visual, cues may also have been partly responsible for these results, given that status cues tend to be visible (see chapter 3 on the role of visibility). Among the other reasons to believe that visible cues are salient is the importance of the subconscious in status consumption.

In the second study, Felson concluded that the increasing diversity of consumer goods had eroded the connection between consumer patterns and class. This inference is unwarranted. Rising incomes will in themselves yield increased variety of goods. An appropriate methodology would have been to test the connection between categories of goods and class; Felson did not do so. For critiques of Felson's research, see Holman (1981) and Semon (1979).

31 "the decline and fall of the status symbol": Blumberg (1974).

32 On the "standard package": see Wittmayer, Schulz, and Mittelstædt (1994). Dholakia and Levy defined the dream as being able "to own your home, nicely furnished, and two cars; to travel and to be a member of local clubs" (1987, p. 437), but club membership is not a universal goal.

32 On residential clustering: see Weiss (1988, 1994).

33 On the match between housing choice and the ideal self: see Malhotra (1988). Sixty percent of the sample matched their housing choice more closely with "ideal social self," 22.3 percent matched it more closely with "actual self," and 17.6 percent chose houses that most closely matched their "actual social self" (p. 17). Malhotra also reports that other researchers have found housing to be the product most connected to self-image.

33 On homeowner associations: see McKenzie (1994, pp. 14–17).

33 On the Chartwell incident: see ibid., p. 17.

33 On the upper-middle-class taste for wood and other natural substances: see chapter 3, "Identity and the New Consumerism."

33 "successful suburbanites": see ACORN (1994). See also similar material from Equifax or a number of other market research companies.

34 On "yuppie" symbolic constellations: see Solomon and Buchanan (1991). They defined "yuppies" as persons 25–44 years, earning

$20,000 a year or more, and living in metropolitan centers of 100,000 people or more. This income cutoff is too low for the true yuppies, but the authors wanted to include aspirants (p. 99).

34 On the importance of how we consume: see Holt (1998, 1997a). One reason the consumption-class connection is more difficult to discern is that consumption patterns have become increasingly complex. Whether or not a family *had* a living room couch was once a status marker, but we now have to differentiate between brands, fabrics, styles, and colors to discern the status differences. Class distance is increasingly created by *how* things are consumed. According to Jager, "the style of consumption itself becomes crucial to the maintenance of social differentiation" (1986, pp. 89–90).

This is a central point of Holt's work. Holt divided residents of State College, a rural university town in Pennsylvania, into those high and low on cultural capital (measured by a linear combination of father's education and occupation and respondent's education and occupation) and found marked differences between the two groups. He found that low cultural capitals (LCCs) emphasized comfort and durability (function) in their furniture and clothing and declared their distance from style and fashion. High cultural capitals (HCCs) revealed more interest in formal aesthetics, the home as a means of personal expression, and "well-made, well-tailored clothes that have absolutely luxurious fabrics." HCCs traveled abroad, subscribed to the *New York Times*, and enjoyed a wide variety of cuisines. LCCs left the area much less frequently, read the local newspaper (which HCCs found parochial and poorly written), and didn't like exotic foods, where Chinese cuisine was defined as exotic. HCCs were connoisseur consumers (in rugs, food, travel), while LCCs were more comfortable with mass-produced, conventional combinations. HCCs craved "authentic" travel experiences, while LCCs liked Disneyland. While both groups were nature lovers, LCCs communed with it and HCCs related to it as a means of personal achievement.

34 On the intrusion of marketing into our lives: see Larson (1992).

34 On the social messages of material goods: the metaphor of material goods as language should be seen as a loose, not precise one, for reasons that have now been elaborated. See McCracken (1990, ch. 4), who argues that material goods are a conservative code that lacks the freedom of language. This is partly why they are so useful as indicators of social inequality. Thus, postmodern approaches that stress the ability of individuals to create personal meanings are often exaggerated. For a survey of coding and decoding, see Holman (1981).

34 For Sidney Levy's article: see Levy (1959).

35 On the symbolic field: see Baudrillard (1988). See also Holt (1997a).

35 For evidence as to whether Americans can "read" the class structure of consumption: see Holman (1981) for an extensive review.

35 On Chapin's findings: see Chapin (1928; 1935, ch. 9).

35 On Davis's findings: see Davis (1956).

35 On the update of Chapin: see Laumann and House (1970). The concept of front and back rooms, and impression management, are from Goffman (1959). See also his treatment of status symbols (Goffman 1951).

36 On occupation and social class: see Cherulnik and Bayless (1986). They depicted middle- and lower-class houses.

36 On living room interiors: see McGrath, Englis, and Solomon (1997), who found that respondents associated modern decor with the homes of high-status people, as well as a variety of other high-status items, such as caviar and champagne.

36 On correlations between Chevrolets and occupation: see Belk, Bahn, and Mayer (1982) and Belk, Mayer, and Bahn (1982).

36 On the connection between purses/wallets and occupation/income: see Belk (1978). This study looked separately at males and females and differentiated by the sex of the owner of the purse or wallet. For all categories except males predicting females, the proportion of the variance in income and occupation that was correctly predicted was quite substantial—ranging from .30 to .59. Males' ability to decode female products is much lower (.12 and .19 for income and occupation, respectively; see Belk 1978, table 5, p. 43.) There is one major drawback to this study. While most of the features presented to the subjects involved fairly subtle differences (business cards from two hair-cutting establishments, two different colors of lipstick, tickets for baseball versus football games, or hockey versus tennis), one differential was very obvious: the wallet was found in either JFK Airport or the Greyhound bus terminal, and the woman's purse contained a ballpoint pen from either the Holiday Inn or the Waldorf-Astoria.

36 On students correlating products to class: see Belk (1981). A 1981 study by Michael Munson and Austin Spivey of two hundred women found that they differentiated significantly between upper- and lower-class brand usage for some types of products deemed value-expressive (autos, magazines, and gasolines), but not for utilitarian products (detergents, deodorants, brassieres, and vacuum cleaners). Gasoline, while functionally utilitarian, was hypothesized to be value-expressive because of its link with cars. Deodorants and bras are social invisibles (see chapter 3).

36 On children's recognition of consumption symbols: see Belk, Bahn, and Mayer (1982) and Belk, Mayer, and Driscoll (1984).

36 On children's differentiation by occupation: see Driscoll, Mayer, and Belk (1985).

36 On the greater status consciousness of higher-class children: see Belk, Bahn, and Mayer (1982). See also Belk, Mayer, and Bahn (1982) for differences among adults.

36 On the British adolescents: see Dittmar (1992, pp. 178–79). Most stud-
    ies have focused on the connection between consumer goods and value
    or personality attributes, rather than class. But these attributes often
    have class associations; for example, autonomy is positively, and
    friendliness negatively, associated with wealth. Dittmar found that pro-
    viding information about a person's material possessions leads subjects
    to significant personality (and hence) class conclusions (pp. 166–68).
    See also Dittmar (1994a, 1994b).

36 On clothing as a symbolic communicator: see Simmel (1957) and
    Sahlins (1976). For an insightful comparison of Weber, Simmel, and
    Veblen, see Mommaas (1990). On Simmel, see McCracken (1990). On
    clothing, see also Davis (1992), Lipovetsky (1994), Craik (1994),
    Solomon (1985), Thompson and Haytko (1997), Rosenfeld and Plax
    (1977), Douty (1963), Rosencranz (1962), and Holman (1980).

37 On sumptuary laws: see Vincent (1934).

37 On the wealthy wearing more clothes: see Lurie (1992, p. 120).

37 On the journalist friend: see ibid., p. 138. On ordinary people decoding
    clothing ensembles, see McCracken (1990, ch. 4, esp. pp. 60–67). Dis-
    cussing congruent clothing ensembles presented to subjects, McCracken
    notes that "informants were swift and sure in their reading of the cloth-
    ing portrayed. Selecting a term from our vocabulary of social types, the
    informant would identify the person pictured as a 'housewife,' 'hippie,'
    'businessman,' etc. Sometimes this term would be accompanied by
    a demographic adjective ('middle-class,' 'uneducated,' 'wealthy')."
    McCracken is interested in the extent to which the metaphor of lan-
    guage can be applied to the decoding of clothes. He argues that in very
    important ways clothing and other material goods are different from
    language. For example, combinatorial freedom is dramatically circum-
    scribed with material objects. Clothing is a "conservative code" whose
    meanings individuals have little control over; they are collectively deter-
    mined. I believe this is one of the reasons clothing is so effective as a
    symbol of social distancing, the point I am arguing.

37 On the survey of middle-class teenagers: see Tefertiller (1994). She
    found that the least degree of uniformity was in makeup brands—
    owing to her choice of brands, I suspect. It is also worth noting that
    teen evidence cannot be automatically assumed to hold for adults.

38 On the boys and LA Gear shoes: for boys, the rank ordering of clothing
    was just short of perfect, perhaps reflecting slightly less emphasis on
    clothes (ibid.).

38 On the PRIZM cluster system study: see Englis and Solomon (1995),
    who used four cluster groups: the group most students aspired to
    (Money and Brains); the group most students were currently in (Young
    Suburbia); the group most students wanted to *avoid* ending up in
    (Smalltown Downtowns); and a group they felt was irrelevant (Middle

America). Because the subjects were third- and fourth-year students, the researchers focused on their anticipated consuming life, that is, on what they "would like to be."

38 "Fine feathers make fine birds": Dittmar (1922, p. 155).

38 On automobile honking: see Doob and Gross (1968).

38 On the phone booth study: see Bickman (1971).

39 On people depicted in front of different houses: see Cherulnik and Bayless (1986).

39 On treatment by salespeople: see Wise (1974), who found that better-dressed people were offered lower prices by automobile salesmen.

40 "I just feel so proud": Nightingale (1993, p. 164). Nightingale argues that "the values of conspicuous consumption as well as the material trappings of those values, became a growing part of poor African American children's upbringing in inner-city neighborhoods" (p. 135).

40 On the sneaker companies' efforts: see ibid., pp. 141–42.

40 For a report on the "Coolhunt": see Gladwell (1997).

40 On the shortening of the fashion cycle: see Nightingale (1993) and Gladwell (1997).

40 On the rise in shoplifting: see U.S. Department of Commerce (1996, table 318, p. 205). See also Cox, Cox, and Moschis (1990).

40 On the personal shoplifter: see van Biema (1996).

40 On the risks of wearing fashionable items, and adolescents' attitudes: see Gonzalez (1990).

41 On high school students' work patterns: see Schor (1992).

41 On the trickle-up process: see Fine and Leopold (1990). See also McCracken (1990, ch. 6) for a revision.

42 On not inferring consumers' motivations: see Campbell (1996).

42 On other sources of meaning in consumer goods: see Belk (1980) for citations of the large body of research supporting the importance of consumer intentionality.

Chapter Three: The Visible Lifestyle

45 On companies' efforts to make products visible: see James (1987). Athletes wearing brand logos is an example of such efforts.

45 For a witty commentary on the "unbearable ugliness of Volvos": see Fish (1994), who argues that academics prefer them precisely for that ugliness.

46 "I can't sell a shirt without a logo": see Underwood (1996b, p. 27).

46 On the meaning of Hilfiger fashion: see Givhan (1995).

46 "These clothes, traditionally associated": Andrew Ross, professor and director of the New York University American studies program. In Givhan (1995).

47 "Upper income fashion is about success": Russell Simmons, boutique owner. In Givhan (1995).

47 "We aspire": Derick Procope, fashion director for *Vibe* magazine. In Givhan (1995).

47 On teens and brand names: see Bradley (1995, p. 32). In answer to "How important is a brand name for the following products?" the following percentages of children answered "extremely" or "very important": sneakers, 59 percent; radios, CD players, 58 percent; video games, 53 percent; underwear, 23 percent; shampoo, 28 percent; stationery products, 12 percent.

47 "The coolest brands are often fashion brands": ibid., p. 31.

47 On peer group influence on consumption of visible products: see Childers and Rao (1992). Childers and Rao were following up on earlier research by Bearden and Etzel (1982), who originally used this methodology to study reference-group influence on product and brand purchase decisions. Bearden and Etzel found that reference groups were more important for publicly consumed goods and for luxuries. (This literature also makes interesting distinctions between brands and products.) See also Richins (1994), who finds that more materialistic people valued more visible possessions and that less materialistic people valued sentimental objects more.

47 On bottled water consumption: see Hamlin (1996), who reports an estimate of $2.5 billion in 1995.

47 "We wanted to make this the Nike of bottled water": Frank Ginsberg, in Khermouch (1996, p. 6).

47 "You could pretty much fake a coat from K-Mart": Merck Family Fund focus groups.

48 On the tripling of fake designer goods: see Grossman and Shapiro (1988) for a 1985 estimate of $60 billion, and Stipp (1996) for an estimate of $200 billion in 1996.

48 For the information on Han dynasty pottery, I am indebted to Russell Belk.

48 On the use of markers in tourism: see MacCannell (1989).

48 "upon being discharged from a tour bus": see Kelly (1987, p. 22).

49 On the beauty industry: see Wolf (1991), McKnight (1989), and Allen (1981).

49 "hope in a bottle": I am indebted to Susan Fournier for this formulation.

49 "If they can't afford a Chanel suit": Underwood (1996a, p. 26).

50 "A classic shade of scarlet": Solowij (1996, p. ; emphasis mine).

51 On the independent quality tests conducted by *Consumer Reports*: the results for eye shadows also revealed no discernible quality differentials. For mascaras, differences were found in laboratory testing, and consumers ranked them differently. See Chao and Schor (1998).

51 On the snob effect: see the classic article by Leibenstein (1950).

54 On the Ethel Klein poll: see EDK Associates poll (provided privately to author), 29 November–1 December 1993. Forty-four percent of women often or sometimes buy designer brands of these products. Twenty percent never buy these designer products. Statistics on quality and on college choice are also from this poll.

55 On differences in status buying: see Chao and Schor (1998) and Duesenberry (1949).

55 On the buying habits of business majors: see Wicklund and Gollwitzer (1982). Belk notes that there is also a "pulling it off" effect: novices are less likely to buy expensive equipment because they cannot pull it off gracefully.

55 In a second study: see Braun and Wicklund (1989).

55 On self-consciousness: see Gould and Barak (1988).

55 On compulsive buying and status orientation: see d'Astous (1990).

55 On materialism and visible possessions: see Richins (1994).

55 On the counterfeiting figures of $200 billion and 5 percent: see Stipp (1996). See also Harris (1996).

56 On the fraction of the U.S. market made up of fakes: see Grossman and Shapiro (1988, p. 81).

56 On fake colognes, baby foods, and Tupperware parties: see Harris (1996).

56 On Cartier watches and Louis Vuitton's withdrawal from the market: see Grossman and Shapiro (1988, p. 81).

56 On the perils of donning a fake: private anonymous communication from overseas garment manufacturer.

56 On instant coffee, Fords and Chevys, and Marlboro men: see the classic studies: on brands and identity, see Birdwell (1968), Landon (1974), Dolich (1969), Grubb (1965), Grubb and Grathwohl (1967), and Higgins (1987). Research on brands and personality has had a mixed track record and has not been pursued much since the 1960s. One explanation for its failure to associate personality with consumer purchases statistically is that the self is not unitary, but made up of many identities. On this point, see Belk (1988) and Kleine, Kleine, and Kernan (1993). Alternatively, the brand-personality relationship may just not be strong.

57 On identity and consumption: the postmodern literature has focused primarily on the relation between personal identity and consuming, rejecting traditional class- or status-based theories. Some of this literature is heavily celebratory, arguing that individuals use consumer goods to create identities in a liberatory and creative way. Some authors have gone so far as to argue that consumerism is a tactic of resistance (de Certeau 1984). On postmodernism and consumer research, see Firat and Venkatesh (1995). As an antidote to the postmodernist view, consider that a majority of Americans say they "don't like to get noticed for the clothes they wear" (reported in Underwood 1995, p. 26).

57 "the brand defines the consumer": Sir Michael Perry, chairman of

Unilever, presidential address to the U.K. Advertising Association; cited in Gabriel and Lang (1995, p. 36).

57 "That we are what we have": Belk (1988, p. 139).

57 On car owners: see EDK Associates poll (provided privately to author), "Attachment to Cars" and "Keep on Trucking," 15–16 September 1994. The question was, "How much do you see your car as a reflection of who you are?" Forty-eight percent of respondents said either "a lot" or "some"; 26 percent said "not at all." The second question was, "If you were a car, what would you want to be?" Only 11 percent of the sample answered "don't know."

57 "When I found that dress": Otnes and Lowrey (1993). On the relationship between consumers and brands, see Fournier (1996).

57 On what we buy affecting who we become: see Kleine, Kleine, and Allen (1995) and Kleine, Kleine, and Kernan (1993). Solomon (1983, p. 323) also makes this point.

57 On clothes "making the man": see Kleine, Kleine, and Kernan (1993, p. 228; figure 2, p. 225).

57 On cosmetic surgery: see Schouten (1991), who presents evidence that people use plastic surgery to literally change who they are.

57 On Harley-Davidson bikers: see Schouten and McAlexander (1995).

57 "Lifestyle advertising": Mort (1988, p. 209).

58 For related evidence on differentiation from a much earlier period: see Sommers (1964), who found that higher-status people gave much more differentiated self-descriptions.

58 On customization: see the discussion in Solomon (1988). One study of newly rich Vancouver women found that they were more likely than the established elite to decorate their homes to make a "creative statement about themselves," relying on interior decorators to do the speaking.

58 On the home as a haven of authenticity: see Wuthnow (1996, p. 247).

58 "We have clients": clerk in Hobbit store, Amsterdam, 19 March 1997.

58 On collecting antiques: see Belk (1995).

58 On antiques: see the fascinating account by Freund (1993).

58 On the bias against national chains: see Holt (1998).

59 On cultural capital and mass produced goods: see ibid.

59 "Although people may claim": Denis Lewis, cited in Dittmar (1992, pp. 13–14). Lewis continues: "Individuality is therefore a sham. Only group identity remains. . . . In the West poverty is expressible not simply in terms of not having enough to eat, but also as being unable to sustain a proper identity through possessions. . . . [Ours is an] identity through possessions model of the world."

59 On the latest twist: some researchers are not so sure. Belk, for example, emphasizes that "uniqueness" has its own properties, which cannot be assimilated to social status (private communication, December 1996).

59 On self-image and status: see Birdwell (1968), who finds, looking at car

owners, that "the degree of congruity between the Owner's Car and himself was the greatest for owners of Cadillac[s], Lincoln[s], Imperial[s], somewhat less for owners of medium-priced cars, a little smaller for those owning low-priced cars, and smallest for the economy-minded respondents." This is, of course, exactly what we would expect. Owners of lower-cost, low-status items have much less incentive to identify with them. Moreover, this finding undermines the idea of self-image as something personal, natural, or asocial. Rather, it suggests that social status considerations shape our self-image.

59   On the increasing importance of spending as a determinant of social status: see Jager (1986).

61   On "taste codes" in some neighborhoods: see McKenzie (1994).

61   On savants in advertising: see Twitchell (1996) for a similar argument.

61   On Nike advertising budget: see Gelsi (1995). The exact figure, in 1995, was $142 million.

62   On vitamins: see NBC-TV *Dateline*, "Consumer Alert: C-ing the Difference," March 30, 1997.

62   On $1 billion spent on fashion ads: see Underwood (1995).

62   On the worldwide jeans manufacturer: anonymous private communication, 1994.

62   On the classic beer study: see Allison and Uhl (1964).

62   On branding: Of course, there is an informational component in some advertising, but in some mediums much of it is directed at creating brand identity, image, and status. Twitchell (1996), on the other hand, claims we get a high entertainment value from the ads.

Chapter Four: When Spending Becomes You

67   On the typical middle-class home: see U.S. Department of Commerce (1996), which includes data on many, but not all, of the above items and activities.

68   "My little girl had a friend visit her": Thompson, Pollio, and Locander (1994, p. 445).

68   "Every time they see new kids with something new": Merck Family Fund focus groups.

68   "Sue, who went with me to submit the application": Fitzgerald (1995, p. 636).

69   On exposure: In my Telecom survey, I found that various sites of exposure are correlated with spending. One site is social: the more often a person visits the homes of friends, relatives, and business associates, the higher his or her spending, controlling for income and other variables. People who report that they are "more aware" of the spending patterns of others also tend to spend more, although both these relationships have low statistical significance.

69 "They will see their friend with one": Stanislas de Quercize, quoted in Underwood (1996a, p. 28).

69 On stimulators of desire: see Fournier and Guiry (1991). They asked one hundred respondents where they thought people got their ideas about the things they "have to have." "What friends or family have" was the most common response (54 percent). The other responses were: TV commercials or magazine ads (35 percent), TV shows (27 percent), shopping malls (16 percent), what strangers have (12 percent), and catalogs (11 percent) (p. 15). The importance of exposure has also been supported in the "standard package" research. Wittmayer, Schulz, and Mittelstædt (1994) found that students training for particular occupations were better able to identify the standard package of their group if they had already been exposed to the occupation through internships or the like. Seeing is not the only sense that stimulates consumer desires, although it is the most powerful. Hearing about products also leads to desires.

70 On the role of imagination and fantasy in consumer behavior: see Campbell (1987). The cultural studies and postmodern literature also emphasize these themes.

70 "*always* have something in mind": Fournier and Guiry (1991, p. 20).

70 "dream about things they do not own": Fournier and Guiry (1993, pp. 356–57).

70 On the size and content of wish lists: see Fournier and Guiry (1991, pp. 11–14; table on p. 13). Jaguar, Safari, and Nantucket house quote is the title of Fournier and Guiry's 1993 article.

70 On imaginary social worlds: see Caughey (1984, pp. 185, 176).

71 "A common daydream of mine": ibid., p. 176.

71 "showing the house to admiring others": ibid., p. 177.

71 "awe and respect": ibid.

71 On the standard "material wealth" fantasy: see ibid., p. 186.

71 On the 60 percent motivated to earn more money: see Fournier and Guiry (1991, p. 30).

72 "I'd better get a good grade": ibid.

72 On household debt of $5.5 trillion: see Ramirez (1997). For the distribution of debt, up to 1995, see Kennickell, Starr-McCluer, and Sundén (1997).

72 On Americans reporting heavy to moderate, slight, or no debt: see Merck Family Fund Survey (1995).

72 On percentage of income toward debt servicing: see Financial Markets Center (1997).

72 On average total household debt: see Singletary and Crenshaw (1996). In 1960 total debt carried by the average household was 60 percent of its annual income; in 1980, 75 percent; and by the end of 1995, 95 percent. Consumer debt alone was more than 20 percent of income in

1995. On debt-to-income ratios, see also Canner, Kennickell, and Luckett (1995). The debt-to-income ratio is only a partial indicator of the severity of debt obligations because it does not include asset holdings.

72 On the doubling of credit card debt: see Singletary and Crenshaw (1996, p. 11). See also Canner, Kennickell, and Luckett (1995) for data between 1983 and 1992.

72 On annual fees and interest of $1,000: see Consumer Federation of America. According to the most recent Survey of Consumer Finances (Federal Reserve Board, 1995), 48 percent of all American households held credit card debts (see Kennickell, Starr-McCluer, and Sundén (1997, table 11, p. 19).

72 On the upsurge in borrowing in the 1990s and solicitations by credit card companies: 40 percent of Americans report that they are solicited to apply for new cards *every week*. Almost half the adult population (48 percent) holds three or more cards (Farkas and Johnson 1997, p. 18). Companies have begun to approach increasingly risky customers, including teenagers and people with bad credit histories. They solicit aggressively on college campuses, even offering free gifts to those who sign up. Mastercard estimates that 80 percent of all college students carry a credit card by their senior year. For many students who have low incomes and are relatively inexperienced in economic matters, controlling their card use is not easy, and the number of students with problem debts appears to have risen (see Bryce 1995).

73 On the influence of Mastercard logos on spending: see Feinberg (1986).

73 Debt among Telecom employees: the survey also asked about people's awareness of others' spending patterns. On a 1–4 scale where 1 equaled "not at all aware" and 4 equaled "very aware," 77 percent reported scores of 3 and 4 for their relatives' spending, 57 percent were aware of their friends' spending, and 28 percent were aware of their coworkers' spending patterns. On the other hand, only 15 percent reported awareness of their neighbors' spending.

74 Neighbors as a reference group: because the Telecom survey was a workplace sample, it cannot be assumed that this distribution of reference groups reflects all Americans.

74 Awareness of neighbors' financial status: only 7 percent said they didn't know when asked how much money they had compared to neighbors. Forty-seven percent reported being not at all aware of their neighbors' spending patterns and lifestyles.

75 For a fuller account of the savings equations: see Schor (1997a).

76 On the impact of educational level on shopping time: see Robinson (1989, p. 50). Women with postgraduate degrees spend 8.4 hours per week shopping, and college graduates 8.0 hours.

76 Commonsense notions about saving: views on the fraction of income saved by income level differ among economists. Neoclassical theories

of consumption reject the idea that the propensity to save rises with income. Keynesian and Marxian theories assume that it does.

78 Downshifters and the upscaling of desire: I want to remind the reader again that my interviews with downshifters were not generated from a random sample.

80 On the impact of television on perceptions of living standards: see O'Guinn and Shrum (1997).

80 On the products and medical conditions publicized on TV: see Shrum et al. (1991), who also discuss the link between television watching and inflated perceptions.

80 On the effects of drama shows versus other types of programs: see O'Guinn and Shrum (1997).

81 On the overstatement of ownership rates: see Fournier and Guiry (1991, p. 21).

81 On the varying impacts of television by financial background: see O'Guinn et al. (1989); see also O'Guinn and Shrum (1997).

81 Inflated sense of consumer norms: among the alternative hypotheses for the association between television watching and consuming is one that draws a correlation between TV watching and depression, which is a common spending trigger.

81 "They try to portray that an upper-class lifestyle": Merck Family Fund focus groups.

81 On the desire for privacy, and historical changes in the degree of privacy in housing and lifestyle: see Halle (1993, ch. 1).

81 "what members of other social classes have": O'Guinn and Shrum (1997, p. 279). The connection to Goffman is theirs; the point about increasing privacy is mine.

81 On the connection between indebtedness and watching too much TV: the Merck Family Fund poll found that 55.6 percent of heavy debtors, 42.4 percent of moderate debtors, 37.3 percent of slight debtors, and 33.6 percent of those not in debt reported that they watched too much TV.

82 On product placements: see Jacobson and Mazur (1995) and McAllister (1996). See also *Brandweek* magazine, which reports on the latest placements and the sizes of the deals.

82 On the increase in larceny: see Hennigan et al. (1982).

82 On the statistical correlation between television and spending: note that other factors that influence spending, as well as TV watching, were controlled for, including income, occupation, education, gender, and age.

82 On TV viewing estimates: see Robinson (1990), who calculated an average of fifteen hours per week from budget diaries. See Nielsen estimates in "The 18-Minute Mile" (1997, p. 2).

83 On the underestimation of credit card debts: see Ausubel (1995, p. 24; 1991). Underestimation is far more severe for credit card debt than other types of debt.

83 On whether consumers intend to borrow: see Ausubel (1991, pp. 70–71), who argues that consumers' underestimation of their debt implies that they do not intend to take on the debt levels they do. He also makes the point that card issuers know that consumers often do not fulfill their intention to pay off their bills quickly (1995, p. 21).

83 On the number who pay finance charges or hold a card balance: see Farkas and Johnson (1997, p. 18).

84 On the dirtiness of money: see Wuthnow (1996).

84 On Elysa Lazar: see Goldberg (1995).

86 "We've had more fights this year": Fitzgerald (1995, p. 634).

86 "housekeeper's child": see Fitzgerald (1995, pp. 635–36).

86 "The wealth of these kids is just mind-boggling": ibid., p. 637.

86 On the pocket money of American children: see Durning (1991, p. 153).

87 "Somebody down the block"; "If you don't provide your child"; "I'm not being a good parent": Merck Family Fund focus groups.

87 "agents of materialism": Wuthnow (1996, pp. 248–49).

87 On the adult critique of youth: data are from Merck Family Fund poll, in which 30.3 percent strongly agreed with the statement and 55.9 percent agreed; and from the Telecom survey, in which 51.7 percent agreed with the statement and 33.1 percent strongly agreed.

87 On the rise in materialism among American youth: see Easterlin and Crimmins (1991) and Rahn and Transue (1997).

88 "You can afford to go to Thom McCann's": Merck Family Fund focus groups.

89 On volume of retail sales at Christmas: see Steinhauer (1997).

89 On gifts for pets: see Bradley (1996, p. 4). Americans spend $20 billion on pet products each year, with $3 billion going for accessories. Hallmark now has 117 greeting cards and 41 specialty gifts for pets.

89 On Karen Greve's findings: see Greve (1995).

89 "I bought a diamond ring for myself": McKeage, Richins, and Debevec (1993, p. 359). On self-gifts, see also Mick and DeMoss (1990a, 1990b) and Sherry, McGrath, and Levy (1995).

90 On the deadweight loss of Christmas gifts: see Waldfogel (1993).

90 On infant formula and the Nestle boycott: see Reinhold (1981) and Hilts (1984).

90 On comerciogenic malnutrition: see James (1987) and the references therein.

90 On painted rocks, tags on sunglasses, and so on: see Belk (1985a).

90 Telecomers "keeping up with the Joneses": I have learned that asking about the "Joneses" is a mistake, because it conjures up a negative, value-laden metaphor from which people dissociate themselves. This interpretation is consistent with the research of Berhau (forthcoming), who suggests that the metaphor is seen as shallow and a bit ugly. Another explanation is that the question may be interpreted as relevant

only to those who are not keeping up very well. People who are not "behind" may report that they don't feel pressure, even if they are significantly involved in positional spending.

93 On resistance to "keeping up with the Joneses" in Philadelphia families: see Berhau (forthcoming).

94 On being taught to repress feelings of jealousy, and so on: see Frank (1985a, pp. 5–7).

94 On the complex cultural message: see Wuthnow (1996), where he discusses materialism as "evil." Berhau (forthcoming) finds that the *source* of one's income matters in how judgmental people are about spending. The spending of those who have worked hard for their money is more condoned, both by themselves and by others.

94 On the shift from traditional to modern consumption cultures: see Campbell (1987).

94 On primitive consumption: see Hirschman (1985).

95 On the shirt label experiment: see Baugh and Davis (1989).

95 On men's slacks and designer labels: see Behling and Wilch (1988).

95 On the $20,000 Rolex: see Underwood (1994, p. 22).

96 "Small" house in suburban Washington: personal anonymous communication (10 October 1996).

96 Lipstick choice and "professional undoing": personal anonymous communication (1996).

97 On the "fear of falling" of the professional-managerial class: see Ehrenreich (1990).

97 On the laid-off plant manager: see Bragg (1996a).

97 On the divorced engraving company employee: see Rimer (1996).

97 On unemployed aerospace workers: see Bragg (1996b). Bragg (1996a, 1996b) and Rimer (1996) were part of the influential *New York Times* series, "The Downsizing of America." For a more in-depth account of downward mobility, see Newman (1989), who describes how visible consumption is maintained as income falls. On this point, see also Roberts (1991).

97 The VALS schema of the 1970s and 1980s: these are author's calculations from data provided by VALS. The original VALS typology data are from 1989, the last year for this classification system. VALS²™ data are from 1995. Percentages exclude the two low-income groups because they are excluded by VALS from the inner- and outer-directed categorization. See Mitchell (1978).

98 "Reasonable comfort" series: data files of Roper Center, University of Connecticut. See also Roper Survey Organization (1993, p. 86). See U.S. Department of Commerce (1996, table 718, p. 466) for median family incomes. See also the discussion and table in Schor (1995).

98 Necessities and luxuries: data files from Roper Center, University of Connecticut.

100 For the classic contribution on market "signaling": see Spence (1974).

100 On personal attractiveness and success in the labor market: see Averett and Korenman (1993).

100 On advertising executives: see Bosman et al. (1997).

101 On male executives undergoing blepharoplasty: see Siebert (1996), p. 34.

101 On plastic surgery: see ibid.

101 On Oxxford suits: see Underwood (1994, p. 22).

101 On Nicole Brown Simpson and breast implants: see Toobin (1996).

102 "[the new laptop computer] is not "outmoded": Mick and Fournier (1996, p. 19).

103 $7.6 billion spent on lawn care: National Gardening Association (Burlington, Vermont), personal communication (July 1996).

103 "'The Joneses' is killing me": Merck Family Fund focus groups.

103 "It's hard, though": ibid.

104 On losing desire for products after purchasing them: see Campbell (1987).

104 "Post-purchase" regret: the Merck Family Fund poll found that only 21 percent of respondents agreed that they often bought things they really didn't want.

105 On impulse buying of clothes: see the references on compulsive buying in chapter 6, "Avoid 'Retail Therapy.'"

106 On the rise in self-storage and transport per capita: see *Boston Globe* (1997).

107 "We'd all be better off": Wuthnow (1996, p. 273).

107 On the changing income distribution: see Mishel, Bernstein, and Schmitt (1996, table 1.6, p. 52).

108 "My dream is to build my own house": Merck Family Fund focus groups.

109 "just don't know when to stop and draw the line": ibid.

Chapter Five: The Downshifter Next Door

113 On the public sentiment that the country had become too materialistic: the fractions in the Merck Family Fund poll who were very or somewhat concerned about the amount of greed and selfishness in our society (81 percent); about the focus on material wealth (73 percent); and about the effect of advertising and television on our values (78 percent). Eighty-two percent agreed that most of us buy and consume far more than we need, to wasteful levels; 91 percent felt that a "buy now, pay later" attitude is leading us to consume more than we need; 72 percent agreed that many of us buy and consume as a substitute for something missing in our lives; 80.5 percent agreed that many of us are addicted to shopping; and 74 percent agreed that the amount we consume is a major cause of many environmental problems. In the Telecom

survey, 90 percent agreed that Americans are too materialistic; 69 percent believed that Americans have too much or buy too much; and 74 percent agreed that Americans shop too much. (For agreement statements, figures are sum of "agreed" and "strongly agreed.")

113 19 percent making a voluntary lifestyle change, and all subsequent data on downshifting: all data are from author's survey (see appendix C).

113 On "always feel rushed" data: see General Social Survey (GSS) (data provided to author). Other figures are from the Merck Family Fund poll, which found that 36.4 percent agree or strongly agree that their life is out of control; 63.6 percent say they want more balance in their life; and 58.9 percent say they would like to simplify their lives. See also Robinson and Godbey (1997, table 22).

114 On the demanding nature of jobs: see Schor (1992) and Hochschild (1997).

115 On simple living in the modern era: besides Shi (1985), see the classic by Elgin (1993). On postmaterialism, see Inglehart (1977, 1990). For the first major statement on downshifting, see Saltzman (1991). For how-to guides and descriptions of downshifters, see Levering and Urbanska (1992), Andrews (1997), Dominguez and Robin (1992), Blix and Heitmiller (1997), Luhrs (1997), St. James (1994) and McKenna (1997). On the politics of simple living, see Segal (1996); see Blanchard (1994) for a case study of the voluntary simplicity movement. The popular press also contains many accounts of 1990s downshifting. For a related perspective, see Ray (1997) on the emergence of "cultural creatives."

135 One, two, or three hundred thousand to retire: at a 5 percent rate of interest, $300,000 generates $15,000 per year.

139 The emergence of a middle-class, but frugal, lifestyle in the Pacific Northwest: The Pacific Northwest has radio shows, newspaper columns, newsletters, college courses, community organizations, and foundations all devoted to the idea of voluntary simplicity. Seattle bookstores devote entire sections to the subject. The public library has a special pamphlet on voluntary simplicity. The rapid growth of the Northwest Earth Institute (NWEI) attests to the rising interest in simple living. Founded in 1993 by Dick and Jeanne Roy, a former corporate attorney and an environmental activist, the institute imports ideas of voluntary simplicity and deep ecology into bastions of consumer capitalism—places such as Microsoft, Adidas, Portland General Electric, and Hewlett-Packard, as well as professional firms, schools, universities, hospitals, religious organizations and other nonprofits, even the Army Corps of Engineers. Since its founding, the institute has formed more than seven hundred study groups, each with an average of ten to twelve members. Volunteers are now working in eighteen Northwest communities, as well as seven more outside the region. "People are drawn to these groups," Dick Roy says, "because they find their daily

lives full of distractions." They are looking for the sense of purpose in life which is denied by our society. They are undergoing a "monumental shift in attitudes from material things to time" and are interested in living frugally in order to gain financial security and freedom. But Roy believes something bigger is happening: "There is a huge subculture of people drifting toward simplicity at different levels." In the Pacific Northwest, he believes, the line between downshifting and simple living is getting fuzzy. By starting with values, and human beings' connection to the earth, the institute is helping people to opt for dramatic life changes (information on NWEI activities from Dick Roy, personal communication, August 1996).

139   On downward income transitions: see Newman (1989).

Chapter Six: Learning Diderot's Lesson

145   "imperious scarlet robe": Diderot (1964, p. 311).

145   the "Diderot effect": see McCracken (1990), who introduced the concept into the contemporary literature.

149   On the Aga: see Rademaekers (1996).

150   On the popularity of holiday spending limits: see the Center for a New American Dream (1997) (data made available to author).

152   On the therapeutic belief system: see Lears (1984) and Leach (1993).

152   On half the population saying they have just enough to get by: Merck Family Fund poll. See chapter 1 for details.

154   On the safety aspects of sport utility vehicles: see Bradsher (1997).

154   On Nike, women's sports and wages: see Greenhouse (1997). See also Herbert (1997).

155   On the Nike boycott: see Johnson (1997, p. 57).

155   On marketing in schools: see Jacobson and Mazur (1995) and McAllister (1996).

156   On the relation between a Vietnamese Nike employee's wages and the cost of a meager diet: see Herbert (1997). Nike spokespeople counter this claim. See Greenhouse (1997).

156   On the environmental impacts of consuming 120 pounds of resources daily and beef and coffee production: see Ryan and Durning (1997), which is an excellent place to begin educating oneself. See also Durning (1992). For the connections to worktime, see Schor (1995).

157   On the lack of household budgeting: see Wuthnow (1996, pp. 181–82). He argues that people develop personal rituals of frugality and splurging that give the illusion of control but often fail to keep finances objectively healthy (pp. 183–87).

157   On saving as "getting a good deal": see Berhau (forthcoming) and Wuthnow (1996).

158   On youth's susceptibility to advertising: see Schudson (1984).

158 On "retail therapy": see Kacen (1997).

158 Compulsive buying: compulsive buyers are considered to be people who engage in "chronic, repetitive purchasing that becomes a primary response to negative events or feelings"; such purchasing "becomes very difficult to stop and ultimately results in harmful consequences" (Faber and O'Guinn 1992, p. 459). Researchers disagree about whether this is an addiction or a compulsion, although the terms are often used interchangeably. See Scherhorn (1990), Natarajan and Goff (1992), and, for an engaging popular account, Goldberg (1995).

158 On oniomania: see Faber (1992, p. 809).

158 On the rise of compulsive buying: see Faber, O'Guinn, and Krych (1987), who report that in the late 1980s Debtors Anonymous, an AA-style self-help group, reported that it was adding new chapters at the rate of about five per month (p. 133). Scherhorn (1990) also argues, on the basis of various pieces of evidence, that addictive consuming is increasing.

158 For paradigmatic cases of compulsive buying: see Christenson et al. (1994, p. 9). On types of products, see table 2, p. 8. The extent of gender difference is somewhat unclear; the literature contains contradictory findings. Self-reported compulsive buyers, however, are very predominantly women.

159 On the importance of acquisition rather than use: see O'Guinn and Faber (1989). The severely addicted person is addicted not so much to the products as to the act of purchasing itself. He or she may well have a cabinet of unopened items and may eventually give some of them away or hold a yard sale.

159 For the typical compulsive buyer spending half her household income on bills: see Christenson et al. (1994, p. 8).

159 On the prevalence of compulsive buying: see Faber and O'Guinn (1992, p. 466). Faber's sample may underestimate prevalence because it is drawn from the Midwest, and this is not a particularly consumerist region.

159 On Arizona college students: see Magee (1994). On general prevalence, see p. 592. Magee did not find a higher incidence among women. Whether the higher incidence among young people is a life-cycle effect or a reflection of greater consumerism among today's youth is not known. Farkas and Johnson (1997) report that young adults (ages 22–32) are more likely than older adults (ages 32–61) to say that "shopping makes me feel good," that "I sometimes buy things without thinking and then realize that it was a waste of money," and that "I don't want to worry so much about saving for my retirement that I end up not enjoying my life now" (p. 19).

159 On innocuous forms of compulsive buying: see Natarajan and Goff (1991). They found that 22–25 percent of their sample indulged in an

innocuous form of compulsive buying (p. 315). These individuals may have strong desires but also have reasonable self-control. Alternatively, they may compensate for lack of self-control by keeping desires fairly limited, infrequent, or inexpensive. Or they may have high desires and low control, but lots of money. On the idea of compulsive buying as a continuum, see also d'Astous (1990), who uses the phrase "generalized urges to buy," and Valence, d'Astous, and Fortier (1988).

159   "shopping makes me feel good": figures from Farkas and Johnson (1997, p. 19).

160   On characteristics of compulsive buyers: see Faber and O'Guinn (1992, table 3, p. 465).

160   On compulsive buying and social status: see d'Astous (1990, p. 24).

160   On New York as a fashion capital: see Goldberg (1995).

160   For a classic statement on impulse buying: see Rook (1987).

160   For information on Buy Nothing Day: contact the Media Foundation in Vancouver.

160   On compulsive buying as an addiction: see Christenson et al. (1994) and Faber et al. (1995). See also Hirschman (1992) and Scherhorn (1990). Because compulsive buyers are more likely than the general population to abuse drugs and alcohol, to be binge eaters, and to engage in other compulsive behaviors such as gambling or shoplifting, researchers conclude that spending can be addictive.

161   "welcome lower holiday spending": the 39 percent figure is from the Center for a New American Dream (1997) (data provided to author).

161   On Montgomery Ward and Rudolph the Red-Nosed Reindeer, and holidays and commercialism generally: see Schmidt (1995). On Christmas, see Miller (1993); see also Twitchell (1996) on advertising and holidays.

161   On $2.5 billion in Halloween spending: see Steinhauer (1997). See also Belk (1990).

161   On Roosevelt and Thanksgiving: see Schmidt (1995, p. 292).

161   On the history of toys: see Cross (1997). See also Kline (1993) and Seiter (1993).

162   Is work-and-spend working?: The strongest argument put forward by defenders of consumer society is that if consumers didn't like it, they could stop buying. Consumption is hardly a forced activity. The fact that people keep buying as they do nearly clinches the case: not only does the system meet their needs, it may well be the best of all possible alternatives. While this is a powerful logic, it is based on unfounded assumptions. The most important is that consumer choice in products is matched with employee choice in hours. Because the vast majority of the income Americans spend in consumer markets is earned in labor markets, the two are intimately tied. If people are not free in one, their freedom in the other is effectively circumscribed. As I argued in Schor

(1992), the market in hours is very limited. Employers set hours, employees do not. And employers prefer, *ceteris paribus*, to have their people working long hours, even overtime, because they are thus able to hire fewer workers and to save on fringe benefits and other costs. To get short hours, a worker must typically make large sacrifices in pay, benefits, and, most important, upward mobility. For most of those who must earn a living, the choice between time and money is skewed. This failure of the "market in hours" creates a structural bias toward spending and against free time. Employers pass on productivity growth in income rather than the option of more free time. Furthermore, people are adaptable in the choices they make around time and money. Contrary to the standard economic story that people are just getting what they want, it is more likely that they are wanting what they have gotten. Once households have earned and spent money, they are highly resistant to doing with less, even if some years before they would have preferred time over money. Thus, the absence of a well-functioning market in hours precludes any interpretation of the current choice for spending over free time as rational, optimal, or even desirable. There may well be an equilibrium that involves lower spending and more free time and is preferable, in the strict sense of the word. To my knowledge, none of consumerism's defenders have responded to this claim. Yet, I believe it to be among the most powerful arguments against contemporary consumerism. Americans don't spend so much because it is their human nature to do so, because advertisers dupe them into it, or because they have a priori chosen money over time. If they are locked into a cycle of work and spend, it is partly because other ways of living have been structurally blocked. For a longer version of this argument, see Schor (1992, esp. ch. 5). See also Schor (1997b, 1997c and 1998).

164 Luxury taxation: I am under no illusion that these proposals, on their own, could radically change spending patterns. Much of what drives the spending–identity–social positioning link is cultural and psychological. Reference group comparisons—or the lifestyles of television characters—are hardly things government can or should legislate about. The issues involved can be addressed only through altering values and norms at the local, national, and global levels, as well as through individuals' own personal transformations. On the other hand, government can be effective in changing the incentives that people face, the basic structures of consumption, and the powerful logics that keep people trapped in competitive spending dynamics.

165 Government policy to affect the income distribution: the government could improve the distribution of income in a number of ways. Most important, it could redistribute assets and economic rights. More conventionally, it could reintroduce progressivity into the tax structure. It could reward companies with a narrower spread in their pay structure

and punish those whose spread is large. Government policies markedly narrowed the spread of income in the middle of this century and have led to its widening in the last three decades. There is now accumulating evidence that more egalitarian income distributions lead to better, not worse, economic performance.

165   Other government initiatives: Government could also encourage saving and free time, which are squeezed out when competitive consumption intensifies. (In the Merck Family Fund poll, more time for family and friends ranked above all other options as something that would make people more satisfied with their lives. Carrying less debt was also highly ranked.) Government could expand its insurance role by expanding collective insurance funds for disability, job loss, and retirement. (Privatized savings mechanisms are regressive, less reliable, and more insecure.) It could also encourage private saving accounts in areas that are not yet the province of public policy, such as vacation financing, parental leave, and employee sabbaticals. The government could even allow some amount of tax-free general saving. These tax breaks could be structured progressively so that the benefits do not accrue mainly to the wealthy, who already do a great deal of saving. Government could also regulate the credit card industry more closely, to make it more difficult for people to accumulate unsustainable debts. Government policy could also facilitate increased downward flexibility in working hours.

165   On 65 percent agreeing that fewer ads would be desirable: Merck Family Fund poll. When asked about a proposal to "eliminate the tax deduction that businesses are now given for advertising expenses," 42.4 percent said "that's a good idea and it would make a big difference," and another 23.1 percent said it's a good idea, "but it wouldn't make much difference." For the view that the public is more positive about advertising, based on other data, see Shavitt, Lowrey, and Haefner (1997). For a review of the literature on advertising effectiveness, see Schudson (1984).

165   Income and well-being: A common argument, which I have made myself, is that over time measures of happiness and measures of consumption are not well correlated. The lack of a correlation is hardly decisive, however, because it does not control for other variables that affect happiness. However, the usual argument is that consumption has a strong effect on happiness. If so, the evidence that happiness and consumption growth move in opposite directions is, at least, very challenging to the conventional view that the consumerist path is a good, or the best, one. For my argument, see Schor (1992); see also Wachtel (1989). For the counterposition, see Lebergott (1993). See also Schor (1997b, 1997c, 1998).

165   The relation between consumption and well-being: This is a complex

issue. On the one hand, being well fed, clothed, and housed has an indubitably positive impact on human welfare, not only for biological reasons but for social ones. Material goods are the building blocks of culture. We construct our societies and lives around consumer objects and products, in fundamental ways. We use goods to create relationships with others, to mark rituals and life stages, and to create social identities. Possessions are integral to our basic sense of who we are. The loss of our possessions can be a devastating event. Beautiful things can also help create human happiness. Thus, I believe modern Americans are no different than most people in most times and places: we experience the acquisition and use of consumer goods and services mainly as positive, highly desirable, and worthwhile.

On the other hand, there is strong statistical evidence that income and happiness are not highly correlated. In data that relate an individual's subjective sense of well-being to his or her income (and by extension, consumption level), we do find a positive relationship; it is particularly strong at low income levels. (Being poor has a very negative impact on happiness.) However, as individuals move up the income distribution, happiness does not increase. One reason is probably that aspirations tend to rise with incomes, particularly for highly educated individuals. With a long-term perspective, we can see that, as countries become richer, their inhabitants do not find themselves happier or more content. In postwar Western Europe, income per person rose between 25 and 50 percent across various countries but yielded no pattern of rising satisfaction. In the United States, decades of increases in consumption have not yielded any improvements in our self-reports of happiness (Easterlin 1995). One study that followed the same people for almost a decade found that rising income had no effect on happiness at all (Diener et al. 1993, p. 208). See also Lane (1991, 1994).

A major reason is probably the prisoner's dilemma associated with positional consumption. (I am not making the strong claim that all happiness is derived from relative position. For the difficulties of this view, see Veenhoven 1991.)

There are other reasons why, beyond a certain point, consuming more does not improve welfare, such as diminishing marginal returns and habituation (see Scitovsky 1976). Finally, the lack of a correlation between income and happiness over time may be the result of offsetting negative factors associated with growth.

Another way to look at these questions is to compare well-being among individuals who differ in how "materialistic" they are. Consumer researchers have done this, measuring materialism as a variety of traits: possessiveness, envy, lack of generosity, orientation to financial success, commitment to acquiring goods. They find that materialists are less content than others with their lot in life. They have less satisfaction in virtually all domains (friends, family life, financial). Furthermore, being envious or selfish is associated with being less happy. People who lay more stress on financial achievement also tend to be more anxious and depressed, in more distress, and not as well adjusted, and they tend to have lower levels of measured well-being (see Richins 1994; Kasser and Ryan 1993; and Belk 1985b).

166 "getting and spending": Twitchell (1995, p. 253).

166 On the 39 percent who say they watch too much TV: see Merck Family Fund poll.

Epilogue: Will Consuming Less Wreck the Economy?

170 On the determination of unemployment: the rate of unemployment also depends on the so-called capital stock, or technology, in use. I assume the capital stock is fixed in the short run.

171 On postmaterialism: see Inglehart (1977, 1990).